The
Summer
of Love
and Secrets

HELENA FAIRFAX

Originally published as

A Way from Heart to Heart

by Accent Press November 2015

Version 2

The Summer of Love and Secrets July 2019

Copyright © 2019 Helena Fairfax

All rights reserved

ISBN: 978-1086154962

To Joe

Wish You Were Here

PROLOGUE

The day Stuart died, everything started out in the usual way. Kate gave George his breakfast and strapped him into the car for the trip to nursery. She never turned the radio on when Stuart was away. If she didn't listen to the news, nothing bad would happen. In any case, she and George had their own routine and some particular songs they loved. That morning he clapped and sang, and Kate joined in, and together they belted out 'The Wheels on the Bus' at the tops of their voices, all the way to nursery.

Later Kate would wonder how it was she could go about her morning so cheerfully and Stuart be dead. But the sun was shining in a cloudless sky, and everyone was going about their usual business. So when she got home she did all the normal things, like tidying away the breakfast dishes and putting on some washing. There was a t-shirt of Stuart's still lying at the bottom of the laundry basket. She held the soft cotton fabric to her face and breathed in the smell of him, but the warmth of his body had gone, and it wasn't the same. She put the t-shirt in with George's things, closed the door of the machine and set the programme. All trace of Stuart was washed away. Kate would wish with all her heart that she'd kept this small link to his living, vital presence in the weeks to come, but early that morning the laundry was just another chore to finish before she started work.

She sat down at her desk in the window and switched on her laptop. Immediately, her Twitter feed sprang into life.

'See what you're missing!! @kate_hemingway
@modelsfirst *#benicassim #greatnight*'

Below the tweet was a photo of four of Kate's friends from
the agency, looking flushed and bright-eyed in a Spanish
nightclub, their arms around each other. The girls were
beaming into the camera, and Kate's heart lifted at the sight of
them. They'd begged her to come and party with them in
Spain, and when Kate refused, they'd teased her she was an old
married woman. Kate's smile became a grin. It was true. These
days she'd rather be at home giving George his bath than out
clubbing with her mates.

Then Kate remembered Stuart, and the smile vanished. The
next three weeks while he was away stretched out interminably.
She felt the familiar tug of anxiety and made an effort to
distract herself, running her eye down her Twitter feed, looking
for anything else of interest. There were a couple of photos
from her friends' catwalk show and news of a fashion gala. She
retweeted the gala and tabbed further down the page, trying to
immerse herself in her own cheerful news feed, but all the
while, on the edge of the screen, the hashtag *#afghanistan* was
trending.

Kate's pulse began to thump. She attempted to ignore it, to
keep scrolling through her colourful images and the sparkling
smiles, but the trending hashtag soon became all she could see.
She made the sensible decision to close her laptop and come
back later. There was no point worrying herself like this, and so
her brain told her hands to shut down and leave her desk.
Somehow, though, before she knew it, her hand had ignored
her message. She clicked. Instantly, a totally different class of
tweet flashed up on the screen, screaming violence.

*3 civilians and a photographer die in Kabul blast. Suspected suicide
bomber #afghanistan #reuters*

There it was. Kate stood, scraping her chair back so quickly
it fell to the floor with a clatter. Her eyes froze on the screen.

Explosion in Kabul market …

4 victims of suicide bomb and several injured …

The page was alive with tweets, but no further mention of a

2

photographer. And no names, either. Kate's mind raced. There were other photographers in Kabul. Or it could even be a mistake. Easily be nothing to do with Stuart at all.

The screen dwindled and receded in front of her. Kate grabbed hold of the edge of the table to steady herself. *Think.* She kicked away the fallen chair and made a grab for her phone. The number Stuart had left her for emergencies rang and rang and rang with sickening futility, until it petered out. His satellite was down. That was surely it.

'If you need anything, phone Paul,' Stuart had told her in the airport, his arms wrapped round her in a fierce hug. Paul was Stuart's closest friend, and besides, he was editor of *The World*. If anyone was in on bad news, it would be Paul. By now he would know all the names of the dead and would be drafting the headlines, in his usual cold-blooded fashion.

Kate fumbled for her mobile with shaking hands. She pressed Paul's number. It, too, rang and rang, before switching to voicemail.

'Hi, this is Paul Farrell …'

Paul's clipped, upper-class voice answered her indifferently. Kate cut the call and stared at the screen. A cold dread seized her. On the rare occasions she'd needed to phone Stuart's friend in the past, he'd always picked up straightaway. Always. Something was wrong. She raced upstairs to Stuart's desk and was rifling through his papers, trying to find the number of his agency, when a loud knock on the door reverberated through the house.

Kate flew down, flinging the door wide to let in a burst of sunlight and a dark figure on the doorstep. Paul. His blue eyes, normally so chilly when they rested on her, were empty. He hadn't shaved that morning. There was a faint line of stubble. That wasn't right. Paul was always clean-shaven. Always correct. Stuffed shirt Paul. Kate's private, childish nickname for him flashed through her mind. She glanced down and was shocked to see that one of his hands was clenched into a fist at his side.

'Kate,' he said.

Kate. Paul never called her Kate. Always Katerina. Always at a distance, with her full name, knowing how she disliked it. Fear and rage ripped through her. How dared he come to her doorstep, alive, and tell her Stuart was dead? She leapt at the sombre figure with fists outstretched.

'No. No! No! Don't tell me!' She beat and beat at his hard chest in a cold frenzy. 'Don't tell me! Don't tell me!'

Paul's head whipped back to avoid her blows. For a few minutes he stood there, silent against her terrified fury. She hammered at him, shouting at him not to speak, ordering him not to say the words she dreaded, until he bent and scooped her up like a child, her head collapsing on his chest as her rage changed to sobbing. He strode into the house with her, still without speaking.

'Please Paul, don't tell me,' she begged, saying the words over and over, clamping her hands to her ears. He sat, pulling her onto his knee, his hands holding her with unusual gentleness, his face frozen.

Time stood still. It could have been hours, or just moments later, that Orla arrived, letting herself in at the front door with her key, rushing in to the room where they were still sitting, Kate, spent, collapsed against Paul's chest.

Kate had asked him not to tell her. During their entire encounter, Paul said not one single word.

*

A month after Stuart's memorial service, Paul surprised Kate by arriving on her doorstep again. He had come to take his godson for a walk. And then every month after that Paul knocked on the door to collect George, and he and Kate had a brief conversation on the doorstep about George's welfare, and neither of them spoke to each other about Stuart or that terrible day again.

In fact neither of them ever said much to each other at all.

CHAPTER ONE

Kate was in the kitchen sorting through her papers when the front door flew open.

'We're back, Mum!' George's footsteps pounded down the wooden hallway.

She stood, catching him in a laughing embrace as he raced into the kitchen. 'Did you have a good time?'

'Yeah. Paul got me these.' He waved a packet of football stickers. 'And we went on a boat ride. The waves were big. I wasn't scared, though. Paul said it was OK.'

Kate felt the usual twist of anxiety and pulled George closer. He wriggled in her embrace. In the months shortly after Stuart's death, whenever Paul came to take George out, Kate had spent the whole day worrying, waiting for their return. As soon as Paul's car pulled up in the drive she would race to meet them at the front door. *Was George all right? Did he cry? Did he enjoy himself? Did he eat his sandwiches?*

If Paul thought Kate over-anxious, he didn't comment. He answered all her questions with matter-of-fact calm. Maybe his unemotional response was a deliberate attempt to reassure her. It was hard to tell, since Paul rarely showed emotion. Whatever the case, since those early days, Kate's fear had abated. Only a residual anxiety remained, flickering inside her, a small, constant presence.

'Did you say thanks to Paul?' she asked.

George pulled out of her embrace. 'Oops.' He looked so like Stuart in that instant, with his blond head tousled, and his blue eyes full of rueful apology. Kate's heart contracted in her chest. She ruffled his curls and gave him a gentle push in the direction he'd come. George turned to run back down the corridor, and Kate followed at a slower pace.

Since that terrible day three years ago, Paul had never once set foot inside her house. He would wait, detached, on the doorstep. Kate heard his deep voice say a few words, and then, when she reached the doorway, there he was, swinging George up in the air.

He placed the boy on the ground at the sight of her.

'Katerina.'

Kate's heart sank. Always her full name. And the distance still there in the way his eyes met hers. Despite everything, nothing had changed.

'Hello,' she said.

'Paul's taking me out again on the seventh of May,' George told her, repeating the date carefully. 'I'll be five then.'

Paul laughed. 'So you will. We'll go somewhere nice. Maybe the seaside, if it's not raining.'

'Awesome.' George waved his stickers. 'I'm going to find my football album. Hope David Terry's in here. See you, bye!'

His feet pounded once more down the hallway and then up the stairs, and Kate and Paul were alone.

Kate shifted her bare feet awkwardly on the doorstep. 'Thanks for taking George out, Paul – '

'It was a pleasure.' Paul cut her off before she could finish. He fished his car keys out of his pocket. 'I'll be back on the seventh. Let me know if you have any problems.'

He was turning away when Kate stopped him, laying her hand on his arm.

'Paul, wait.' He looked down in surprise at the hand on his jacket, and she withdrew it swiftly. 'I mean, have you got a minute? There's something I'd like to ask you.'

'Is everything all right?' His cool eyes met hers immediately, searching her face.

'Yes, it's – ' She broke off, waving her hand in the air. 'Oh, come inside for a minute, Paul, for goodness sake. You make me nervous.'

There was a flash of vivid green, and Paul stared at her fingernails. She snatched them down, curling them into her palm.

'It was for a shoot yesterday,' she said, embarrassed. 'I just forgot to wipe it off.'

'Ah.' He glanced up at her. 'Frozen pea ad?'

There was a taut silence. Kate drew her brows together. Then, despite herself, she began to chuckle. She'd forgotten how ridiculous Paul's deadpan humour could be sometimes. She tilted her head back, gazing up at him in amusement, and wiggled her fingers in front of him. 'It's a new make-up range, Paul. People pay a fortune for this stuff.'

'Really? Good Lord.' Paul smiled. The creases that ran either side of his mouth deepened attractively, and the colour of his eyes shifted to warm blue. It was such an unusual sight, Kate's laughter died, and she found herself staring at him.

The light left Paul's features abruptly, and the tightness around his mouth returned. 'I need to be off,' he said. 'So if there's something you wanted to ask …?'

'Oh. Of course you do.' Kate folded her arms, tucking the painted nails into the crook of her elbows. Paul was a busy man. 'I was wondering if I could ask you a favour, but if you haven't got time to talk to me, maybe we could meet up next week instead?'

An odd expression came over Paul's face. He frowned, seeming to deliberate, before reaching for the phone in his jacket pocket. He flicked through the screens.

'I have Friday evening free,' he said eventually, dropping his phone back in his pocket. 'Would you like to go for dinner?'

Kate stared at him. Was he crazy? 'Oh no, it's just some business, that's all,' she said. 'It's for a charity I'm promoting. Maybe I could come to your office? Or just lunch?'

Her protest was sharper than she intended.

Paul's mouth became a straight line. 'I have a full schedule. The economic summit starts in a few days' time. Friday's my only free night for weeks.'

Of course. The world's heads of state would soon be

arriving in London, and Paul would be working long hours in the press office until it was all over.

'Dinner it is, then.'

Paul must have caught the woodenness in her tone. He hesitated for a couple of seconds, before saying, 'Maybe you might find I'm not such terrible company. I've been thinking about asking you out to dinner for a while.'

Kate's eyes widened in stupefaction.

There was a split second of taut silence. Paul dropped his gaze to the car keys in his hand. 'Well, that's settled,' he said, when she failed to reply. 'I'll pick you up at eight on Friday.'

The noise of tyres on gravel brought the awkwardness to an end. Paul turned his head. An ancient red car pulled up, slamming to a halt inches from his. Orla, sporting a brilliant blue afro, swung open her door, narrowly missing Paul's expensive car.

'Hey, Paul,' she called out cheerfully.

'Hello, Orla.' Paul answered in his usual measured fashion. He set off down the drive. As they passed, he glanced over. 'Nice blue. But did you know pea green is trending?'

Orla flicked a sidelong look at Paul's waxed jacket, his conservative haircut, and his dark chinos. 'Thanks for the fashion tip.' She gave him a mocking grin and sashayed on towards where Kate was standing.

Paul laughed. A light, relaxed, laugh – the sort of laugh he rarely shared with Kate. He turned as he reached his car, and sobered. 'See you Friday, Katerina,' he said. '8 p.m.' He lifted a hand in farewell and climbed into his car.

Kate watched him disappear down the drive, returning his farewell with a droll wave. 'That's twice Paul's laughed today,' she said. 'A miracle. Should be headline news in his own paper.' Then she ran her eyes over Orla's hair, and broke into a chuckle. 'Let me guess. It matches your book cover.'

Orla patted her curls. 'Yeah, I've got a poetry reading next week. It cost a fortune, but it's been worth it already for the look on Paul's face.'

Kate's smile faded. She turned to go back into the house,

automatically pushing George's discarded trainers under the table in the hallway.

'So what was that about Friday?' Orla tried to find room for her jacket on one of the hooks. 'You got a hot date with Paul?' She caught sight of Kate's expression, and her coat dropped to the floor. 'Wow. A date. Really?'

'What? No,' Kate exclaimed. 'Are you crazy?'

To her vexation, she felt herself redden under Orla's intelligent gaze. George chose that moment to stick his head over the banister and shout down a greeting.

'Yo, Orla!' He proceeded to embark on a long-distance, excited conversation with Orla about his day out. Kate went through into the kitchen, where she began tidying her papers.

'Sounds like George had a grand time with Paul,' Orla said, following Kate a few minutes later. 'He's bursting with it.'

Kate muttered something non-committal. Then a thought struck her. She put down the satchel she was filling with her papers. 'Is *that* what it is?'

'What's that, hon?' Orla had her back to her and was filling the kettle at the sink.

'I wanted to ask Paul about putting a piece about At Home in his paper. You know, just for some publicity. But then he asked me out for dinner. It was weird. Do you think it's because of George?'

Orla caught the note of anxiety in Kate's voice and turned round to face her, the kettle dripping water. 'We've been through all this, Kate.'

'I know.' Kate lifted her shoulders. 'I can't help it. But I mean, why ask me out for dinner? It just seems strange, that's all.'

There'd been a time just after Stuart's death when Kate had been terrified George would be taken away from her. She was a young, single parent. Stuart had left her well provided for, but she still needed to work full-time in order to make ends meet, and George spent his days in a nursery. Stuart's parents had hinted several times that George 'might be better off' under their care, and Kate had spent months, more than a year, desperately anxious that Stuart's well-to-do family and friends might somehow be able to make good on their hints.

'No one is going to take George away.'

'I know that now.' Kate fiddled with the strap on her satchel. 'But maybe Paul has some concerns about him. Something he wants to discuss. Maybe he thinks I'm doing something wrong.'

Orla flipped the switch on the kettle. 'There's absolutely nothing wrong with George.' She reached up into the cupboard and took out a couple of mugs. 'Do you know, Kate, does it ever cross your mind that Paul might just want to get to know you better?'

Kate blew an unladylike raspberry and pushed all her papers into her bag. A couple of George's crayons fell off the cluttered table and rolled underneath it. She knelt to pick them up, her voice coming muffled. 'Paul's barely spoken a word to me since the day we met. He always calls me Katerina, even though knows I hate it. On the day I married his best friend he was silent all day, to the point of rudeness. He collects George once a month, and he never comes into the house.' She stood and looked at Orla. 'He just hovers on the doorstep, looking like he can't wait to be gone. I think I'd know by now if he wanted us to get to know each other better.'

'Hmm.' Orla opened the cake tin, the choice between Battenberg and carrot cake seemingly a more important consideration. Kate waited patiently. Despite appearances, her friend was giving the comment careful thought.

Orla finally plumped for the Battenberg. 'Who knows what goes on inside Paul's well-groomed head? All I know is, maybe he isn't such a cold fish as you think.' She brought their mugs to the table. 'To be honest, I quite like him.'

Kate gasped. 'You *like* him? Since when? "A buttoned-up shirt" – that's what you said. "So full of reserve you could stuff him and put him in the British Museum". Remember that one?'

Her friend gave an unladylike guffaw. 'Well, he does talk to us both like he's got a silver spoon rammed in his mouth.

Sometimes I get an urge to stick a fork in him, just to see if upper-class blood really does run blue.' Kate started to giggle at this, too, but stopped when Orla sobered. 'I know he seems off-hand, Kate, but you have to admit he's always sort of been there for you. Ever since Stuart died. And George worships the ground he walks on.'

'Oh, George thinks Paul's the best thing since David Terry.'

'All I'm saying is perhaps you should give him a chance.' Orla's voice dropped a little, and she reached over to touch Kate's hand. 'He was Stuart's best friend, after all. Stuart must have seen something special in him. Maybe it's time you actually got to know each other, instead of not speaking on the doorstep.' She stopped for a moment, and her brown eyes twinkled naughtily. 'Anyway, you've got to notice Paul's fit as a butcher's dog.'

Kate dropped her gaze. 'I hadn't noticed,' she said. 'All I know is, since the day we met, he's always been really distant.' She pulled out a chair and drew her mug towards her. 'Actually, sometimes I'm convinced the only reason he visits is to make sure I'm looking after Stuart's son properly. To be honest, when he looks at me, I feel about this high.' She swept up her finger and thumb, held closely together. 'Like I was never good enough for Stuart.'

The laughter in Orla's eyes vanished. Kate took in the twist to her friend's mouth and sighed. 'I know what you're thinking, Orla, but it's fine, honestly. When Stuart and me first met, I was hardly the answer to all his friends' prayers.' She kicked the leg of the table. 'Or his family. Anyway, it doesn't matter what any of them think. George is my only worry now.'

'I know, love. I just thought since George gets on so well with Paul, maybe he's more fun than he seems. George thinks he's fun, anyway.'

'Fun?' Kate placed her mug down abruptly, spilling some of the liquid. 'Paul Farrell wouldn't know fun if you made him join a circus. Sometimes I wonder what on earth he and Stuart ever had in common.' She dropped her eyes, suddenly full of tears, and mopped at the spilt tea with a tissue. 'But then Stuart saw the best in everybody.'

Orla began to speak, but her reply was cut short by the sound of George charging down the stairs.

'I've got it,' he shouted, racing into the room. His cheeks were round and red with excitement, and he was flapping the pages of his sticker album in the air.

'Slow down, slow down.' Kate laughed. 'No need to shout from the hall. What did you get?'

She put her arm around him and peered down at his book.

'David Terry,' he cried, shoving the album under Kate's nose. The England captain's unfeasibly blond head was now stuck at an angle on the page. 'I knew if Paul chose the stickers David Terry was bound to be in there. Paul is *awesome*.'

Kate caught Orla's look and rolled her eyes with a grin.

*

George chattered away about Paul's awesomeness for the rest of the week. Paul could head a ball more than ten times; Paul knew a brilliant place to get jam doughnuts; Paul interviewed Batman once in New York (not the real Batman, the actor who played Batman). Apparently there was no limit to Paul's all-round greatness. By the evening of their so-called 'date', Kate was more than a little tired of hearing Paul's name. She got George ready for his bath, pouring some bubbles into the water and sloshing it round, before hanging his pyjamas on the towel rail to warm.

'Paul said he never has a bath,' George said, lowering himself gingerly into the water.

'Did he?' Kate answered faintly. She stood in front of the mirror, ready to put on her make-up. In the reflection, George began happily zooming his toys about in the bubbles.

'Yep. He always has a shower.'

Condensation was beginning to cloud the mirror. At George's words, Kate had a sudden image of Paul in her mind, standing behind her, a towel wrapped around him and his smooth, naked chest damp with moisture. She wiped at the condensation furiously until her flushed reflection reappeared. What a ridiculous image. A tingling spread through her, and she bent quickly to pick up her make-up bag.

George gave a loud splash, banishing the unwanted picture. Kate began applying her mascara in practised strokes and noticed her fingers weren't steady.

I've been thinking about asking you out to dinner for a while.

Paul's curious comment ran through her head. And then it came to her in a flash of recall. The look in Paul's eyes when he'd spoken reminded her of another time, the day they first met, that time by Stuart's fishpond.

That was it. That was why she felt so unsettled. Kate put down her make-up and gazed unseeing at the steamy mirror. She hadn't thought about that day for a long time, but suddenly there it was, the memory clear and fresh, as if it were yesterday.

She'd been in Stuart's garden, kneeling by the pond. It was a summer afternoon, and the surface of the water was hazy in the sun. She heard Paul approach, and stood. This must be Stuart's friend. For a moment or two they stood there, without speaking. In the heat, with the sun beating down on her, perhaps her imagination was playing tricks on her that day. Whatever the reason, the harsh lines in Paul's unsmiling face, and the blue of his eyes, glittering in the sun, affected her powerfully. He spoke her name, and she stumbled back towards the pond. She recalled the swiftness and strength in his arms as he caught hold of her, the intensity in his gaze as he searched her face. Then he released her, and all trace of emotion was gone.

Despite the warmth of the bathroom, tiny goose bumps appeared along the length of Kate's bare arms. Her reflection was a pale blur in the mirror. Some more furious splashing and a loud whoop from the bath recalled her to her senses. She sighed and replaced her make-up bag on the shelf. When she turned round, there was a little puddle on the floor next to the bath, and two plastic dinosaurs were just visible in the soapy water.

'You look lovely and clean, George,' she said. 'Let's get you out, before you shrivel up like a turnip.'

Half an hour later, Kate had shrugged herself into her dress and was getting George into his pyjamas when she heard Orla open the front door. She checked her watch. One minute to eight. Mr Punctuality. She heard the murmur of voices in the hallway followed by the sound of Orla slamming the door shut. At least, Kate guessed it was Orla who had closed the door. Paul had far too much restraint to do any slamming.

'Is that Paul?' George rammed his head through his pyjama top at the sound.

'Yes, it is.' She ruffled his head. 'And what's he going to say if he finds you're not even ready for bed yet?'

'I *am* ready,' he protested, tugging his pyjama top in evidence. 'Can I say hello?'

'Fine. But only for a minute. And don't ask him a million questions.'

Paul's firm tread could already be heard on the stairs. George shot out of the bedroom door.

'Paul, I've got a lightsaber,' he cried.

'Have you, old chap?' She heard them hug each other, Paul patting George's back. 'Keep it by your bed, then. That should see them off.'

'Yeah.' George reappeared through the door, tugging Paul's hand. 'That's what Mum says.'

Kate drew herself to her feet from her kneeling position. She'd tucked the plastic lightsaber between the bed and the wall, where George could easily reach it. As soon as he turned it on, and its pink light flashed, she'd told him, the 'monsters' that gave him nightmares would flee the room. But how Paul guessed what the toy was for, she didn't know. She looked up as he filled the doorway.

'Katerina.' He nodded.

In his crisply ironed shirt, with his face clean-shaven and his neat haircut, he brought with him a sense of orderliness that made Kate feel at a distinct disadvantage. She nudged aside a few of the scattered toys that littered the floor. In her bare feet, she was smaller than Paul. It was an unusual feeling for Kate. There weren't many men taller than she was.

'Can I show Paul my bedroom?' George tugged on her arm.

'Absolutely not,' she said, guiding him towards his bed. 'It's bedtime.'

'Oh, but he's never come inside and seen my bedroom before. And last time when we went to the zoo I told him he could look at my tigers.'

'Paul has come inside before. It was just before you remember.'

Paul crouched down by the bed. 'I saw your room when you were a baby, old chap. You've got a lot of toys now.'

'I don't remember.' His face was on a level with Paul's, and he looked at him seriously. 'Did you see it when my dad was alive?'

Kate tensed, staring down at Paul's shoulders, but he responded to the mention of Stuart as evenly as he did to everything.

'Yes,' he said in his quiet way. 'That's because your dad and I were friends.'

'Aren't you my mum's friend?'

Kate rolled her eyes. 'Honestly, George, I said don't ask a million questions.'

Paul stood up, saying gravely. 'Well, of course we're friends.'

She stole an ironic glance at Paul's back before stepping forward. 'Time for bed now, George.'

George leapt onto his bed, turning to give Kate such a pleading look, she was forced to smile. 'Can I ask him just *one* more?' he said.

She heaved an exaggerated sigh. 'OK. But this is absolutely the last.'

George's head swivelled straightaway. 'Why do you call her Katerina? Orla calls her Kate.'

'*Everyone* calls me Kate.' Her muttered aside concealed her curiosity. She found she was as eager to know the answer as George. She wondered how Paul would answer and turned curious eyes on him, expecting him to be discomfited.

Paul gave the question serious consideration. 'Katerina's

your mother's full name,' he said eventually. There was a pause, and then his eyes came to rest on Kate. 'It's a beautiful name, and I like it.'

Kate felt her cheeks go pink under his steady gaze. Because he liked it? She checked his features for any hint of irony, but there was none.

'I like it, too,' George broke in. 'But I have to call her Mum.'

Paul gave George a smile that made him appear years younger. 'That's because she's your mother and she looks after you. And now I'm going to take your mother out for dinner.' He bent his tall frame over George's bed, and kissed his head. 'Sleep tight.'

George lay back, checking automatically for the lightsaber. 'Are you going to take me out for dinner another time?'

'George,' Kate remonstrated, but Paul merely laughed.

'Fine. If your mother says you can, we'll go for pizza. Just the two of us. Your mother doesn't like pizza.'

Kate stared at Paul again. Fancy him remembering that.

'No, she says it's like cheesy cardboard.'

Paul laughed at that beside her, and Kate began to feel strangely excluded in this masculine exchange. She realised how much her son was missing out, not having a father to share secret jokes with, and her heart twisted.

'Lie down then, George.' She smoothed his hair before giving him a kiss and a hug. 'Orla will be up to say goodnight in a bit.'

George was a good sleeper. His monsters no longer troubled him so much since Kate had bought him the lightsaber, and now he snuggled down contentedly beside it.

Out on the landing Kate looked at Paul and put her fingers to her lips, motioning him to be quiet until they were out of earshot.

'Thanks,' she said quietly as they descended the stairs. 'For offering to take him for a pizza, I mean. He likes you.'

She realised she probably sounded surprised, but she couldn't help herself. George looked forward to Paul's monthly visits with an enthusiasm that flummoxed her. It had been easy to see why people loved Stuart. He was charming and engaging, and always the first to strike up a conversation. Whereas when Paul was with her, he was just so ... *silent.*

Orla waited in the hallway, her beautiful blue afro a stunning contrast to her dark skin. Her sleeveless dress revealed the tattoo of a large Celtic cross running the length of one bare arm, and an eagle's head adorning the other arm above the elbow. She'd had the tattoos done years ago, as symbols of her Nigerian and Irish heritage.

Kate glanced at Paul, who was dressed in a neat, dark blue shirt and dark trousers. He nodded at Orla, who returned his greeting with a friendly grin.

'I just need to find my shoes.' Kate bent to feel under the hall table, moving aside George's trainers. Too late, she thought of the view she was presenting as she fumbled around on her hands and knees. In the eight years since she began modelling, she'd gone from a size six to a plus size. The rear she was presenting to Paul's view, clad as it was in a figure-hugging plum silk, was an ample one.

Great, she thought. Orla in full regalia, and now an eyeful of my finest feature.

She retrieved her stilettos and stood up straight. Immediately she felt better. Nothing like the extra inches provided by high heels to make you feel more in control. She picked up a lilac satchel stuffed with papers from the table and saw Paul lift one neat eyebrow. She raised the satchel half-defiantly.

'I told you it was work. And if dinner is all you can fit in your schedule, I'll have to bring my papers to the restaurant.'

Paul nodded. His reasonable response left Kate with the uncomfortable feeling she was being a little childish. As usual he managed to make her feel ill at ease just by being polite. And then she felt guilty for being irritated.

She swung her briefcase down from the table. 'Orla, I'm sure Paul's far too busy to keep me out late.'

She knew she sounded churlish, but Paul always brought

out the worst in her. It seemed the constraint was mutual. By the time Kate climbed inside their waiting taxi, there was not even a trace of a smile on Paul's cool, cleanly shaven features. He gave the name of their restaurant to the driver and leaned back in his seat, stretching his long legs in front of him in the roomy cab. As he did so, Kate suddenly became aware of him; really aware of Paul's physical presence. The sleeves of his jacket brushed against her bare arm, and she felt the warmth of his body as he shifted. The tingling, heady sensation she'd experienced earlier that evening in her bathroom returned, sweeping through her with a strength that took her by surprise. His hand brushed her thigh as he reached to attach his seat belt, and she drew in her breath. Instantly, he raised his head to look at her. She drew back, afraid he would read the heated thoughts rushing through her mind.

'What's wrong?'

Kate's reply came swiftly. 'Nothing.' She swept her gaze down the length of his legs. 'I just wondered how you got such razor-sharp creases.' She lifted her eyes to his. 'Or was it your butler?'

Immediately she regretted her impulse. She'd said the first thing that came into her mind, but her retort was childish and rude. Instead of seeming put out, Paul merely shifted his legs. His lips twitched a little. And his legs, on closer inspection, were actually far more muscular than she'd realised.

'Maybe I'm just not used to socialising with the fashion crowd. Next time I'll wear my sarong.'

Somehow, Kate couldn't bring herself to smile at his joke. Stuffed shirt or no stuffed shirt, the thought of those long, hard legs in a sarong was doing nothing to quell her body's heated reaction. What was the matter with her? The nearness of him, the clean smell of his body, the lines in that smooth-shaven face so close to hers, had provoked a reaction that took her totally by surprise. She felt a momentary sense of panic. This was stuffed shirt Paul, for goodness sake. Definitely weird to be thinking about his bare legs.

She made her voice a deliberately cool drawl, trying to

match his humour. 'Darling, sarongs are so nineteen-nineties. It's all about the leggings. Next time I'm at a shoot I'll pick you up a pair, and you can wear them for *Newsnight*. They'll think you're the shizz.'

He broke into a laugh, and the two creases in his cheeks deepened. Kate turned away, disconcerted. What was happening? A Paul who was relaxed, and who laughed at her jokes. A Paul who told her that her name was beautiful, and actually seemed to mean it. A Paul who looked at her as though he might even like her. It was as though she had stepped into a parallel universe, where everything bad was good.

At this rate, she, too, might actually start to believe Paul was fun.

.

CHAPTER TWO

The taxi pulled up outside the restaurant, and Kate's sense of disorientation increased. She'd assumed Paul would take her to the sort of place she went to with the clients from her modelling agency. The sort of place Orla said was 'for grown ups'. One of those vaguely chilling restaurants, perhaps, with black lacquered tables and bright lighting, where everyone recognised each other but pretended they didn't, because they were all far too cool.

Instead, she climbed out of the taxi onto a dingy pavement. A yellow light spilled from the restaurant window, and the delicious smell of spices filled the street. She breathed in the aroma in hungry anticipation as Paul paid off the driver.

'I think I may be a little overdressed,' she said, thinking of her designer silk.

'You look great.' Paul gave a small smile, as though at a secret. 'And trust me, no matter what you're wearing, the staff will love you.'

He gestured for Kate to precede him up the narrow threadbare staircase, his cryptic comment adding to her sense of bewilderment. When Paul pushed open the glass door at the top, the head waiter came forward to welcome him, holding out his hand. His expression changed into one of genuine delight.

'Paul. As-salamu 'alaykum.' He took Paul's hand in his, and Kate watched in astonishment as the two men embraced.

'Wa alaikum assalam.' Paul stood back, clasping the older man's arm. 'Good to see you, Adeeb. How is your family?'

'They are very well. It is good to see you, too.' The restaurant owner's lined features were alive with warmth. 'How are you?'

'I'm well. And hungry.'

Adeeb laughed. 'Come inside.' He waved them both into the room, greeting Kate with a speculative nod.

'Adeeb, this is Katerina Hemingway.' Paul ushered her forward. 'Stuart's wife.'

Adeeb's brown gaze softened, and he held out a hand to Kate, placing the other hand over his heart. 'I am pleased to meet you. And I am sorry for your loss. Your husband was a good man.'

Kate took his hand, struck by that terrible mixture of joy and pain on meeting a friend of Stuart's. 'You knew my husband?'

Adeeb bowed his head. 'We met in Kabul. Many years ago. His death was a tragedy.' He spoke matter-of-factly, as though Stuart's death were a natural event, one of many of the unfathomable mysteries of life. His philosophical manner was strangely comforting.

'Thank you.' Kate put her other hand over Adeeb's. 'I'm glad to know Stuart had a friend in Afghanistan.'

'Your husband had many friends.'

Kate swallowed. Paul touched her elbow, smiling down at her. 'Adeeb tried to teach Stuart how to cook. It was enough to test any man's friendship.'

Stuart's lack of skill in the kitchen was legendary. Kate's sorrow was diverted, as she suspected Paul intended. The lump in her throat dissolved. For a couple of seconds, all three of them shared a smile at the thought of Stuart actually standing still long enough in the kitchen to cook anything.

Adeeb led the way to their table. After he left to organise their drinks, Kate was able to take in her surroundings. The tiny restaurant was noisy with diners, the tables covered with sizzling dishes and great piles of naan breads. It was cramped, and condensation fogged the windows, but the waiters swung busily from table to table, and the noise of cheerful voices could be heard in the kitchen.

'Thanks for bringing me here,' she said. 'It's a lovely place. I had no idea.'

Paul followed her gaze around the wooden tables and the fading wallpaper. 'Adeeb is a good friend of mine,' he said. 'I didn't know if it was quite the style you're used to now. But the food is delicious.'

Not her style? Paul turned his attention to the menu and Kate stared at his bent head in astonishment. What on earth did he mean? Did he think she thought herself too good for the place? That she'd gone up in the world? That was rich, considering –

She bit her lip, caught up in the irony. It was exactly what she herself thought about Paul. She examined his dark head, wondering if she'd always underestimated him, as Orla kept telling her. Kate was used to George's constant chatter, and Orla's ebullient spirits, and Stuart had always worn his heart right out there on his sleeve. Maybe it wasn't surprising she found Paul's reserve more difficult to fathom. She remembered how Orla had told her she ought to try and get to know him after all this time, and immediately she felt guilty.

'Adeeb's your friend,' she said. 'And he was a friend to Stuart, too. I wish –' She broke off, fiddling with her napkin. Her thoughts were carrying her down a bleak avenue. Paul waited. She raised her gaze to his. 'I wish I could have got to know Stuart's friends better, as well as you do. Sometimes –' She took in a breath. 'Stuart was away so often, and George was just a baby. I never really socialised with his friends. Sometimes I feel I've missed out on the world he knew, and now the chance to get to know it has passed me by. Everything's just gone.'

Paul didn't answer for a moment. He regarded her intently. 'I wish you'd got to know his friends, too,' he said eventually. 'You know, it's three years since Stuart died.' A shadow crossed his face. 'I'd often wondered about bringing you here since then, but I guessed you wouldn't want to come. After Stuart died, you cut yourself off from everyone, except Orla. '

A chill of astonishment ran through Kate. Cut herself off? That wasn't true! Paul was the one who'd always been distant. Wasn't he? She stared at him, and he held her gaze, the blue of his eyes deepening in the candlelight. Kate remembered how Orla had told her she needed to get out more often, meet up with the girls from the agency, make a new set of friends, even. But the years since Stuart's death had gone by in a fog –a dense mist she'd been only too happy to hide in.

Paul's gaze seemed far too piercing. She looked down at her menu and began to study it. Luckily a waiter appeared shortly afterwards to take their order, because Kate was struggling to think of a single reply to his astonishing statement. After the waiter left, taking their orders with him, Paul turned to Kate, and she wondered uneasily whether he was about to utter some more home truths. The evening wasn't going at all as she'd expected. But the hollows in Paul's cheeks softened as his eyes met hers.

'It can't be easy bringing up a child alone,' he said. 'George is a great little chap.'

It was the perfect comment to set Kate at ease. She gave Paul her first genuine, grateful smile of the evening. For a while they talked of George's good nature, how much like Stuart he was in looks and personality, and the way, just like Stuart, he leapt from interest to interest, buzzing around like an enthusiastic bee.

After the waiters removed their first course, Kate took a small sip of her wine. She stole a look at Paul, who was gazing at the tablecloth, lost in thought.

'It was good of you to keep in touch with George,' she said. 'You know, after Stuart died. Not many men would have taken time to spend time with a toddler for their friends.'

Paul gave her a quizzical look. 'It was a pleasure. I like George. On the days when I take him out we have tremendous fun. He's full of beans. And he makes me realise there's more to life than all the political egos and in-fighting I deal with as part of my job.'

Kate had never considered Paul's personal life before. Now

it seemed a shame he didn't have his own family. He'd had a few relationships over the years, but none of them seemed to last.

'Did you never want to settle and have children of your own?'

Paul wiped his fingers on his napkin and shrugged. 'Maybe my work has always come first.'

The warmth had vanished from his expression. His dismissive answer frustrated Kate. Some devilment made her want to prod him into opening up.

'Work came first? Even with perfect Joanna?'

Her barb hit home. Paul's heavy brows rose in astonishment. A dull flush mounted his cheeks, and Kate wondered if she'd gone too far, but then he surprised her by breaking into a laugh. "Perfect Joanna", he repeated. 'Good God. Is that what you called her?'

Kate felt her own cheeks warm and was a little ashamed. 'Well, she did appear to be perfect.' She caught Paul's raised eyebrow. 'Stuart and I thought she was nice.'

'Yes, she was nice,' Paul agreed amiably. 'But the only reason our relationship lasted so long is that we hardly saw each other. I was wrapped up in work, and Joanna wanted a relationship that was more committed.'

Kate tried to think of an answer to this, but failed. Paul's reply seemed typically cold and remote. What was the matter with the guy, that he couldn't settle with a perfectly nice girl like Joanna? Although she could definitely see why so many women found Paul attractive, despite his inability to commit. Her gaze fell on Paul's hands, resting loosely on the tablecloth, and the thought came into her head of those hands around her, and how it would be to feel again the strength of his embrace, as she had done that time by the fishpond. Her eyes flew up to his, and she found he was looking at her attentively. Aghast at the direction her imagination was taking her again, she looked away.

'How did you know about George's lightsaber?' she asked, on safer ground. 'When you were in his bedroom, you said it should "keep them away". Has George told you about his monsters?'

'No. I just assumed –' Paul halted for a moment, his mouth curving into a self-deprecating smile. 'I just assumed he saw monsters because it's exactly what I used to do. My mother gave me a torch. To ward off ghosts.'

Kate was taking a sip of water and almost choked on it. It was hard to imagine Paul ever frightened of anything. Beneath his upper-class accent, everything spoke of tough resilience. The image of him actually scared of ghosts was so incongruous she began to chuckle. An answering smile lit Paul's face, and they both laughed out loud.

Paul sobered quickly, saying, with unexpected seriousness, 'You know, I didn't keep in touch just for George's sake.'

Kate raised her eyes quickly to his. She was saved from answering by the arrival of the waiter with their main course. Paul looked away to pass some remark to him, and the strange moment was gone. Kate shook herself. Of course, Paul was bound to stay in touch with George, for Stuart's sake. That's what friends did.

She turned her attention to the plate in front of her, feeling on edge again. Nothing about Paul was ever direct, and she was always trying to second-guess what he was thinking. It was time to get the subject off the personal. She indicated the satchel on the seat next to her.

'Let's talk about why I've come. Have you heard about my work with the charity At Home?'

He nodded. 'Is this what you wanted to see me about? There was a piece in one of our rival papers.'

'Yes.' She dismissed his rival with a wave of the hand. 'A few months back. And that piece was OK. It brought us some publicity. But we're looking for something a little more in depth.' She put down her fork. 'I've been helping out at this charity for a few years now. I don't know how much you know about it?'

'Maybe not as much as I should.' He was smiling now.

'OK. At Home works with teenage girls, and they've got

half a dozen drop-in centres round London. It's for girls who find themselves in a crisis. They come to us for all sorts of reasons. They might be living in poverty, homeless, getting themselves into drugs, or maybe being bullied at school. Perhaps they're being abused at home, and have nowhere else to go. Or maybe they just want to drop in and talk. At Home provides a safe place for them, whatever their problem, where people listen.'

She stopped for breath and took a sip of her water. She wasn't a natural at asking for help, of any kind. She was conscious she may have rattled out her words too quickly, but Paul was sitting perfectly still, giving her his full attention.

She replaced her glass on the table. 'There are a few girls – around thirty or so – who the charity feels would really benefit from something extra. Something more than they can get from us in London.' She pulled her lilac satchel towards her and began to rifle through it. 'We've raised enough money to take them away for a week. Because of my background, the organiser has asked me to go with them as a sort of role model. Someone the girls can relate to. And of course to raise publicity.' Paul continued to watch as she flipped through her papers. 'Here it is,' she said at last, pulling out a crumpled brochure. 'There's a hostel in Yorkshire. We're going to take them up there – into the countryside, which most of them have never seen – and while we're there we're going to run a programme to give them some skills, help them with their confidence, and help them think about their future.'

Paul took the brochure from her and glanced at it briefly.

'Very good. So you've already got the funding,' he said. 'What do you want from me?'

'Publicity,' she said, matching his directness with her own. 'We've got the funding for a one-off, but we want to make it a regular event.'

He nodded. Then he turned his attention to the brochure and studied it in silence, turning the pages, taking his time in his usual thorough way. Kate bit down her impatience.

'You know this isn't really the type of thing for my

newspaper,' he said eventually, looking up. 'We cover political and financial stories.'

Kate raised her chin. 'But you run social stories in your magazine on a Sunday. Chloe – the head of At Home – told me your paper did a piece of journalism years ago with a group of teenage girls in Afghanistan. That was a social piece. Chloe said it won your paper an award.'

It was Chloe's mention of that article in the *Sunday Magazine* that prompted Kate to suggest asking Paul for help, despite her reservations and the awkwardness between them.

He gave her another one of his infuriatingly slow, assessing looks. 'Someone's been doing their research.' He looked down again at the crumpled pages Kate had passed to him, relapsing once more into silence.

'And social stories like this are political, anyway,' Kate carried on insistently, worried he was about to turn her down. 'These girls are –'

'OK.' Paul held his hand up with a laugh. He lifted his head and Kate saw that his eyes were actually twinkling. *Twinkling*. It was so unusual, she stared at him with a mixture of astonishment and relief.

'OK,' he said again. 'Let's get some coffee and go through everything else in that Mary Poppins satchel you've brought with you. Then I'll have a think about it.'

Kate smiled. 'Great. And I'll get dessert as well.'

Paul caught her note of excitement, and his mouth turned down in a smile. It was years since Kate had experienced real hunger. Even though nowadays she could buy as much food as she wanted, she would still experience a feeling of childlike anticipation at the mention of a rich dessert.

An hour, a bitter chocolate ice and an after-dinner cognac later, Kate was getting on better with Paul than she'd ever thought possible. He pulled out the photos of Yorkshire, agreeing that the inner-city teenagers' reactions to this windswept landscape would make a great article. Then he asked pertinent questions about the girls and the volunteers, listening to Kate speak without adding any of his deadpan jokes or relapsing into awkward silences.

Finally he slipped her papers back over the table.

'Fine,' he said. 'There might be some potential.'

'Fabulous.'

He held up a hand. 'But don't get too excited. I need to think a few things over.'

She took hold of the papers and returned them to her bag, stealing a couple of glances at Paul as she did so. He was gazing down at the table, expression hooded. She bit her lip. Had she lost him? Should she press him again? She was opening her mouth to speak, when he raised his eyes to hers.

'Right,' he said. 'I sympathise with the aims of At Home. And I'll even make a personal donation. But my newspaper is a business, not a charity fundraiser. If I run a story, I have to be certain it will interest my readers. There are a lot of other charities out there helping disadvantaged teenagers. So what is there to interest my readers about this one?'

Kate's heart sank. Paul was gazing at her expectantly. It had been a mistake to ask him herself. She was no good at this sort of thing. She should have let the charity organiser do the job. Chloe was a much more persuasive speaker. Kate closed her eyes momentarily. She didn't want to let Chloe or the girls down. It was time to lay down her last card.

She opened her eyes, quelling the anxiety that clenched her stomach. 'I know what could make this stand out for your readers. What if I gave you an interview?'

There'd been a time – and not that long ago – when the tabloids couldn't get enough of the teenage Katerina Rudecka. Photographers had stalked her, journalists had pestered her agency, but Kate had never given any personal interviews in the press, despite some mind-boggling offers and her agent's urging. After Stuart died, interest in her had rekindled briefly, but Kate had ignored it. Since she had no qualifications, modelling was one of the few careers open to her. She did it because she was good at it, and to earn money. She hated being recognised, and would do anything to keep George's name out of the papers. Offering herself for an interview was an enormous step.

There was the tiniest flicker in Paul's expression, but otherwise no surprise. Had he expected her offer, Kate wondered? Manoeuvred her, making her think it was all her own idea? She studied his features carefully, but as usual, it was impossible to guess.

He studied the table, as though considering her suggestion, and Kate continued. 'You know what happened to me,' she said. 'Or most of it, from Stuart. And if it hadn't been for his photos, maybe I'd still be homeless, living in a squat with Orla.'

Paul looked up then, shaking his head. 'I don't believe that. You were always going to get out of there, with or without Stuart.'

His unexpected faith in her – after all the years she'd suspected him of thinking she'd taken advantage of his friend – moved Kate to the heart of her. She dipped her head, twisting her spoon in her fingers. 'The fact is, you know I got lucky. Stuart's photos of me and Orla got us out of there. Those other girls aren't so lucky. I'd like to help them. And if giving a personal interview is the way to do it, then that's what I'll have to do.'

Paul leant across the table and gently took the spoon from her hand. 'You understand it's going to stir up press interest in you again?'

She swallowed and nodded. 'I know,' she said, in a voice that didn't sound like hers. Her fingers were trembling a little.

'I want you to think about this carefully.' His expression was serious. 'You remember what it was like? Photographers following you, calling your name? The tacky shots and the intrusion? Stuart told me how much stress all that caused you. Are you sure you want to put yourself through all that again?'

Kate gave him a wry look through her lashes. 'That was when I was a teen sensation. I'm an old has-been now. I don't think people will be quite so interested.'

'That's rubbish. You're incredibly beautiful.'

Kate felt the blood begin to mount to her cheeks. Was this really how he thought of her?

He sat back in his chair abruptly, bringing her back to earth with a thump.

'Fine,' he said.

'Fine?' She stared at him, disorientated. 'Does that mean you'll let your paper run a piece on us?'

'Yes.'

She leaned forward, anxious to make sure he'd got the point. 'I mean an extended piece? We can have a journalist with us in Yorkshire for the full week? Not just bobbing in for an hour and scribbling something?'

'Yes,' he said again, with a grin.

'Brilliant.' She beamed at him, and the corners of his lips lifted momentarily, his eyes reflecting her excitement, before the old seriousness returned.

'But I want to be the one to interview you.'

'What?' Kate stared at him, aghast. 'But you're the editor. Don't you have important editing stuff to do?'

It was bad enough talking to any journalist, but as far as Kate was concerned, baring her past to stuffed shirt Paul would be like standing before a judge and jury.

'Don't look so terrified. If anyone interviews you, I want it to be me.'

'I'll have to run it by my agent first,' she said, with a hint of desperation.

A flicker of amusement crossed Paul's face. He and Kate both knew her agency would bite his hand off at the chance of exposure for one of their models in the *Sunday Magazine*.

'Agreed,' Paul said. 'Ask your agent first. But I don't want anyone from your agency hanging around while you do the interview. It has to be one-to-one, with you only. All your agency wants is to promote Kate Hemingway, the model, and that's not the story either of us need.'

Kate frowned, thwarted. Her agent would have been a prop and a shield. But Paul was right. Her agent's presence would put a totally different slant on the interview. She bit her lip, thinking things over. Then she had the flash of an idea.

'OK. I'll come alone. But I have some conditions.'

Paul leaned forward a little, listening.

'I don't want any questions about George or Orla,' she said. 'Their lives are private.'

'Of course.' He gave a small nod.

'And I want to meet the journalist who did the piece on the Afghani teenagers. The one Chloe told me about, that won an award. If she still works for you, she'd be perfect to come with us to Yorkshire.'

It was worth a try. For all Kate knew, the journalist might have left Paul's paper to work for someone else. Or maybe she might be a freelancer, or away on assignment abroad. Kate studied Paul's face for his reaction, and was surprised to see a slow smile spreading.

'The same journalist?' he repeated. 'Actually, it was a man who wrote that piece. Would your charity object to a male journalist going on the trip?'

'No, it's fine,' Kate beamed with relief. 'Chloe will be over the moon.' She picked up her coffee cup. 'Funny,' she added. 'I would have thought it was a woman who wrote the article. Chloe told me the questions were so –'

She broke off. To be truthful, she hadn't really listened when Chloe enthused down the phone. She'd been too preoccupied with George at the time, who'd brought a group of friends round for a sleepover. She caught Paul's eye and realisation dawned. She put down her cup.

'That journalist in Afghanistan,' she said. 'Don't tell me.'

Paul lifted his glass to drain the rest of his cognac. 'First rule of journalism,' he said with a smile, replacing his glass on the table. 'Always do your research.'

Kate felt her heart do a strange slide into the pit of her stomach. She stared at Paul across the table. '*You* interviewed those girls in Afghanistan?'

His eyes seemed to be twinkling again. 'Correct.'

'I don't believe it.' She closed her eyes briefly. Not only had she agreed to bare her soul to Paul Farrell, now it seemed she would be spending a whole week in his company in the wilds of Yorkshire. She tried a last ditch effort to shake him off.

'How will you possibly find the time to come with us? It's a full week up north. What will they do at the paper without you?'

He shrugged. 'Well, I suppose ordinarily it might be difficult to arrange, but since your week away is the quiet season in parliament, it shouldn't be a problem. And thanks for your touching faith, but believe it or not, I'm not totally indispensable.' He caught Kate's look of chagrin and leaned back in his chair with a smile. 'I've been sitting behind my desk for far too long. It will be a chance to do some proper journalism for a change.' He signalled to the waiter for the bill, and turned to face her, his smile deepening the creases in his face. 'And I've always loved Yorkshire.'

CHAPTER THREE

'So, tell me again.' Chloe said. 'Paul Farrell, editor of *The World*, is actually coming up to Yorkshire *himself* to write up about us? He's not sending one of his underlings?'

Kate was sitting in the small, cluttered offices of At Home, clutching a mug of tea. She'd spent the past few days wondering if she could really go through with Paul's interview. It wasn't the fact that her private history would be picked over in *The World* for the whole of the country to see – although that was bad enough. It was the thought of Paul looking at her in that impassive way of his, like a priest hearing a sordid confession. It was almost more than she could stand.

Now Kate took in the expression on Chloe's face and knew she couldn't possibly let her down. The manager of At Home usually appeared harassed. Today she was leaning forward, staring at Kate in eager astonishment.

Kate gave her a tight smile. 'That's what the man said.'

Chloe leapt to her feet with an almighty whoop, scattering papers onto the floor. 'Wonderful! I can't tell you what this will mean for publicity. I *love* you.' She reached over to wrap her plump arms around Kate, pulling her close in an ecstatic embrace.

'I love you too, Chloe,' Kate said, her voice muffled by her friend's baggy cardigan. 'Only this dress is one of my designer freebies.'

Chloe released her. 'I'm just totally gobsmacked. I can't *wait* to tell the girls. Oh,' she added, as a thought occurred to her. 'Do you think Paul Farrell might help us with our classes while we're away?' Her eyes grew even wider behind her glasses. 'That would be brilliant.'

'I'm sure he'd love to.' A mischievous smile crossed Kate's face. There was a certain consolation to be found in the thought of upper-class Paul spending a week confined in a hostel with a boisterous group of teenage girls. 'So, only a few weeks to go,' she said. 'How's the planning? Anything else I can help with?'

'We're not doing too badly. The hostel has been booked for ages. I've almost finished writing up the programme for the week, and the girls are all giddy with excitement. You must have a lot to do, too. How's George going to cope without you?'

Typical of Chloe, Kate thought. She remembered every detail of the girls' family lives. It was no wonder they all loved her.

She smiled at her fondly. 'Orla's planning to take him on holiday to the seaside while I'm away, and they've been talking about it for weeks. I expect Orla will spoil him rotten as soon as my back is turned.'

'We haven't seen Orla for a while. How's she doing?'

'She's well. Sends you her love. She's working on the next book and she's got more hours at the college, plus some work giving poetry classes in schools. She's loving it. Oh, and she's just dyed her hair blue to match the cover of her last book.'

'Oh, that's wonderful.' Chloe laughed out loud. She'd been like a fond aunt to both Kate and Orla, and her delight was genuine. 'And what about you?' she continued, studying Kate attentively. 'How have things been?'

'It's been OK, I suppose.' Kate shrugged. 'Work keeps me busy. And George,' she added, with a little more of a smile.

Chloe leaned forward and touched her arm. 'He's a great little boy. He does you proud.' There was a silence for a second or two, and then Chloe added, 'And how about outside work? Are you having much time to yourself? A social life?'

Kate pulled a face. 'Now you're starting to sound like Orla. She's always on at me to get out more. Hinting at setting me up on dates. Even hinted about me and Paul Farrell last week.' Kate laughed out loud at the thought, but Chloe didn't join in. She just looked at her thoughtfully.

'Paul still takes George out from time to time, doesn't he?'

'Yes, that's right.' Kate didn't elaborate. Chloe had a sharp mind, and Kate didn't want her putting two and two together and making anything except four. But Chloe didn't add anything else. She merely stood, retrieving her empty mug from her desk.

'Do you know, I think this week away will do you good, Kate,' she said, looking down at her. 'It will be a break for you, too, and maybe it will give you some time to think about things.'

She didn't expand on what the 'things' were that Kate needed to think about. She just collected Kate's mug with her own and took them both into the kitchen.

After she'd left, Kate felt that unpleasant prickle again. She'd managed to get a safe, comfortable routine in place for herself and George in the years since Stuart died. But now that prickle of unease seemed to be constantly under her skin. It had been there ever since she'd asked Paul for help, and she couldn't seem to shift it.

*

The next two or three weeks were busy ones for Kate, and she had little time to dwell on the interview she'd promised Paul. Her agency had landed her a contract with a cosmetics company, and she was in the process of doing a few retro-themed photo shoots round London. She had a new hairstyle – a sixties-era geometric bob – especially to fit in with the theme. George loved it, and told her she looked like one of the space women in his sci-fi annual. Orla, who seemed a little harassed these days, told her she was looking more and more like Julie Andrews every day.

In the world of high fashion, it was good to have friends and family who kept your feet on the ground, Kate thought.

Paul was also busy, but of course he was bound to be. Eight heads of state had arrived in London, amidst massive security, and Paul's job was far more important than selling make-up. At least, he always made Kate feel as though it was.

One evening Orla and George were in the living room, squabbling companionably over a board game. Kate was in the kitchen making them all some cocoa and biscuits, when George suddenly shouted through to her.

'Hey, Mum! Paul's on telly again!'

Kate hurried through in her dressing-gown, her wet hair dripping down her back. Paul's heavy-browed, unsmiling face filled the room. He was answering a question on the effectiveness of the summit, which Kate had heard ended badly, with a bitter disagreement over the Middle East. There were faint shadows under Paul's eyes and the creases that ran down his cheeks were more pronounced. He seemed even more remote up there on the big screen than he did when he stood on Kate's doorstep. She barely recognised him as the same man who crouched down beside George's bed to talk to him about his lightsaber. And as for the man who once soothed Kate in his arms while her heart broke inside her, he could have been just a figment of her imagination, part of the nightmare of losing Stuart.

Kate stood in the middle of the room, watching Paul's head on the screen, and wondered how it was that you could know someone for eight years, and they could still appear like a total stranger to you. She was so wrapped up in the direction her thoughts were taking her, it was a couple of seconds before she registered that her mobile phone was ringing. She fished it out of her dressing-gown pocket, saw the name on the screen, and did a total double-take.

'It's Paul,' she told Orla and George, with a startled laugh. His phone call, combined with his face still gazing down from the television screen, only increased her sense of unreality. She pressed a button on the phone, and began to leave the room. Behind her, Orla laughed, and Kate heard her start to explain to George how Paul could phone and be on television at the same time. George was probably even more convinced his godfather had superpowers.

She stepped into the hallway, which felt chilly after the warmth of the front room.

'Katerina. How are you?'

'I'm fine,' she said. Her answer sounded a little curt. The thought of doing an interview with the unsmiling and serious man she'd just seen on the television caused her to tense up, and the wet hair shedding cold droplets down her back was making her shiver. 'And how are you?' she continued, trying to inject a little more courtesy into her voice. 'I just saw you on television. You must be glad it's all over.'

'Yes.' There was genuine relief in his voice. 'Now I can concentrate on more interesting things. I was wondering if we could do your interview next week.'

More interesting? Was he being sarcastic? 'Well, I'm not interviewing the chancellor next week,' she said dryly. 'I'm just making adverts for face cream.' Her diary was on the hall table. She opened the cover and began flicking through the pages. 'We're shooting in the Ritz on Wednesday. How about meeting me there? We could do the interview over tea.'

'We could,' he said. 'But I don't like interviewing in hotels. Too impersonal. How about Wednesday evening? Are you free?'

'Yes,' she said, without thinking.

'Fine. You can meet me at my flat. I'll make you dinner.'

Kate caught her startled reflection in the mirror. She stood open-mouthed, trying to think of some way to wriggle out, but her mind was a blank.

'Katerina?'

'OK,' she said grudgingly. Then she r realised she sounded like a moody teenager and was cross with herself.

'Good.' There was a tense pause. 'It won't be as bad as you imagine, Katerina. I'm not the big bad wolf.'

She shrugged, even though she knew he couldn't see her. 'That's OK, then. I'm not Little Red Riding Hood.' Her hands were still gripping the phone.

'And if you're worried about my cooking, I haven't poisoned anyone yet,' he continued. 'And you won't be short of dessert. See you on Wednesday.'

He cut the call. Kate stared moodily at her phone's screen, lifting her head a few minutes later to see her drooping face looking back at her in the hall mirror.

'Buck yourself up,' she whispered furiously.

'What?'

Kate turned with a start. Orla was standing behind her, a puzzled expression on her face.

'I was just coming to help you with the cocoa,' she said. 'Everything all right?'

Kate dropped her phone back in her dressing-gown pocket and sighed. 'It's this interview with Paul. Now he wants me to go to his flat to do it. On Wednesday evening. Is it all right if you stay with George again?'

'Yes, of course.' Orla regarded her friend for a minute steadily, and then she reached over and gripped her shoulder, giving her a gentle shake. 'You think too much, that's your trouble, Kate. Paul's only trying to make you feel relaxed. Give the guy a break.'

Kate slid her eyes in her friend's direction. 'Guess I don't have much choice. Chloe's all excited about this interview for At Home. I can't let her down.' She brushed back the damp tendrils of hair from her forehead. 'Maybe you're right. Maybe I'm worrying too much. But I'll be glad when this whole thing's over. Everything's changed. Wish I'd never asked Paul Farrell in the first place, and we could go back to how we were. Ignoring each other.'

*

On Wednesday evening, Kate stood for a couple of minutes outside Paul's building, clutching an expensive bottle of wine. It was a quiet street, in an affluent part of London. A line of sycamore trees ran down each side of the road, screening the exclusive apartment buildings from the view of common people. It was the sort of street that should have old-fashioned nannies strolling up and down it, pushing silver prams with big wheels. Instead, the road was empty apart from a gleaming line of cars parked alongside the kerb.

Kate stepped into the lobby and pressed the bell for Paul's flat. Years of modelling gave her an instinctive feel for where a camera would be. She turned her head and watched the CCTV swivel round to examine her. She glared at it, then dropped her gaze, feeling a little foolish for challenging an inanimate object. There was a click on the intercom, followed by Paul's deep voice. 'Hi. Come up.'

The door buzzed. Kate pushed it wide and found herself in an art deco hallway, with a marble floor and giant chandelier. She gazed about her curiously. It wasn't the type of building she'd imagined would appeal to Paul. Not that she'd ever really thought much about his home. If she did, she always imagined him living in a minimalist loft conversion somewhere. The hallway was quiet as a library, and there were letters and even a parcel lying untouched on the hall table. Kate could never quite get used to this subtle signifier of wealth. In the places she lived in as a teenager, the postman never left any mail out because someone was bound to nick it.

She made her way to a clanking lift. After a shuddering ascent, she pulled the gates open with a rattle. Paul was waiting for her outside the door to his flat. She took the few paces across the corridor, calling into play her model's training. It was an effort of will to try and look more confident than she felt.

'Katerina.'

She looked up into his unsmiling face, wishing the heels on her boots were higher. She felt disoriented in the unaccustomed surroundings.

'Hello.' She held out the wine. 'I brought you this.'

The straight line of Paul's mouth curved, and the tension in her spine relaxed a little. And then to her utter surprise, he leaned forward and kissed her cheek. For a fleeting second she felt the heat of his body and glimpsed a pulse beating in his strong neck, so close to her own mouth. Then he moved away, as though his greeting were nothing out of the ordinary; as though he was in the habit of kissing her every day. She lifted a hand to touch her skin, where his lips had rested.

He went inside. 'Put your jacket on a hook,' he said, over his shoulder.

She stared at his shoulders as he retreated down the narrow hallway. First he kissed her, and now he walked off abruptly, as though the touch of her skin had burned him. And leaving her to take off her own jacket, when he was normally so punctiliously polite. Kate watched him disappear into what must be his kitchen, and rolled her eyes.

She shrugged off her fake fur wrap and tried to find a hook for it. The hallway was another surprise. Instead of the regimented neatness she'd expected, there was a jumble of masculine jackets and overcoats. An indefinably male aroma rose as she pushed the coats aside, and for a couple of seconds she breathed in the comforting smell. She'd forgotten just how much she missed a male presence. The paraphernalia of handbags and high heels in her own hallway seemed ultra-feminine in comparison.

'Can I get you a drink?' Paul's head appeared around the kitchen door. 'Glass of wine?'

Kate turned her head and nodded. Hopefully he hadn't caught her sniffing his clothes like some sort of freak. It seemed he hadn't noticed. He merely waved a hand to indicate the next room. 'Go on through. Make yourself at home. I'm just stopping dinner from burning.'

'Can I help?'

'Definitely not. Sit down and relax. Put some music on if you like.' He drew his head back, disappearing into the kitchen.

Relax. That might be funny if Kate thought about it long enough. She went through into Paul's living room. There was a wide settee and a couple of deep armchairs, the worn red fabric partly concealed with throws. An Afghan rug covered most of the wooden floorboards. In one corner stood an old-fashioned lampstand with a tasselled shade, from which spilled a comforting yellow glow, and along the whole of one wall was a bookcase crammed with books, with the overspill carefully piled up on the floor.

Kate took it all in with a growing sense of wonder. This threadbare cosiness was so unlike the clean lines she expected, she was thrown off balance. She crossed the room, her boots sinking into the deep pile of the rug, and studied the collection of books. Here at least was evidence of Paul's ordered mind.

Political and economic non-fiction took up one shelf, and fiction another. In alphabetical order, Kate noted with a smile.

It was no surprise to find Paul's taste in fiction was very similar to Stuart's, and seemed to consist mainly of thrillers. There were a few photos, too, on the shelves, lined up in plain white frames. A black and white picture of a young smiling couple – possibly Paul's grandparents – standing on the steps of an enormous house; a colour photo of Paul as a boy, sitting on a beach, a wide grin on his sunburned face. He was flanked by two smaller girls. Kate picked this photo up and studied it. She guessed the girls were Paul's younger sisters. Paul's slim face already had the two creases which deepened when he smiled. It was a joyful photo that lifted Kate's spirits, and at the same time made her feel a little envious of his happy childhood holiday. She replaced the frame carefully and moved along to the next, which was angled away in the corner of the shelf.

Kate turned the frame towards her with a finger, and her breath caught in her throat. It was a picture of herself and Stuart on their wedding day. It was no surprise that Paul had kept a photo. He'd been best man, after all, and Stuart was his closest friend. The strange thing was that Stuart's back was angled to the camera. The photographer's focus was on Kate, and she was gazing up at Stuart with an expression that radiated pure love and happiness. Her eyes were wide in her face, her lips parted in a small, joyful smile. The image wrung Kate's heart.

She picked up the frame and gazed at her younger self. Why had Paul framed this photo, out of all the dozens that were taken that day? It was a puzzle typical of him, and Kate was so involved in trying to decipher it that when he spoke her name behind her she started, almost dropping the frame. She replaced it quickly and turned to find Paul setting down her glass on a table in the corner.

'Here,' he said. 'I'll bring dinner through. Hope you're hungry.'

He left without further comment. His abrupt behaviour wasn't helping Kate relax. She crossed over to the table and picked up her glass. Maybe wine might be the answer. Then she remembered she was about to be interviewed, and set the glass back down. Better to keep her mind clear.

Paul reappeared, this time carrying two steaming plates. 'Come, sit down,' he said. 'I don't know about you but I could eat a horse.'

The meal certainly smelled inviting, and Kate's stomach rumbled, despite her tension. The shoot had left her little time, and she hadn't eaten much since giving George his breakfast. Paul laid the two plates on the table and pulled out Kate's chair for her. As he tucked her into her seat, she looked down at her plate, curious to know what he had made for them.

'Spaghetti Bolognese,' she said in surprise, gazing at the inviting twirls of pasta. She didn't know what she'd expected Paul to cook, but certainly not this nursery staple. 'It's one of my favourites.'

Paul pulled out his own chair, sinking down opposite her. 'I know. That's why I made it. Comfort food, you once said.'

'Did I?' Kate picked up her fork and spoon, and began to twist the pasta. 'I don't remember.'

This was the second time Paul had confounded her. He remembered she didn't like pizza, and now he remembered her favourite meal. She thought about it for a second or two, before dismissing it as just a trick of his journalistic mind. He probably filed even the minutest trivia away in that brain of his.

As she began to tuck in, Paul laid his tablet on the table and pressed a button.

Kate eyed it with misgiving. 'Is that thing recording?'

'Relax,' he said, edging his pen and notepad to one side.

Relax. Kate would stab Paul with her fork if he said that again.

He picked up his cutlery and began to eat, unconcerned. Kate eyed him for a moment, but it seemed when he said he was hungry he wasn't exaggerating. He was making great inroads on his meal, and paying no attention whatsoever to his recorder. So far this evening he'd ignored her, or if he addressed her at all, it had been in monosyllables. Strangely, Kate was beginning to find his odd behaviour reassuring. If Paul found nothing to get worked up about, then everything must be OK.

'Do you have to worry about what you eat?' he asked, without looking up from his meal. 'For your job, I mean?'

'Not really. I try to eat sensibly, three meals a day, but I work quite hard, and I do a lot of running round after George, so sometimes I miss a meal. I've never understood why they call me a plus size model. I'm five foot ten, and the correct weight for my height.'

Paul raised his eyes a moment, and then returned to his meal. 'But you didn't start out as a plus size model.'

'No. I was seventeen when I started out. A modelling agency saw the photos of me that Stuart had taken.' She looked up, half-defiantly. 'You know all this already. The photos Stuart took of me and Orla when we were living in the squat. The ones that were plastered in your newspaper.'

Paul nodded without rising to her hint of challenge. 'I know. I wasn't editor then. I was just a journalist, in Afghanistan. But I saw the photos.' He raised his gaze to Kate. 'They caused a stir.'

Stuart was a gifted photographer. The photos he'd taken that day in the squat were arresting. Orla and Kate had their arms around each other and were gazing defiantly into his camera. Kate's hair was cropped short and ragged, close to her skull, and together they looked like a couple of Dickensian urchins, one white skinned with dirty blonde hair, the other dark with an almost skinhead razor cut. The girls' underlying anxiety was clear, despite the defiance. Stuart's images were powerful and had attracted widespread attention. Questions had even been asked in the House about why two teenage girls had to resort to living in conditions of such squalor.

'Orla wasn't sure about having our photos taken at first,' Kate said. 'But I trusted Stuart right from the first. After that a lot of people were interested in what happened to us. People actually seemed to care.'

She made to raise a fork to her mouth. When Paul made no response, she thought better of it, replacing it in her bowl almost angrily. 'I was a size zero when I started modelling because when Stuart met us I was literally starving.' She glared at Paul, as though somehow it was his fault. 'But fashion people thought I looked great.'

Paul raised his eyes briefly, but the meal in front of him seemed to be taking all his attention. Kate stared at him. Was he even listening to what she was saying? All he seemed to care about was clearing his plate. She thought she'd try and shock him.

'And do you remember how I had my hair then?' she said. 'All cropped? After those photos, I set a new trend. I used to see women in suits getting on the tube with my hairstyle. They thought it looked edgy. Used to make me laugh. What no one knew was Orla chopped my hair off for me with some kitchen scissors because we thought it would get rid of my lice.'

Kate thought she had him then. There was the merest downward turn to his lips, but in the dim light cast by the lamp it was hard to tell if his expression was one of amusement or disdain.

He reached across the table and picked up a side-dish. 'Yes, I got nits at boarding school,' he said, in his deep, posh voice. 'Couldn't get rid of the blasted things. Would you like some more parmesan?'

Kate eyed the dish he was proffering, incredulous. He wasn't even listening. He replaced the dish on the table.

'You're like a kitten on hot coals,' he said, as though reading her mind.

'I hope you're not going to tell me to relax again,' she burst out.

He looked up then. 'Look, everything I've asked so far is common knowledge,' he said. 'Well, maybe not the nits,' he conceded, after a little thought. 'But all kids get nits. I don't get why you're so prickly about mentioning them. In fact I've been scratching my head wondering about it.'

Kate looked at him blankly.

'Scratching my head,' he repeated, leaning forward, with such a mischievous smile Kate was forced to chuckle. At the sound of her giggle, Paul's face crumpled with mirth, and the next minute they were both laughing out loud.

'It's not funny, Paul,' Kate protested through her laughter. 'It's horrible finding insects in your head all the time.'

'I know,' he said. 'It's louse-y.' Somehow, the fact that they'd both suffered the same affliction seemed hilariously funny. They continued laughing for a while, until Paul finally straightened up.

'OK,' he said, returning to his meal. 'Let's not talk about you for a bit. There's no rush. We've got all evening. Tell me about your parents.'

Kate groaned. 'OK. I suppose we might as well start at the beginning.'

A flicker of satisfaction crossed Paul's face, and he nodded once briefly. Kate looked down into her meal. The delicious sauce no longer seemed as appetising. She laid down her fork. In the corner of the table, the tablet's red light blinked.

CHAPTER FOUR

'I suppose the beginning is when my dad met my mum.' Kate brought her hands down onto her lap, and gripped them together. 'My dad was an engineer. He was Czech, and he came over when he got a job in London for the railways. Anyway, he met my mum, they got married, and then they had me. And even though things were hard moneywise, everything was great. I thought it was, anyway.' She uncurled one tense hand and reached for her wine glass. 'But then my dad decided we'd be better off if we lived in Australia. He got a job in Victoria, and went out there by himself to find us all somewhere to live. We were supposed to follow.' Kate shrugged, as though what came next was no big deal. Paul was leaning back in his chair, his fork lying on his plate. He was listening intently.

Kate met his gaze. 'I guess this must seem odd to you. You've travelled the world, but my mum had hardly ever been outside London. Going to Australia was a massive step for her, and she got cold feet. She kept putting it off and putting it off. First of all, she wanted me to finish primary school. Then her work was too busy, and she needed to stay on a bit longer. Then the months turned into years. My dad came back every six months. He told us he was always waiting for us. Then when I was thirteen, out of the blue my mum decided we'd pay my dad a surprise visit. We flew out, just the two of us.' Kate studied the wine in her glass. 'When we got to Melbourne, we found my dad was living with another woman, and I had a one year old step-brother.' She took a small sip and replaced her glass on the table. 'It was a bit of a surprise.'

Kate could see a muscle move in Paul's cheek. His eyes were on hers, but he said nothing.

She frowned. 'I loved my dad. I wrote to him every week, and sent him cards and parcels. Stuff I'd made. He sent me photos. But funnily enough, no photos of his girlfriend, or my new brother.' Her head drooped. This was where it started to get harder, but she swallowed down the unpleasantness and carried on. 'So, there was a massive row, but I really took to my little brother when I saw him. He was cute. I liked the town my dad was living in, as well, and it was hot and sunny. My dad and his girlfriend had a swimming pool and a massive garden. It was nothing like our tiny house in London. I asked my dad if I could stay and live with them, but he said no. He said his girlfriend wouldn't like it. Two days later me and my mum were on a flight home. That was the last I ever saw of my dad. I waited for him to get in touch with me when I got back, but he never did.'

There was a moment or two of silence. Then Paul reached out over the table, and his hand touched Kate's lightly. Suddenly it came to her that she didn't actually care about baring her soul in a newspaper. She didn't care about anyone else's opinion, but she cared deeply about Paul's. Before this strange, new realisation of Paul's importance to her could mute Kate's voice, she lifted her head and began to tell him the rest.

'After we got back to England, nothing was ever the same again. My mum wasn't happy because I told my dad I wanted to stay with him. In fact, she was really furious about it. Now I look back on it, deep down of course she must have been really hurt. But I didn't understand at that age. I just saw how angry she was with me, and I thought she didn't want me, either. Our relationship went downhill pretty quickly. And then my mum started seeing other men. Not just one, there was a whole string of different guys. She dressed a lot younger, got a taste for going clubbing. She never seemed to want to spend time with me anymore, like we used to, and sometimes a whole weekend would pass and she hadn't even been home.'

Kate's gaze stuck at a point just below Paul's chin.

'After a while I started to think, what's the point? I gave up on a lot of things, my self-esteem was at rock bottom, and I began to drift in with totally the wrong crowd. I started bunking off school, because none of it seemed like it mattered.' Her gaze was still fixed on Paul's shirt button. 'Then when I was fifteen, my mum finally found a guy she wanted to be with. She got married again.' Kate swallowed. This was painful.

'Do you want to take a break?'

Paul's quiet voice brought Kate to earth. She thought of why she was doing this. Thought of the ecstatic look on Chloe's face when she'd told her about the publicity, and the misery she'd seen in some of the girls from At Home when they first visited, and shook her head.

'No. Let's carry on.' She was about to reach for her wine glass again, then decided against it, and took a sip of her water. 'After my mum got married, things were all right for a while. I got on OK with my stepdad. He didn't say much. Kept himself to himself, watched television, did jobs round the house. Sometimes he would watch me, though.'

Paul made no sound, but Kate sensed his body coil. She twisted her lips.

'Anyway, to cut a long story short, one day, when my mum wasn't in, he came in my bedroom and tried it on. I pushed him off, but I was frightened. I told my mum, but she wouldn't believe it. All the old arguments came out. I was plain jealous, I never wanted her to be happy, I was just like my dad, blah, blah. I finally had enough. I packed my bags. My mum said good riddance, and don't come back.'

Paul caught Kate's fingers in his. She jerked her head up and found his normally smooth features were twisted and harsh. The shadow he cast behind him loomed large against the wall, rising to the ceiling and towering over them. In the quiet of his flat he radiated tension. The change in him was so great, for a fleeting instant Kate recoiled.

'Paul.' She returned the grip of his hand. 'It's all in the past, now.'

The tension in his fingers relaxed very slightly under hers.

'So what happened then? Where did you go?'

Slowly, Kate withdrew her hand. 'I went to stay with a friend from school at first. But that couldn't last. I couldn't live there forever. I went round from friend to friend, staying where I could. I didn't want to go home. Not with my stepdad lurking about. Sometimes no one could have me, so I slept in a bus shelter, or maybe someone said I could sleep in their car. Then I met some older guys, and they said I could stay at theirs. They were nice guys, but they were really into drugs.'

'Was there no one you could talk to about what was happening? Any of your friends' parents?'

Kate shrugged. 'Not really. They were all wrapped up in their own problems, and anyway –' She frowned and shook her head. 'It's hard to open up to people you don't really know. It's like you feel ashamed. Like it must all be your fault.' She lifted her chin. 'That's why I feel so strongly about getting publicity for At Home. Maybe someone there could have helped me if I'd known about it. I don't know.'

He nodded. 'So what happened after that?'

Kate blew out heavily. 'OK,' she said, looking at Paul. 'I'm going to say all this in one go, but don't interrupt or ask any questions until I get to the end.'

He gave another grave nod.

'I started doing drugs as well. I wasn't really into it like they were, it just helped me take my mind off things. I didn't often go to school. I was being bullied, and I hated it. I can see why the other girls picked on me. I stood out. I was tall, skinny, and a lot of the time if I had nowhere to stay I probably didn't smell too good.' She fiddled with the pristine tablecloth. 'Anyway, one day I decided to show up at school, but I was pretty high. One of these girls started hassling me, and I just don't know what happened.' To her horror, Kate felt as though someone suddenly poured a hot bucket of shame all over her. Her face flamed. She forced herself to continue. 'Something just snapped. It really was like a red mist that fell down and blinded me. I grabbed her sharp compass off her desk – that one you use for maths? – and I just ran it into her shoulder.' Kate closed her eyes, remembering the girl's screams, the compass sticking out of her flesh, the horror of the teacher and the rest of the class. 'Later the police came, I got arrested, and had to spend a night in the cell.'

'Good God.'

Kate's face whipped up. Paul was looking at her with an expression of horror. Her shame increased. She stiffened, and glared at him defiantly, but his next words threw her off balance. 'You were only a child. Still at school, for God's sake. What did they hope to achieve by putting you in a cell?'

She searched his face and realised his horror was directed at her situation, and not at her. She read compassion in his features, and for a couple of seconds she was silent. Then she straightened, and gave a slow shake of her head. 'I don't know. I was sixteen by that time, anyway, and pretty much off the rails. They didn't press any charges. Maybe they didn't know what else to do with me. Perhaps they thought they were doing me a favour giving me a bed. Anyway, then the social workers got involved, and they sent me to a hostel. They tried their best, but the hostel was even worse than the guys I'd just left. But the absolute best thing was, that's where I met Orla.' Kate's face brightened. 'She's far more savvy than me. She found us both some other places to live, and then after a while we ended up at the squat, where Stuart came to take the photos.' She looked up again, and smiled. 'I hit it off with Stuart straight away. He was funny. Talked to me like I was a person, not just some chavvy kid. Stuart was always interested in everybody, it didn't matter who they were, a politician or the cleaner. He talked to everybody like they mattered.'

'Yes, that was Stuart.' Paul looked down at the table, and for a moment neither of them said anything more. Paul's face was dark, his long fingers curled around the stem of his wine glass.

Kate's tension ebbed at the memory of her first meeting with Stuart, and her voice softened. 'I hero-worshipped Stuart right from the start, but I was way too tongue-tied at that age to say anything. I didn't even tell Orla. I thought she'd just laugh in my face. Anyway, Stuart treated me like a little sister. He told me later he felt responsible for me, after the photos in the paper, and all that interest that was stirred up in me. He even came with me when an agency got in touch, just to make sure they looked after me properly. He didn't have to do that.' She rested her hand on her chin. 'After I started working, I didn't see much of Stuart for ages, but he still kept in touch from time to time. My modelling career took off, and I did a lot of travelling. And Stuart worked abroad for most of the time. But I never forgot him, and I followed all his photos, and always knew where he was. Sometimes he'd send me an email, checking everything was going OK. He even sent a postcard, once, to my agency.' She smiled at the recollection. 'Then three years later we met again at a party. Stuart was still the same.' Kate raised her gaze to Paul's. 'But I'd grown up,' she said softly.

Paul was completely still. Only the blue of his eyes shimmered in the half-light. His gaze held hers. 'He told me how you'd met again,' he said quietly. 'I was in the States at the time. He emailed me.'

'What did he say?' Kate asked curiously.

Paul smiled and shook his head. 'Let's just say I couldn't believe –' He broke off, looking a little discomfited.

'Couldn't believe what?' Kate stared at him. 'Oh my God,' she said slowly. 'I was right all along. You disapproved of me, didn't you?'

'No,' he said sharply. 'No. I'd been away a long time. All I'd seen of you were those first few photos he'd taken. Of course, when I met you, I realised –' He stopped again. 'As you say,' he went on quietly. 'You'd grown up.'

There was a tense silence. Paul dropped his gaze. Kate remembered again their first meeting in Stuart's garden, and wondered if Paul, too, recalled that day with the same intensity. She opened her mouth to speak, but couldn't think of the words to frame the question, without it sounding odd. In any case, the moment passed and was gone. Paul flicked his head in the direction of his recorder.

'We'll just do a couple more questions, if that's all right?'
Kate stiffened again, and gave him a short nod.
'What about your parents after that?' he asked. 'Haven't
they ever tried to get in touch?'
She drew her brows together. 'My dad, no. I don't think he
even knows what's happened to me. I'm Kate Hemingway
now. Katerina Rudecka has totally disappeared. And I'm pretty
sure he'd never read any gossip mags or look at fashion pages
in Oz, so I'm sure he's never seen a photo. And if he did, he
probably wouldn't even recognise me.'
'And your mother?'
She swallowed. 'I found out my mum and my stepdad went
to live in Spain, about a year after she told me to leave home.
Ironic she left London to go with my stepdad, when she
wouldn't leave for my dad. Anyway, she's never written. Even
when I started modelling. I'm sure she must have known ...'
She looked down at the tablecloth, which was now creased and
twisted in her fingers.

To find yourself rejected by both your mother and father
wasn't a very salutary tale. She'd thought sometimes about trying
to contact her parents – of being the one to take the first step –
but she couldn't face the possibility of being rejected a second
time.

Kate couldn't imagine George doing anything, under any
circumstances, where she would just leave him. But no matter
how many times people told Kate it wasn't her fault, deep down
she'd always felt there must be something wrong with her, to be
just abandoned like that. To her great horror, she felt tears
prickle behind her eyelids and tried desperately to pull herself
together. This was what she'd been terrified of. She was
supposed to put on a brave front, not let Paul see her weak like
this. She bent her head quickly, pretending she'd dropped her
napkin on the floor, but Paul was before her. Like a shot, he
reached his hand over the table to cup her cheek, keeping her
gaze on his.

'You know none of this was your fault, don't you?' he said.
Kate didn't answer. A large, fat, stupid tear rolled slowly

down her cheek and dripped onto his fingers.

'Katerina, listen to me. You were a child. Nothing that happened was your fault.' He shook her face, his touch warm and gentle.

Kate leaned a little into his hand. 'I try to think like that,' she said. 'But it's hard. Stuart persuaded me to see a therapist for a while. But sometimes you just can't help feeling if you'd only been a bit different, if you'd just been a different person, people wouldn't have just left you.'

Her voice quivered.

Paul tightened his grip. 'The people who left you were the ones who lost out.'

Kate said nothing, and he dropped his hand.

'Do you know what this calls for?' he asked solemnly.

She shook her head.

'This calls for a massive bowl of chocolate and almond pudding, hot chocolate sauce, and whipped cream.' He stood, removing their plates. Kate rose to help him, but he waved her away. 'Stay where you are,' he said. 'Help yourself to more wine while I'm in the kitchen.'

He moved past her, and Kate cast a glance at her half-full glass on the table. She'd barely drunk a drop. And the bottle was still nearly full, which meant Paul had drunk even less. His mind must be razor clear. And he certainly knew how to get people to talk. All the time he'd been pretending to concentrate on his meal, he must have been listening to her intently. Her eyes fell on Paul's notepad, which was full of some scribble. How had she not noticed him writing? She twisted her head to make sure he was out of the room. Then she reached a hand out swiftly over the table and picked up the pad. It appeared to be full of some form of shorthand, interspersed with question marks. She replaced it on the table, disappointed.

Trust me, Paul had said. Funnily enough, this evening he'd made her acknowledge what she'd always known deep down. Whatever he might think of her, Paul was a man she could rely on totally.

When he returned, he was carrying two enormous bowls of

chocolate and cream. He placed one of them in front of her, leaning over to move her glass as he did so. He had rolled up his shirt sleeves and his bare arm grazed hers briefly. He smelled deliciously of almonds and chocolate.

'Did you make this?' Her eyes were wide as she gazed into her bowl.

'Yes.' He gave her a grin. 'I took it out of the packaging and switched the microwave on, all by myself.'

Kate grinned back. She realised Paul was now also completely relaxed. The arrival of dessert seemed to signal some sort of finish to his interview. The intensity had left him, and when he sat at the table he leaned back a little, holding his bowl in one hand and looking at her with his attractive smile. 'I've never known anyone enjoy a dessert as much as you do, apart from maybe George.'

'Oh, George loves his pudding!' Kate laughed and licked her spoon. 'Actually, I do have to watch what I eat a little, for my job. I can't eat the amount of dessert I'd like every day, but when I go out I make up for it, and enjoy it as much as I can.'

'How much dessert do you think you could eat, if you allowed yourself?' he asked, tucking in to his own bowl.

'I'd eat it for breakfast, dinner, and tea.' Kate suddenly remembered something, and broke into a chuckle. 'For Christmas dinner, George and I have a chocolate starter, followed by turkey dinner, followed by chocolate pudding. It's heavenly.'

She gave a satisfied sigh and filled her spoon. Then greed got the better of her. As she was lifting the loaded spoon to her mouth, a small dollop of cream fell off the edge and dropped. 'Oh.' She slid her finger into the neckline of her dress and scooped up the cold cream from where it had fallen on the top of her breast. She lifted her creamy finger to her lips and raised her head, to find Paul had gone totally still. His gaze was fixed on her mouth.

It was many years since Kate had thought of her body as desirable. Ever since Stuart had died, she'd thought of it as merely a tool of her profession. Her torso was moved this way and that under the camera by people who had no interest in her as a real woman. Clothes were put on and removed from her with clinical dispassion; make-up and hair were styled by people who talked over her head. Her body was an object, advertising clothes for other women to admire.

The intensity in Paul's expression caused a jolt of awareness of herself. A powerful heat spread throughout her body. Paul's eyes were fixed on her, dark and intense, and her skin flamed and burned under their scrutiny. He lifted his gaze from her mouth, and the throbbing hum of her pulse sounded in her ears. There was complete silence in the room, apart from their breathing. Then Kate's fingers relaxed their hold, and her spoon dropped from her hand with a clatter, bouncing from the table to the floor.

'Oh,' she cried again, standing quickly.

Paul stood as swiftly, pushing his chair back. 'Leave it,' he commanded. 'I'll fetch another.'

He took a step towards her, and she drew back. She remembered kicking off her boots under the table, lulled into relaxing by the dessert and Paul's good-humoured conversation. Now she stood in her stockinged feet, feeling exposed, forced to tilt her head slightly to look at him. The heat had vanished from his expression, as though she'd imagined it. He was looking down at her gravely.

With a rising feeling of unease – the same unease she'd felt the day she first met him, that time beside Stuart's pond – Kate finally understood that Paul wasn't the stuffed shirt she'd always dismissed. The Paul Farrell she had just glimpsed was an unknown force.

He bent to retrieve her fallen spoon. She felt the air move around her feet and took a small step backwards.

'I'm sorry.' Her apology was ambiguous. Whether she was apologising for her clumsiness or for her heated reaction to him was not clear, even to her.

Paul pulled himself upright in a slow movement.

'Don't apologise.' His eyes met hers, and then he moved past her.

Kate looked at her bowl, still lying on the table. Suddenly the delicious dessert no longer seemed so appetising. She ducked her head under the table to retrieve her boots. When Paul returned from the kitchen, she was sitting in her chair, pulling up the zips. She lifted her head and saw him standing motionless in the doorway.

'Actually, Paul, it's getting late,' she said. 'I think I'd better get back, if we've finished?'

There was a short silence before he answered. 'Yes, I think I have everything. For now.'

Kate wasn't sure about the sound of 'for now'. She stood, looking up at him uncertainly. He made no move to persuade her to stay, simply turned in the doorway.

'I'll phone for a taxi,' he threw over his shoulder, and a chill descended.

What was the matter with him? Had she imagined the heat in Paul's eyes? She certainly hadn't imagined her response to him. It had come out of nowhere, with overwhelming force. Now she felt vulnerable and exhausted. She wanted to leave, but perversely, she hoped Paul would persuade her to stay.

He returned, carrying her jacket.

'Here,' he said. 'The taxi's on its way. I'll walk you down to the street.'

He settled the jacket around her shoulders.

'Thanks.' Kate hesitated a moment, before adding, 'And thanks for your thoughtfulness. With my favourite dinner, and everything. It was nice.'

Paul smiled, then. 'Yes, it was nice,' he repeated. 'I'm glad you enjoyed it. Next time I'll make you something different.'

Next time. Kate shrugged herself into her jacket without acknowledging his throwaway statement. A terrible awkwardness descended, and now she couldn't wait to be gone.

Paul accompanied her across the corridor and into the clunky lift. They stood together in silence as the lift rattled its way to the ground floor. By the time they stepped out of the building into the cool night air, it seemed all the tension of their relationship had returned. The taxi was waiting at the kerbside.

Paul took hold of Kate's elbow and turned her to face him. 'I know how much you hated it, giving this interview.' His quiet voice was clear in the night air. 'But what you said will help those other girls of yours. Stuart would be proud of you.'

Kate gave a small smile. 'Thanks. For trying to make it easier, I mean.'

He ducked his head swiftly and kissed her cheek, as he had done when she arrived. This time, instead of drawing back quickly, he pulled her to him in a brief embrace, and she caught the scent once more of almonds and chocolate.

'Don't worry about my write up in the paper,' he said. 'Everything will be fine.'

He released her and stepped back.

Kate climbed into the waiting taxi, and gave the driver her directions. Then she turned to wave to Paul, but he'd already gone.

.

CHAPTER FIVE

Paul made his way home from work across Southwark Bridge in his shirt sleeves, his tie loosened, his jacket held in one hand. Normally at this time of day he would still be buzzing. The highly charged atmosphere of the press office, the stresses and strains of his job caused a mental high that he usually enjoyed. Today, though, he felt overwhelmingly tired. The evening was unseasonably warm. The streets had thinned out, and most of the city's commuters had long since left for home. A cruiser passed beneath the bridge, and the sound of music and laughter wafted upwards. To Paul's left the dome of St Paul's gleamed in the setting sun; to his right Tower Bridge lowered its arms, and a line of waiting cars rumbled across. The scenes of the city unfolded all around him, but Paul was oblivious. When a tourist stopped to take a photo, stumbling into him, it barely registered.

The all-consuming nature of Paul's work stopped him having to reflect on the past, but this evening he was weary, and random memories were seeping into his brain. His intention on leaving the office had been to make his way home, but somehow he found himself leaving the bridge and running lightly down the steps onto the Thames embankment. The wooden tables of the local pub were spread out on the concrete flags. Paul bought himself a pint at the bar and went to sit by the river.

Sometimes the sight of the Thames flowing past and the indifference of hordes of Londoners would ease Paul's mind in times of stress. The world flowed on around him regardless, making him feel the insignificance of his own concerns. Today, though, wasn't one of those days when ease came readily. His interview with Katerina was ready for the night's press. He had spent the entire day consumed with thoughts of her.

Paul understood only too well how Katerina had come to think of him. He could see it in the way she spoke to him briskly on the doorstep, on the days when he came to collect George, and in the way she looked at him sidelong through her long lashes, her blue eyes wary. He saw it in the way she rushed to leave him after their interview, her fingers fumbling at the zips on her boots.

Paul had succeeded in what he set out to do, all those years ago, ever since they first met, that time in Stuart's garden. He had set Katerina at a distance. And he had managed so successfully that now he was in a position to change things, he had no idea how to begin.

He raised his head to find the dying rays of the sun twinkling and dancing on the Thames as they had done that day, eight years ago, on a smaller expanse of water. That afternoon, in the heat of summer, when the light had glinted off the glassy pond, making Paul's head ache.

There were times even now when certain events in Paul's life replayed in his head. Mainly they were times of high stress. The time when he and Stuart were on assignment in West Africa, and Paul had been gripped by his fear of flying. The time in Afghanistan when he'd come across dead bodies swinging from a bridge, bloated and fly-ridden. These scenes would burst into his head at the most inconvenient moments and play themselves out there.

And then there was the day he met Katerina. In the quiet evening as he sat by the Thames, the scene began to play out in his mind again, unstoppable, with painful familiarity. He was standing by the French windows. Stuart's garden was a large, rambling expanse, slightly overgrown, and Katerina was nowhere to be seen.

Stuart called out from the kitchen. 'She'll be round by the pond. Go and introduce yourself. She won't bite.'

Reluctantly, he pressed down the door-handle. He was just back from Afghanistan, and his spirits were depressed and strained. Half his mind was still on the scenes he'd left behind. Stepping out onto Stuart's green suburban lawn was unreal, as though he'd entered a world of surreal colour. Paul tried to shrug off his tension as the effects of jet-lag, but as he strode down the long path to the end of the garden, he was filled with a sense of foreboding. When he reached the corner where the fishpond was situated, behind a sheltering willow-tree, he stopped dead.

Kate was kneeling on the low stone wall of the pond, cropped blonde head bent over the water in an attitude of intense concentration, one slender hand slowly skimming the surface. There was something self-contained about her absorption. The movement of her hand was graceful on the water. Heat shimmered on the pond's surface, giving her outline a dreamlike quality.

He must have given some signal of his presence –drawn in his breath a little sharply, perhaps – because her hand jerked with a startled, wet slap on the water. She scrambled to her feet.

'I thought you were Stuart.' Her voice was another surprise. Deep and slow, and older than her years. And her eyes – a striking blue, reflecting the late afternoon sky above them – were level with Paul's chin, even in her bare feet. The dreamlike illusion vanished with her words. She had presence, and she was staring at him with an unnerving curiosity.

'You must be Katerina.'

And then it happened. Something Paul could never explain to himself afterwards, no matter how often he thought of it. Whatever it was, he could swear it affected her with equal strength. Her eyes widened. She took a clumsy step away from him, stumbling against the low wall of the fishpond, her bare arms spread. Before she could fall, he caught her to him, pulling her slight body with ease into his arms.

Her hand, cool and damp from the pond, pressed against the muscles of his chest; her body was fragile in his embrace.

He was conscious of an overwhelming desire to hold her safe.

He looked down into her startled expression and realised she was gazing at him in some trepidation. Of course. The way she regarded him made him feel ashamed of his response. With an effort of will he released his hold, schooling his expression to one of polite enquiry. 'Are you OK?'

She nodded. He wanted to reach out again to reassure her, but kept his arms by his sides. He stepped back, increasing the distance between them.

She raised her gaze to his. 'My friends call me Kate.'

Paul opened his eyes with a start. He looked around him uncertainly before picking up his glass up from the table and taking a long pull on his beer. He could hardly believe he was alone. The air around him seemed to tremble with ghosts of the past.

He'd visited this pub many times with Stuart. Once they'd sat outside after work together, at this same table. Now he felt Stuart's presence beside him, shirt-sleeved, legs stretched out in front of him on the flagstones.

'Is it your round, mate?' Paul said sidelong to his long-dead friend. Trying to make a joke of it, as they used to joke with one another all those years ago, two young trainees out in the city.

All of a sudden the view of the Thames swam in front of Paul's eyes. 'I miss you,' he continued into the empty air. 'And some days I don't know how I'll get through the rest of my life without you.' When his friend didn't reply, Paul rose to his feet. His fingers were trembling slightly as he placed his empty glass on the table. 'Whatever happens now, Stuart, you know I'll always look out for her.'

There was a gentle rustling, and Paul turned. The leaves of a discarded newspaper lifted in the breeze.

'I'm so sorry you're gone,' he whispered.

A passer-by turned to stare at him for a couple of seconds before walking away with quick strides, the heels of her shoes sounding hollow on the flagstones. Paul waited for a while, the

sounds of the city flowing around him. Then he turned to
make his way to the tube station, and home.

*

On Sunday morning Kate was up early, ready for a trip to the
gym. She liked to take George swimming first thing, when the
pool was nice and quiet. Sometimes it was an effort to drag
herself out of bed so early at the weekend, but this morning –
the day her interview with Paul was to appear in print – she
was glad of an excuse to leave the house.

Kate had come to an arrangement with Orla the previous
night, whereby Orla would stay over and read the interview in
the morning, while Kate was out. Then she could prepare Kate
for any 'bad stuff' before she read it herself.

'What do you mean, "bad stuff"?' Orla had asked, looking
at Kate in that way she had when she thought Kate was being
an eejit.

'I've bared my soul,' Kate said. 'And Paul seemed OK while
I was baring it, but you just never know. He's a good journalist.
He got me to say loads, but none of what I said was good. I'm
worried he might tear me to shreds.'

Orla just rolled her eyes. 'You worry too much.'

Kate knew Orla was right, but nevertheless she woke up
that morning actually feeling queasy. As she came downstairs
carrying her gym bag, the letterbox opened with a loud,
metallic thwack, making her jump. Paul's heavy newspaper
spilled through onto the doormat, followed by the sound of
the paper boy's feet crunching down the gravelled path.

Kate reached the bottom of the stairs and scooped the
paper up. She carried it into the kitchen, placing it on the table,
and as she did so the newspaper uncurled, revealing a small
black and white photo of herself, staring back at her from the
headlines.

*Who is Kate Hemingway? Paul Farrell interviews the widow of his
friend, award-winning photographer Stuart Hemingway.*

The photo showed Kate gazing off camera, her head turned
away a little. The fringe of her geometric bob fell over her
brow, hiding her expression.

Kate studied it with a professional eye, and guessed her hidden features were meant to be symbolic, to entice the reader to open up the paper, where all would be revealed. Then she wondered which of her photos Paul had chosen for the inside spread. After her interview, he had surprised her by phoning to arrange for a shoot with his staff photographer.

'I have memory sticks full of studio photos,' Kate had told him. 'Can't I just send you one of those?'

Paul laughed. 'Of course not. We want you to be yourself.'

'Myself?' Her heart quickened. 'I'm never myself in photos. I don't know how to be myself. No one's photographed me as *me* since Stuart died. I'm just there to promote a product.'

There was one of Paul's silences. Then he said, 'OK, I'll come with you.'

Instead of infuriating her, as this statement from Paul might have done only recently, Kate felt strangely reassured. 'Won't you be busy?'

'Come to our offices. It won't take long. We'll shoot round the corner, by the river.'

And so Kate had arrived straight from taking George to nursery, in her leggings and boots, as 'herself'. And instead of it being awkward having Paul there, he'd actually helped her relax. He discussed the shoot with the photographer in that calm way he had, and cracked his deadpan jokes, and then it was all over.

She left the paper on the table and went to the fridge to get herself a glass of juice. The cool liquid eased her throat a little. Orla was right. Just because Paul came from a privileged background, and was lucky to have a happy childhood, didn't mean he was going to look down on her for growing up someone else entirely.

So why did she feel so nervous all the time?

She closed her eyes, leaning back against the fridge. Suddenly she was back in Paul's flat, feeling again the heat in his gaze as she scooped up the cream from her bare skin. She remembered the way his eyes darkened, how he had stared at her parted lips, and she felt her response to him surge anew, warm and quick through her veins …

She lifted the cool glass to her cheek and pressed it there. Behind her, the door crashed open, bringing her to her senses.

'Ugh,' Orla groaned. 'It's Sunday morning. I can't believe you've got your gym things on.'

Kate fluttered her eyes open. 'I know,' she said, shifting herself away from the fridge. 'It's rubbish. But if we go any later the pool is rammed, and then sometimes there are people who sort of recognise me, and they stare. And anyway, George likes space to learn to swim. Speak of the devil,' she added, her smile widening as the door slammed open again, and George tore into the room.

'I've got my things.' He held his sports bag aloft.

'Good work.' Kate ruffled his head. 'Let's just get some cereal and a drink, and we'll be off.'

She began opening cupboards and getting George's breakfast ready. Behind her she heard Orla give a long yawn. Then she heard the sound of the paper rustling.

Kate whirled round. 'Don't open it yet.'

Orla dropped the paper on the table. 'OK, OK.' She held up her hands. 'I will read your interview after you've left the house. Not a moment before.'

'What's an interview?' George broke in. 'Is it bad?'

Orla laughed and shook her head. 'An interview is when someone from a newspaper or the television asks you some questions so they can get to know you. And Paul asked your mum some questions, and now he's written all about her in the paper.'

'Oh.' George's freckled face creased in thought for a moment. 'Well, that won't be bad. Paul likes Mum. He told me.'

'Well, there we are then, nothing to worry about.' Orla turned to Kate with a grin. 'Paul likes you.'

Kate forced her lips into an answering curve. 'You're right, George. Paul said he was my friend, didn't he? So let's let Orla read the paper in peace, and we'll get off to the gym.'

As always, George was the perfect distraction. Whenever

Kate found herself dwelling on memories of Stuart, or worrying about a situation, as she was now, George's boundless zest for life always pulled her out of it.

They spent a long while in the pool, splashing each other and playing around in aimless fun. George could swim well enough to get himself across the smaller pool with his armbands on, and what he lacked in technique he more than made up for in enthusiasm. By the time they'd showered and dressed, both of them had worked up a healthy appetite. Kate had skipped breakfast, and while they were in the changing rooms her tummy rumbled loudly, making George laugh. George himself was on a growth spurt, and seemed to be permanently hungry. They decided they couldn't wait until they got home to eat, so they would go to the gym café and get some scrambled eggs on toast.

Kate had chosen her gym because it had an excellent attitude towards privacy. She still hadn't forgotten the lessons learned at the height of her celebrity, when she first started working as a model. Although nowadays people were far less likely to recognise her, there were only a few places open to the public where she felt comfortable taking George. Everyone had a camera on their phone these days. It wasn't that Kate minded being recognised herself. Her photos were out there, and that was all part of the job. It was just she hated to see strangers snatching photos of her son. Mobile phones were banned in her gym, and had to be kept in the lockers at all times. Anyone caught taking a photo would have their membership withdrawn immediately. So Kate didn't think twice about taking George into the café.

She pushed open the glass doors, and was met with the welcoming smell of toast and coffee.

'Yum,' cried George, taking a small leap. 'Can I get a milkshake?'

There were already a handful of gym goers in the café. They all turned their heads at George's loud exclamation, and several pairs of eyes stared at Kate.

'Shh,' she whispered, half laughing. 'No need to shout. Yes, you can have a milkshake. Good idea. What flavour?'

They crossed the café to the food counter, and as they made their way up the room, the place fell strangely quiet. Kate took a sideways glance, and her heart lurched. Of course, how stupid she was. On almost every table was a copy of Paul's newspaper. Everyone in the café came to relax after their workout and to read the Sunday papers. And there was her photo across the top of every one, and whatever Paul had written about her for all to read inside.

Her throat went dry as she approached the counter. She gave her order and pulled out a tray, wishing she'd thought to put on her baseball cap. George was wearing his, so that was something, at least. Once her tray was loaded, she made her way to a table in a far corner, making sure she and George were both sitting with their backs to the room. Immediately, she wished she hadn't. Now everyone's eyes must be on her, while she was unable to see what was going on.

She bent to blow on her steaming coffee. 'Let's eat up, George, and get back to Orla.'

Fortunately, George didn't need prompting to eat quickly. He polished off his eggs before Kate had taken more than a few bites of her own meal. She decided to leave the rest and was just gulping down the remains of her coffee when she heard footsteps behind her. She stiffened.

'Excuse me.' A girl's voice, shy and tentative.

Kate turned her head. Standing awkwardly behind her was a teenager, aged thirteen or fourteen, clutching a pen and a copy of the *Sunday Magazine*. Kate's eyes dropped to the proffered pen, and the girl blushed.

'Can I have your autograph?' she said. 'I wouldn't normally. It's just I really like you, and when I read your interview … I think what you do with At Home is brilliant.' The girl's eyes failed entirely to meet Kate's. Her gaze fell somewhere between the floor and the table.

'Sure,' Kate answered. 'What's your name?' She took the magazine from the girl's hand and found herself rewarded with eye contact.

'It's Charlotte. Thanks.'

'Did you know about At Home and what we do?' Kate asked.

'Yes. I went –' Charlotte blushed furiously and cast a glance behind her. 'I mean a friend went a few times. 'Cos of bullying, and that.'

Kate signed her name across the cover of the magazine without saying anything. It was clear Charlotte didn't want to say she'd been herself, and Kate respected her privacy. 'You know you can always drop in at any time. And I asked them to print the phone number in the article.' She met Charlotte's gaze. 'Give it a ring if you have any problems.'

'I will.' Charlotte took the paper from her. 'Thanks, Kate.'

The girl return to her table, where a woman Kate took to be her mother was waiting for her. The older woman raised her hand and smiled, and Kate smiled back. Maybe the interview was working already in raising the charity's profile. Chloe would be pleased.

'Why do people want your autograph?' George slurped the remains of his milkshake. 'I don't get it.'

Kate turned back to the table and began stacking the tray with their empty plates. 'George, it's a good job I've got you to talk to,' she said, laughing. 'Otherwise I might start thinking I was important. I bet if David Terry was here, you'd want his autograph.'

'Yeah.' George's eyes lit up. 'That would be awesome. I wish David Terry came to this gym. Paul said he might take me to see a game. Paul said if he takes me in the press room after, we might get to see Terry, and then I could get his autograph.'

'Did he?' Kate stood. 'Well, Paul is very kind.' Her heart began that sinking thing again. It seemed, in George's eyes at least, Paul could do no wrong. Instead of comforting her, the thought only reinforced her sense that Paul's influence on her life seemed to be growing stronger every day.

*

When Kate arrived home with George, the kitchen was empty, the breakfast things tidied away, and there was no sign of Orla or the newspaper. George was eager to go up to his bedroom to play one of his video games. Kate watched him run off up the stairs. The house fell still. She put their wet things in the washing-machine and wandered into the living room. It was all unnaturally quiet.

Orla was sitting cross-legged on the settee, her notebook in front of her, writing furiously. The window to the garden stood open, and the warm summer breeze was lifting the leaves of the newspaper scattered all around her, half on the floor, half beside her on the settee.

Kate's hair was still a little damp after her swim. She shivered in the draught and crossed over to the window to pull it close. Orla raised her head, only just becoming aware of her friend's presence.

'Hey,' she said. 'Back already?' Her expression was a little dazed, as though she'd just come up from a deep sleep. Kate knew how her friend could be once immersed in her writing. It was as though the rest of the world didn't exist.

'We've been gone for hours,' she said, with a smile. She bent to pick up the *Sunday Magazine*, which was lying open and creased on the floor. 'Did you read it?'

'Read it?' Orla laid down her pen. 'I practically bloody well devoured it. Seriously, Kate, do you really have no idea?'

Kate's unease increased tenfold. Her eyes dropped to the crumpled magazine in alarm.

'Sit down and read it.'

When Kate didn't move, Orla raised herself off the settee and came towards her. She took Kate by the arm and steered her gently into one of the armchairs. The expression on Orla's face was no help at all. Her beautiful brown eyes were heavy with emotion, and she stood uncertainly in front of her chair. Kate's heart leapt into her mouth. Now she knew it was something bad. Orla was absolutely never at a loss for words.

'Kate, I don't know how you're going to take this,' her friend said eventually. 'But when I read it, I was actually moved to tears.' She crouched down, laying a hand on Kate's arm. 'I really can't believe I never guessed what was going through that guy's mind, after all these years. He keeps his feelings close.' Her last words came out in a rush. 'I think Paul's in love with you.'

'*What?*' Kate sat up straight, her disbelief ringing round the room. 'Are you crazy? In love! He's so damn polite and stiff. In fact, he's so bloody polite it's intimidating. You've got it way, way wrong.' She shook her head vehemently, staring at Orla in astonishment. Her friend was normally so astute about people.

Orla stood. 'I'll leave you to read it. Tell me then if I'm wrong.'

There was no hint of teasing in her words. Her expression was perfectly grave. The anxiety Kate had experienced ever since asking Paul for help pressed on every nerve ending. There was a terrible sick feeling in her stomach, as though the ground she took for granted had suddenly opened up. She wanted to quiz Orla again, but her friend passed her the magazine and left the room, without saying another word. When Kate lifted it up to read it for herself, she found her hands were shaking.

On the cover of the magazine was a full-length photo of herself, dressed in her dark blue tunic top and black leggings. She was leaning back, one leg bent at the knee, with the high heel of her boot resting against the red brick wall behind her. The photographer had stolen this photo during what was supposed to be a break in the shoot. She'd been caught looking slightly off camera. There was no trace of anxiety in her features. Her eyes were a bright blue in the morning light, and she was laughing.

Kate bent forward. On the day the photos were taken, it hadn't taken long for her to realise Paul had no idea what was involved in a fashion shoot. During their break, he'd claimed her attention for a minute, holding up his mobile and pretending to be one of the paparazzi. He was an excellent mimic, and Kate guessed immediately which one of the tabloid reporters he was taking off. He shuffled forward, and his cry of '*Oi, Kate, over 'ere darlin'!*' made her laugh out loud. That was when the photographer had snapped her.

Kate stared at the photo for several minutes. Of all the photos that were shot that day, Paul had decided to use the one where Kate was smiling directly at him. In that moment she looked more unguarded than she had for a long time. Her features were open, and she looked vulnerable, something she was usually at great pains to conceal. Compared to her usual stylised fashion shoots and cool poses, this photo was a revelation.

Kate chewed her lip, turned the cover and flipped through the pages until she reached the interview.

Who is Kate Hemingway?

Kate Hemingway arrives on my doorstep, fresh from a photo shoot at the Ritz, an expression of wariness on her face. She is wearing a short grey flannel dress and high black boots. A fake fur jacket is wrapped around her shoulders, and there are tiny pearls in the lobes of her ears. Her face is scrubbed of make-up, and her skin so perfectly clear it seems almost radiant. Kate Hemingway is far more beautiful in the flesh than she ever appears in her photographs. She is also thoughtful, and has brought me a bottle of wine ...

Kate's lips parted in amazement. When she'd arrived at Paul's flat that evening it had been shadowy in the corridor. They'd exchanged barely a couple of sentences of greeting before Paul turned to go inside. And yet here he was, with this detailed first impression. She reread the first few lines again, picking out the words he used to describe her. Wary, thoughtful ... *beautiful.*

When she first came to media attention, it seemed every journalist wanted to project something different onto Kate Hemingway. According to which article you read, she was either a heroine of the underclass or a scrounger off the state; a grasping wannabe or a helpless victim of an uncaring society. After her husband, photographer Stuart Hemingway, was killed by a suicide bomber in Kabul, all the labels were forgotten. Everyone unanimously decided Kate was a brave widow and an ordinary working mother.

Kate seems to have remained impervious to public opinion and has never once spoken to the press. The reason she is reluctantly here with me today is to promote her charity, At Home, for whom she works tirelessly. I switch on my recorder, and Kate turns her head in my direction. She meets my gaze squarely, but as soon as the tablet begins to record, I sense her retreat. I've devised a plan to help bring Kate out of her shell. I've made her favourite meal of spaghetti Bolognese. Her beautiful face lights up like a child's, and she smiles.

Kate Hemingway was born Katerina Rudecka twenty-five years ago, in south London …

Kate read on slowly, stopping to read and re-read the same words. Gradually, the interview unfolded before her, not exactly as she remembered it, but from Paul's perspective. It was all there, all the story of her teenage years in their banal and sordid detail.

When Kate tells me of her outburst of rage and her arrest for assault, her expression challenges me to comment. Maybe she expects my reaction to be one of disgust. Instead, I think of the terrified, angry and lonely child she was, and I'm filled with sadness for her.

Kate let out the long breath she had been holding. She put the magazine down for a moment and squeezed her eyes shut. For years, she had thought Paul looked down on her. She felt unexpected tears well. She blinked them away, then stood quickly, taking the magazine to the window, where she stood, breathing in the fresh air as she read on.

The rest of the interview dealt with the time Stuart had come to photograph the squat, the happiness of Kate's marriage, which was all too short-lived, her grief and her devotion to George, and her work with At Home. Chloe had provided Paul with some eloquent quotes in praise of Kate, which dried her tears and brought a smile to her face.

Then came the final paragraph.

So, who is Kate Hemingway? Beneath the reserve she likes to adopt in public – and maybe not as far from the surface as she imagines – lies the teenage Katerina Rudecka: a brave, lonely, and determined young girl who was dealt the wrong cards in life.

As Katerina rises to leave our interview, she gives me one of her rare smiles. It's a smile that transforms her. On the inside and on the surface, Kate Hemingway is quite simply a beautiful person.

And let no one convince her otherwise.

Kate returned to her chair, placing the magazine on the table beside her. Orla's words rang in her head. *The guy's in love with you.* How had everything changed? Had it really changed, or had Paul always been in love, and Kate just blind all these years?

She stared ahead, revisiting every recent conversation, her mind a jumble of emotions in which shock and sadness were uppermost.

'*I've been thinking about asking you out for a while…*'

Paul's comment resurfaced in Kate's brain. She shook her head. Had she really seen nothing?

Orla entered the room, her footsteps unusually quiet.

'Hey,' she said. 'I brought you a cup of tea.'

Kate's turbulent feelings must have been reflected all too clearly, because Orla left the mug on the side table and dropped down beside her.

'Oh, Orla. I really think you're right. He's been in love with me for ages. How could he have hidden it for so long?'

Orla's full mouth curved down. The fact that she felt the misery of the situation only increased Kate's unhappiness.

'All these years I've been thinking he was looking down on me. That he thought Stuart had made a big mistake. Stuffed shirt Paul.' She gripped the arms of the chair. 'And all along – Oh Orla, it's all just too sad. What on earth am I going to do?'

To the horror of both of them, Kate burst into tears, covering her face with her hands. Orla put her arm around her.

'Nothing, hon, nothing. Why do you have to be the one to do something? He's a big tough guy.' She gave one of her rumbling laughs, shaking Kate's shoulder. 'You must have noticed that, at least. Whatever there is to be done, Paul will think of something. Don't upset yourself, Kate. That's the last thing he'd want.'

Kate shook her head. Paul was in love, and none of his feelings were reciprocated. She couldn't begin to imagine how much misery his unrequited love for her must have caused him all these years. She was taken aback at the depth of her compassion for him. It felt almost as though Paul's pain was her own.

Kate dried her tears, brushing away that thought as quickly as it had come. Orla was right about one thing. Paul was a strong person, and he was also resourceful. His write up of her interview had been masterful. No doubt he knew very well what his next step would be, but Kate no longer had any idea what he was capable of, and she was filled with terrible uncertainty. Ever since asking Paul for help, her carefully ordered life since Stuart's death had started to unravel.

Kate drew herself together. She couldn't just wait for Paul to act. Goodness knows what he might do next. It was time to try and wrest back control. Time to get her safe, controlled life back where it was before Paul started to mess with it.

CHAPTER SIX

Kate pressed the bell for Paul's apartment. The camera above whirred round slowly to study her, and she looked up into its unwinking eye. Somewhere on the other side of the lens Paul was able to see her. Which meant Paul saw Kate, but she didn't see him. A reflection of all the years they'd known each other, and she appreciated the irony.

The door buzzed, and Kate stepped inside, as she had what seemed like an age ago. Was it really only a few weeks? The Victorian lift clanked its laborious way upwards. Kate clutched her heavy bag to her, the nerves in her stomach made worse by the swaying lift. The doors rattled open, and she made her way across the corridor.

Paul's head appeared around the door of his flat. This time there was no half-light to hide in. It was Saturday morning, and a bright sun poured through the arched window on the stairwell. When Paul stepped out, his black shadow met Kate's, entwining with it on the wall behind him.

The sunlight lit his serious features. 'Katerina. Good to see you.'

He stepped forward to kiss her, his lips brushing her cheek. The warmth of his body radiated out to her briefly, before he released her. He opened the door wide to let her in.

'Can I get you a drink?' He moved inside. 'A cup of tea?'

He headed away from her down the corridor. Kate stared after him. This was the man who had revealed his affection for her to the nation. And he was talking about tea. It was no wonder she had never once guessed at the depth of his feelings.

'A cup of tea would be nice,' she said faintly. She hung her jacket in the hallway. Paul turned into his kitchen, and Kate stepped through into his living room, in a repeat of her previous visit, only this time by day, and with the light shining clearly on everything.

The curtains were wide, and the sky over the city was a mesmerising blue. Kate crossed the room and gazed down. The River Thames was visible through a break in the surrounding buildings. The surface shone silver today in the sun, with flashes of light in the ripples. As ever, Kate found the sight of the river reassuring. So much trouble and pain and suffering it had seen in this frantic city, and still its waters flowed on. Her own troubles paled beside it. The slow river would be chugging past centuries after she was gone. She gave herself a mental shake at the morbid way her thoughts were taking her. Paul's reflection appeared behind her in the window, and he touched her shoulder.

'I've brought you a drink,' he said. 'Come and sit down with me.'

She took the steaming tea from his hand, but instead of moving to sit beside him on the large settee, she retreated to the armchair opposite, placing her tea on the table beside her.

Paul dropped into the settee, stretching out his long legs. For a couple of minutes there was silence. Only a few weeks previously, Kate would have put the awkwardness down to Paul's reserve. Now she realised there was far more to the constraint between them than that. Paul's feelings for her were now almost tangible in the room. Kate wondered how he had coped all these years with this burden of not being able to express himself, even to his best friend. She stole a glance at him as he sat there, gazing at the coffee table. The weather had been warm recently, and Paul's face was tanned against the cream of his T-shirt. His brow was a little furrowed, but other than that, he seemed at ease. Kate remembered Orla's description of him as a tough guy, and it seemed to her then that Orla was right. He turned his head and caught her studying him. Straightaway, the harshness in the lines of his face softened, and she wondered how on earth she could ever have imagined that he thought of her with disdain.

'What's George up to today?' he asked. 'Is he dragging Orla out in the fresh air?'

It was just the right question to break the ice and dispel the awkwardness a little. Kate laughed and shook her head. Orla was noted for her ability to stay indoors all day scribbling, oblivious to what was happening around her, even on the sunniest of days. If it weren't for George begging her to play ball in the garden, Orla might very well never see daylight at all.

'Orla's gone to Dublin. She's giving a workshop for children as part of their poetry week, and then she's off to Kildare to see her mum. And George is away for the whole weekend with Stuart's parents. They came to pick him up yesterday.'

'That's good of them.' Paul's voice gentled. 'How are they doing?'

Kate reached for her mug and considered the steaming depths for a while before answering. 'They're doing better than they were. George is a great comfort to them.' She lifted her eyes and gave a small smile. 'He's a comfort to me, too. He's always cheerful. Like his dad.'

'Yes.' Paul dropped his head to stare at the legs stretched out in front of him, and for a moment or two they sat in silence. There was nothing else to add. Stuart had been a ball of energy. Everywhere both Kate and Paul looked, he was missing.

Kate took advantage of Paul's silence to resume her covert study of him. His body was motionless as a painting, his chest barely rising and falling under his t-shirt. He had an uncanny ability to remain totally still. Living with Orla and George for so long, restfulness was not a quality Kate was used to. And Stuart, too, had never been able to sit still for long.

In the past, Kate had found Paul's ability to remain quiet unnerving – intimidating, even. Now she found there was much about his stillness that was tranquil. He raised his eyes and caught her watching him again, and she looked away quickly.

'Thanks for your write up,' she blurted out, then kicked herself mentally for her gaucheness. 'I mean, for all the things you said about me. I was really touched.' She felt her cheeks go warm. Really touched. Was that the best she could do? His eyes were on her, unmoving. She reached down to the bag at her feet and pulled it onto her knee.

'And thanks for seeing me today.' She clutched the closed bag. 'I've brought you some things,' she continued, her grip tightening. 'Some things of Stuart's. I'd like you to have them. I-–I'd been meaning to give you them sooner, but –' She stopped. It had taken her years to go through Stuart's things without her heart breaking inside her again.

The lines in Paul's brow deepened.

'Of course if you'd sooner not –' she faltered.

He leaned forward. 'No, of course. Thank you.'

She held the bag towards him wordlessly. It swayed a little in her outstretched hand.

Paul reached forward to take it, his fingers brushing hers. 'Are you sure?' he asked. 'Sure they aren't things you'd like to keep for yourself? Or pass to George?'

'They're yours.' Kate shook her head, leaning back in her chair. 'You should have them.'

He placed the dark cotton bag on the seat next to him and pulled out the first item he found. He gazed at it for a second or two, then leaned forward, resting his elbows on both knees.

'Good times,' he said, lifting his head to Kate with a small smile. In his hands was a framed photo of the two friends standing together in a garden. They were each holding a pint of beer, and they were grinning at each other, eyes alight with mischief. Kate had often wondered what the joke was. If Paul remembered, he wasn't telling. He stared at the photo before putting it down on the floor, propped against the settee.

Then he felt again in the bag, this time bringing out a vinyl record in a monochrome sleeve. It was a band they'd both loved. Paul had once managed to blag his way backstage, using his journalist's credentials. He'd given Stuart the autographed album one birthday.

'Wow,' he said, studying the sleeve. 'I'd forgotten all about this.'

He kept his gaze on the record, lost in thought, until Kate broke in on his abstraction. 'There's something else in the bag.' He propped the record against the settee with the framed photo. The last item was a red jewellery box. It had got lodged in a corner of the bag. Paul drew it out and flipped open the lid. Inside was a pair of gold cufflinks. He lifted them out with his finger and thumb. The cufflinks clinked together gently when he placed them on his palm.

'My wedding present to Stuart.'

'Yes,' Kate said quietly, searching his face. 'He wore them the day we got married.'

'I remember.' Paul turned them over and read out the inscription. '*Man up.*' His smile grew a little wider, deepening the creases either side of his mouth.

Paul had had the words engraved specially. Kate remembered how the present had made Stuart laugh out loud. Now in the quiet of his living room Paul gave a quiet laugh too as he touched the cufflinks with one finger.

'Stuart never would tell me what the joke was,' Kate said.

'No.' Paul met her curious gaze. The amusement in his eyes shifted to something a little more sheepish. 'Maybe he didn't want to embarrass me.'

'To embarrass *you*?' Kate stared at him as though such a thing were impossible, and he gave a short laugh.

'Yes, me. Is that so hard to believe?' His long fingers curved over the cufflinks, hiding them in his palm. 'Shall I tell you the story?'

She nodded. She'd always wondered what Paul meant by the inscription. Whenever she'd tried to wheedle the truth out of Stuart, he'd just laughed and said nothing.

'It was on one of our first assignments together.' Paul leaned back against the worn cushions of his settee, stretching out his legs again. 'We were reporting from West Africa and we'd gone behind rebel lines. Our story made a stir at the time, and Stuart got some really excellent shots. Later he won an award for one of them. You might remember. Anyway, to cut a long story short, we knew we weren't in a great position.'

Kate frowned. She knew just how dangerous the 'position' would have been, as Paul euphemistically called it. Was this why Stuart wouldn't talk to her about it? Because he thought she would worry?

Paul continued talking, matter-of-factly, as though he was describing one of their days away to a rugby match. 'Word got out about us, and our location became known. We got advised by our contacts behind the lines to get out.' He heard Kate's involuntary intake of breath and looked up. 'Don't worry, we were safe. It wasn't as bad as I'm making out.'

She raised her eyebrows. If it had been Stuart, she would have pressed him; would have made him tell her the truth about just how serious it had been. On the other hand, Stuart had never even mentioned this incident to Kate at all. He tended to hide things from her. Even after they'd been married for years, Kate would discover something that Stuart had failed to tell her, and when she questioned him about it, he would say he didn't want to worry her. At least Paul was talking to her about their assignment, even if he was making little of the danger.

'So how did you get out?'

'We got some help.'

'Some help?' Kate shook her head. 'You make it sound so ordinary. Like you got a taxi home from the pub.'

Paul grinned. 'Well, in a way. The army sent a helicopter to pick us up. Me and Stuart and our translator, and a couple of other guys.' His smile faded, and he picked up one of the cufflinks and studied the inscription, not speaking for a while. Then, as though it was an afterthought, 'Stuart knew perfectly well I'd be terrified.'

Kate's jaw dropped. Was this Paul speaking? Paul admitting he was frightened? 'Well, of course you were,' she exclaimed. 'Anybody would be. Wasn't Stuart frightened?'

He looked up at that and caught her expression. He gave a short laugh. 'No, we weren't scared of getting shot.' He laughed again, and Kate wondered what on earth was so funny. Paul jingled the cufflinks in his palm. 'It wasn't the rebel army I was afraid of. I was terrified of getting on a plane.' Kate's eyes widened in astonishment. He gave a wry, twisted smile. 'Getting into a helicopter is a particular nightmare. When that damn tin machine landed to pick us up, blades whirling so you could hardly hear yourself speak, and all that dust blowing everywhere, into your mouth and in your eyes, we went running towards it like a scene from a hellish film. I got all the way up to the open door –' He released a shuddering breath, closing his eyes for a second. 'I can still feel it now. Army guys shouting down, all that dust and racket. The thought of having to take off in one of those blasted machines again was more than I could stand.'

'So what did you do?'

Paul looked down at his fingers, wrapped once more around the cuff-links. 'Everyone else scrambled in until there was just me, with Stuart at my back. I was just going to turn round and tell him to forget it, to go on ahead without me and I'd make my own way through the hills, when I felt his hand grab the scruff of my neck. He looked livid. You know Stuart, he never swore and he never lost his temper, but he did this time. He shouted right in my face: "Man up and get in the sodding chopper!"' Paul burst out laughing. 'I was so surprised, I just did it. I scrambled in, with him pushing me by the seat of my trousers. And then when he got in, we looked at each other and just laughed our heads off. The crew were staring at us like we were nuts. We laughed and laughed about it pretty much all the way back to the station. And then every time one of us wavered about something after that, no matter what it was, the other one would say "man up and get in the sodding chopper!"'

Paul's laughter dwindled to a smile. Then his mouth turned down in a deep curve, and his expression grew distant, lost in the past. For a while they both sat there in silence. Kate watched Paul, deep in his thoughts, and realised she'd never in her life seen him open up like this. For so long she'd wondered what Stuart had loved about his friend, and now she was finally beginning to understand.

As she watched, the curve of his mouth became a thin line. He bent forward. When he lifted his gaze, the softness had disappeared, and his eyes were bright and harsh.

'You know the real reason why I gave him these for a wedding present?' The cufflinks were hidden in his clenched fist.

Kate frowned, puzzled. 'Was it not what you just said? That story you just told me?'

Paul shook his head. 'A few weeks before you got married, Stuart got cold feet.'

Kate sat forward quickly

He held up his hand. 'It's not what you think. But one night he came round to the flat. Came to tell me he didn't think he should go through with it.'

'What?' Kate stared at him open-mouthed. 'I don't understand.' This was the first she'd ever heard of it. Stuart had never whispered a word about this conversation in the entire time they were married. 'What did he mean? If he said he loved me, why didn't he want to get married?'

'Well, that was the reason. He loved you too much. Said he thought he'd make you unhappy. Said he thought you might be too young, that you'd grow up and get tired of him –'

'That's rubbish. I knew from the start I loved him. Right from when we very first met. I never wanted to be with anyone else.'

'I know.' Paul raised his hand palm up and gave a rueful smile. 'But that didn't stop Stuart worrying. He thought you might change your mind later, when it was too late. And he worried he'd be spending too much time away from you on assignments, that he'd be leaving you alone too much, and – and that something might happen to him.'

Kate shook her head violently. 'I understood all that and I didn't care. I wasn't a child. I wanted to be with him, no matter what. Right from the start –' She gave a painful gasp and looked down at her hands, which were clenched tightly on her lap. 'I loved him more than anything.'

'Yes.' Paul stopped for a moment, and dropped his gaze to

the cufflinks. 'I knew right from when I first met you how much you –' A muscle worked in his jaw. Then he carried on. 'I told Stuart the same,' he said, measuring his words slowly and carefully. 'I said I could see how much you were in love with him, and that to walk away from you would cause you unbearable pain. I told him not to be an ass and to stop worrying. That's when I told him to man up.' He let out a harsh laugh.

For a moment, there was silence in the room. Kate was incapable of replying. There was a terrible constriction of grief in her throat, and she couldn't make a sound. She kept her eyes resolutely on her own fists clenched on her lap, swallowing several times. Out of the corner of her eye she noticed Paul's fingers uncurl. The cufflinks fell on the rug, clinking softly before rolling still. She raised her head, and saw that the balls of his palms were pressed to his eyes.

'If I'd had any idea –' He spoke with head bowed, his voice coming clearly, with desperate control. 'If I'd had any idea how much pain Stuart was going to cause you, I would have throttled him then and there with my own bare hands.'

He gave a bitter laugh at the irony of his words.

Kate stared at his covered face, appalled. His hands were screwed into fists, and his shoulders shook. She started up from her chair.

'Paul!'

She gazed horror-struck at his bent head. This was Paul, and he was *crying*. Stuffed shirt Paul, who always seemed capable of anything, who never for an instant lost his cool, who even at Stuart's memorial service had given a measured eulogy, and had never so much as bowed his head in grief. His shoulders continued their terrible shuddering, and she ran forward to kneel beside him.

'Paul, Paul,' she whispered urgently. She tugged his fists from his face. 'Paul, what you told Stuart was right. They were the best years of my life. I wouldn't change them for anything in the world.'

'Have you any idea –?' he began, his fingers tightening on

hers so that she almost cried out. 'Have you any idea how hard it's been to see you in such pain, and not be able to do a single damn thing to help you?'

She caught Paul's face in her hands, and then somehow she was sitting on his knee, cradling his head, soothing him as he had once soothed her. All the misery of their loss flooded through her, and her face crumpled. She murmured Paul's name again and again, as much to reassure herself as to calm him, holding him helplessly while his shoulders shook. The muscles in his back were rigid. She reached her fingers to the back of his head, pressing them into his short cropped hair, pulling him closer to her, trying to soothe the terrible shaking.

She bent to drop a gentle kiss on the top of his head, and at the same time he moved, so that his mouth was close to hers. In tense silence, they gazed at each other, their brows almost touching. In the depths of Paul's eyes, Kate saw her own turbulent emotions reflected. And then his hand moved to cradle the nape of her neck, and he pulled her to him. His lips found hers. Kate's fingers twined around his head. He shifted her on his knee, and one of his hands fell to her waist to curl around her in a gentle hold. His lips were warm, and she returned their pressure. He held her to him with care, as though afraid of hurting her. His strong hand was gentle on her waist. When she opened her mouth under his he gave a groan and pulled her to him more firmly, running his hand from her waist to her thigh. For a long while their kiss held, and then Paul's hand shifted on Kate's body, and his warm, gentle fingers moved under the soft linen of her skirt to caress her naked skin.

She lifted her head, breaking their kiss, and rested her brow against his. His eyes shimmered, and his quick, warm breath caressed her cheek.

His hand stilled on her bare skin. 'Should I stop?' he asked quietly.

The question hovered between them in the stillness of the room. The blue of Paul's eyes darkened. A pulse was beating urgently at his temple. Without speaking, Kate moved her hand from where it lay on the nape of his neck, to place her palm gently against his hard chest, as she had done once before, that day they first met. She felt his heart leap again beneath her fingers, as it had done all those years ago. As perhaps she had known deep down his heart would always leap for her. She shook her head slowly, moving her fingers on his chest to open the buttons of his shirt. She placed her hand on the smooth skin beneath and heard him draw in a breath.

'Don't stop,' she said softly.

His hands tightened around her, and he bent his head to take her mouth in his, bending her back in his arms until he blotted out the light with the depth of his kiss.

CHAPTER SEVEN

Violet-tinged dusk drifted over the streets and filtered through the slatted blinds of Paul's room, casting a gentle haze over his sleeping figure. Kate lay for a while with her head turned towards him, gazing at him as he slept. The sheets were round his waist, and the light fell in soft stripes on the outlines of his torso, smoothing the planes of his features. She reached out a hand to touch the downward curve of his mouth, then withdrew it, afraid of waking him.

Afraid. She pondered the word and knew that wariness wasn't an emotion she felt with Paul any more. She was no longer cautious of him, as she had been when she was a teenager. Now she wondered what it was about him that had filled her with unease, for all those years, and a terrible thought entered her mind. Was it *this*? Was it because deep down she'd known, all this time, how her body would react to him? Even when she was married to Stuart? Was this what she'd been frightened of, all that time?

The thought hit her with a sickening thump, making her feel dizzy, even though she was lying with her head on the pillow. It seemed only a short while ago she was standing awkwardly with Paul outside her house, willing him to be gone. Now she was willing him to wake, to hold her in his arms and make love to her again, with all the passion she knew him capable of. She turned her head to stare at the ceiling. How was it possible to feel this way? She wondered if she had betrayed Stuart, and the thought caused the ceiling to swim above her.

She rolled over carefully on the bed, moving Paul's hand from her waist slowly so as not to waken him, and swung her feet over the side. For several minutes she sat there gazing at the wooden floor, wanting to stand but somehow unable to make her limbs do as she wished.

She didn't heard Paul stir, didn't hear so much as his breath quicken. Nothing to indicate he was awake. Then his voice came softly from behind her on the bed. 'Don't tell me you're regretting it.'

Kate pressed the tips of her fingers to her mouth and averted her head, looking down at the floor. She had no idea how to respond.

Paul too was silent for several minutes. Then he took in a deep breath. 'You know I would never do anything to hurt you. I think you must know by now how much I've always loved you.'

Kate moved her hands upwards to cover her face. She tried to bank back the sobs but they came in an unstoppable well. She longed for Stuart to return, and for the comfort of their relationship. Now everything was uncertain, and she had no idea what she was supposed to do. And then she thought of Paul, and the burden of unrequited love for her that he had carried for years, and her misery increased.

All of a sudden he was there, sitting beside her. He scooped her up onto his knee and held her, their naked limbs entwined. Her hot tears dripped through her fingers and onto his chest.

'I'm sorry,' she said after a while, when the sobs seemed to be subsiding. 'I always seem to be sitting on your knee, one way or another.'

'My knee is at your disposal,' he said gravely.

'It's a good knee,' she agreed, with the last of her sobs.

Lying against his chest, she felt the vibration of his quiet laugh. 'I'm glad you think so. But if you ever find you don't like my knee, I'll have it cut off. Just say the word.'

Kate breathed an answering chuckle into his chest and he went still.

'Stay with me tonight,' he said softly.

She pressed her face closer into him.

'Stay with me,' he repeated. He threaded his fingers through her hair, and caressed her. 'Sleep next to me. Just this one night.'

The green shoots of a new, fragile emotion stirred within

Kate. She nodded. Immediately, Paul's arms tightened around her. She felt his strong heart beat against her breast. For a while they sat there in the fading light, until finally Kate lifted her head to wipe her wet cheeks with the back of one hand.

'You know, you're not really a stuffed shirt, after all,' she said.

There was an ominous silence as both Kate and Paul realised what she'd just said. She sat up straight on his knee, turning a horrified gaze to his.

Paul gave her a small, incredulous shake. 'Did you just call me a stuffed shirt?'

'It's what Orla says, not me,' she said quickly.

'You little fibber.' He squeezed her rib cage, and she laughed with relief. 'Don't blame Orla.'

He turned and pushed her onto the bed, tickling her ribs until she laughed out loud.

'I'm sorry, Paul!' She tried to wriggle away from him but he held onto her, his fingers working their way inexorably up and down her ribs until they found her most ticklish spot. She began to laugh and shriek out loud, her legs thrashing under him in a vain attempt to throw him off. Eventually he caught hold of her hands and pinned them above her flushed face.

'Let's see if you think I'm a stuffed shirt by tomorrow.' He lowered his head to hers and she breathed in, a most delicious thrill of anticipation running through her.

*

Kate stood by her kitchen window gazing out into the garden. Behind her, Orla was at the table, typing into her laptop. Kate listened to the sound of the rhythmic tapping and tried to choose the right words to begin a conversation. Several times she had run an opening sentence through her mind, imagining how it would be if she actually broke in on Orla's concentration and said the words.

'Orla, you know last week when you were in Ireland? I slept with Paul.'

She tried that one out for size in her head, and came to the conclusion that it had way too much shock value. It went nowhere near explaining the shift in the relationship between herself and Paul, and would provoke only amazement.

She tried another. 'Orla, you know you said you thought Paul was in love with me? Actually, you were right, and we've slept together.'

That one was pretty good, but again held a bit too much surprise in it. She decided on a gentler approach, and turned. Orla was deep in thought, staring at her screen, a cooling mug of tea next to her.

'Orla, are you doing anything on Friday? It's just that I was going to meet Paul for a drink after work, and I wondered if you'd be able to have George.'

Orla raised her head absently. 'OK, love. I expect you have a lot to talk about.'

She turned back to her screen, without adding anything more. Kate stood beside her, gazing down at her in astonishment. It was so unlike Orla not to leap on what she'd said and press her for all the details. Kate and Paul had never once been out together alone, apart from the time they met for dinner, and that was only business. Maybe Orla hadn't registered what she'd said.

'I went over to Paul's at the weekend,' she continued. 'While you were in Ireland. I wanted to thank him for the interview. Actually, we got on really well. You'd be surprised how well.'

Kate twisted her fingers as she gazed down at Orla, waiting for her reaction.

'Uhuh.' Orla continued to stare at her screen, and then typed in a couple more words without looking up.

Kate leaned forward. 'Are you all right, Orla?'

Her friend turned to her then, focusing sharply. 'Yes, why?'

'I don't know. You just seem a little out of it. Is everything OK with your family?'

Orla snorted. 'Yeah, right as it ever will be on the funny farm.' She finally closed the lid of her laptop and stood, patting Kate's arm. 'I'm sorry if I seem a bit off. It's just this deadline I have for my latest book. And a couple of other things with my publisher.' She shifted her gaze.

'Oh.' Kate wrinkled her forehead. 'Is it too much, having George so often? I can see about the after school club. Or ask one of the other mums for help.'

'You know I love looking after George.' Orla patted her arm. 'But maybe you should look into getting some extra help once in a while.' She turned to the table and began fiddling with her papers. 'Just in case.'

'In case of what?' Kate studied her friend, puzzled. There was something going on that wasn't quite right. Their eyes met, and she realised Orla was returning her gaze with an amused look of her own, as though she knew Kate, too, had a secret she wasn't telling.

'I may have to take on some extra work,' she explained, still vague. 'It's not that I don't want to have George. I just think it's best to be prepared for the times when I can't.' Then she added, 'I'm glad you're seeing Paul on Friday. Didn't I say it would do you good to get out more?'

Kate felt herself blushing. 'It's only a drink,' she said. 'Don't get any ideas.'

Orla's teasing look faded, and she laid a hand on Kate's arm. 'I'm glad you're getting to know him. He's a great guy, under that stiff upper lip. And he's been a loyal friend. Just try not to break his heart.'

Was there nothing Orla didn't guess at? Kate's cheeks grew warmer. 'Paul's much tougher than I am. We both know that,' she said.

Orla dropped her hand. 'I suppose you're right. You will be careful, though, won't you hon?'

Kate nodded, although often she felt no matter how careful she was, her life was just whirling around her, beyond her control.

*

The days leading up to Friday were among the hottest London had ever known, and Kate had difficulty sleeping. Each night, her thoughts chased each other round and round in her sultry room. Sometimes she would wish her relationship with Paul could go back to how it had been, with their polite, chilly exchanges on her doorstep. She had known where she stood then. But mostly she lay awake thinking of Paul, of his arms around her, of the way he had spoken her name with such low and urgent passion. *Katerina* ... Her heart would jump, and she would be forced to throw off the thin sheet covering her, and to try and cool her burning skin in the fitful draught from the window. When Kate dwelt on the tenderness in Paul's embrace that night, on the intensity of his feelings for her, an answering emotion reared up inside her, wild and irrepressible.

On the night before she was due to see him Kate swung her legs over the side of her bed and sat up, abandoning the struggle to sleep. Her exhausted mind blazed with conflicting emotions of desire and doubt. For a long while she sat there, gazing out at the city through her window, the sound of her heart's rapid beating thudding in the quiet of the room. The wail of a siren in the distance brought her to her senses, and she wrapped her arms around herself. She glanced at her bedside clock, and her eyes fell on her wedding photo. Stuart had his arm around her waist and was smiling down at her. Kate felt all the loss of those uncomplicated days, and a swell of sadness rushed through her.

She picked up the photo and held it in her lap, bending her head over the frame. Stuart's face was averted, looking down at her younger self. She ran her finger gently down his cheek.

'What should I do, Stuart?' Her whisper threaded through the room. Minutes passed, and somewhere a church clock struck the hour, the chimes sounding clearly in the heat of the night. Stuart didn't answer. Kate laid down on her bed, and squeezed her eyes shut.

*

On Friday evening, Paul sat in the shade of the hotel garden where he was to meet Kate, a glass of cold beer in one hand. The heat wave blanketed the city. His tie and jacket lay discarded on the wooden table, and his shirt sleeves were rolled to the elbows. Behind his chair a bank of heather was alive with bees. The sweet scent of the herbs and the gentle sound of their humming completed a relaxed Friday evening scene. To an outside observer, Paul appeared totally at ease, his legs stretched out in front of him. On closer inspection, the hand holding the glass was gripping it a little too firmly.

He took a slow sip. Ever since the weekend with Kate, his heart had beat a little too rapidly. At work, his secretary had noticed that underneath his usual calm decisiveness he was distracted. Twice he had forgotten to return a call. He laughed off her concern, telling her his uncharacteristic lapse in concentration was due to the oppressive heat.

When Kate appeared in the doorway to the garden, looking deliciously cool and fresh in her white sundress, he placed his beer on the table and stood. 'Katerina.'

She drew near, and he bent to kiss her cheek. The clean, fresh scent of her skin drew him close, and it required a huge effort of will not to pull her into his arms there and then. He took a step back, looking down into her upturned face, so tantalisingly near to his.

'How are you?' he asked.

'I'm well, thank you, Paul.' Her eyes were hidden behind her sunglasses, but Paul sensed immediately that she was teasing.

He laughed. 'It was a serious question,' he said. 'Here, take a seat.'

He drew forward one of the wrought-iron chairs and helped her into it, before sitting himself. Kate was still smiling, that small, teasing smile she gave, when she was part laughing at him. He leaned forward, propping his arms on his knees.

'What's the joke?' He felt himself beaming like an idiot. He was intensely happy to see her.

'Nothing. That is, it's not a funny joke, as in ha ha. It's just something that makes me smile.'

'So, what? Tell me.'

'It's just I like how you're always so polite. You ask me how I am, every time, even when I've only just seen you. And you stand up, and you wait to sit down again until I'm sitting. You're always so considerate. I used to think you were stiff, but now ...'

'But now you know me better, and you see what an awesome kind of guy I am, in every way,' he finished for her. She laughed, her red lips parting. 'And now you know I'm definitely not a stuffed shirt,' he added, in a low voice.

He watched her cheeks turn a delicious shade of pink. Then the waitress approached and Paul drew back, allowing the young girl to place a tall, ice-filled glass on the table beside them. She stared at Kate as she did so, eyes widening in recognition. Kate responded with a friendly smile, and was rewarded with a beaming grin. Then the young girl glanced enquiringly in Paul's direction.

'Could I have another beer please?' he asked. 'Thank you.'

Kate cast him another teasing glance as the waitress disappeared. 'Even when people are staring, they still get the Mister Farrell courtesy.'

Paul laughed and lifted the remains of his beer. 'It's really good to see you.'

Kate took off her sunglasses and raised her cocktail, returning his toast. Then she bent her head to drink. Paul's eyes fell to her full mouth around her straw. She drank thirstily, releasing the straw with a sigh, before running her tongue over her lips. She caught him looking and went perfectly still. Her blue eyes, which so readily reflected the heat-filled sky, fastened on his.

'Paul,' she said quietly. Their eyes held for several seconds. He saw only too clearly the desire and doubt chasing each other on Kate's expressive face.

'Don't tell me you regret it.' He repeated the same quiet words he had spoken in the dusk, in the shadows of his room. He wanted to take her in his arms as he had done that night, to make her feel the passion he knew she shared with him. If he could pull her closer, if he could seal in the doubts he knew were troubling her, and not allow them to escape …

A burst of laughter arose from a nearby table, and he cursed the lack of privacy. It was a mistake to meet Kate here. A movement over her shoulder caught his eye. He looked up and gave another inward curse. Now he knew for certain that arranging to meet in this public place was definitely a bad decision.

*

When Paul leaned back in his chair there was a chilly expression on his face that Kate recognised, and her heart sank. Then she heard a smooth, rather sardonic voice above her head.

'Paul.'

She turned. Standing just behind her, and a little too close for comfort, was the journalist Barrie Dickson. His gaze dropped to Kate's, and she tilted her head. His small eyes gleamed in recognition.

'Katerina, I'm sure you know Barrie.' Paul's tone was polite, as always. Only those who knew him closely would recognise the lack of warmth.

Of course Kate knew Barrie. He worked for the *Shaftesbury* – or the *Shaft*, as it was known. The derogatory abbreviation summed up Barrie's style of tabloid journalism. He'd spent some time stalking Kate before her wedding, at the height of her unwanted celebrity, trying to find any dirt he could. When it was clear Kate wasn't going to be falling drunk out of any night clubs or sleeping with someone she shouldn't, Barrie had got bored and moved on. It appeared Kate led too dull a life for Barrie's brand of journalism. Or maybe until now. The way the journo's lizard-like eyes were flicking from Kate to Paul, it was obvious she had rekindled his interest.

'Yes, I –'

'Mrs Hemingway,' Barrie said. There was a light, lingering emphasis on the *Mrs*. 'Is it OK if I call you Kate?' His mouth widened in a smile. He moved to Kate's side, looking down at her. She sat up straight.

'Barrie, you've always called me Kate,' she said tartly. 'All the times you were shouting out my name in the street. The times you kept trying to look up my skirt. Remember?'

Barrie's dark eyes remained fixed on hers. He laughed, not unpleasantly. 'Good times, weren't they? But there was never anything to find on you, Kate. Squeaky-clean Kate, we used to call you.' He made the nickname sound something to be ashamed of. Kate bit down her anger and he turned to Paul. 'Maybe we were looking in the wrong direction, Paul, eh? Nice interview in your Sunday rag.' His quick gaze flicked once more between them. 'Good to see you're looking after Stuart's widow.'

The insinuation was unashamed. Kate felt her face flush with anger. Paul leaned back in his chair, one arm propped on the table, the picture of ease.

'Nice try, Barrie,' he said. 'I'd ask you to sit down, but Katerina and I are discussing her project with At Home. See you around.'

Barrie merely laughed. Paul's dismissal pinged off his thick hide.

'Yeah, maybe you will at that,' he countered. He lifted his hand in a mock wave, before moving off to join his colleagues.

Kate sat back, rubbing her brow with her fingers.

'Don't let him rile you. He's just an annoying little gnat.' Although Paul appeared relaxed, and his long legs were still stretched out in front of him, his eyes were hard as he watched Barrie walk away. 'Although I wonder what he's up to.'

'What do you mean?'

Paul shrugged. 'Sometimes I just get a hunch. But maybe it's nothing.'

'Do you mean they're going to be gossiping about us?' Kate persisted.

He turned at that. 'About you and me? I don't know. That's not what I meant. But if they did, would you mind?'

Kate left it slightly too long before answering.

'I see.' His eyes were watchful. 'You don't want us to be seen together.'

Kate shook her head vehemently. 'That's not it. It's just that I need some time to think.'

The waitress chose that moment to reappear, carrying Paul's beer, and Kate cursed the interruption. Now it was impossible to gauge Paul's reaction. He had his polite mask back on as the waitress placed his beer on the table.

'Thank you,' he said. The waitress nodded, and smiled, and walked away.

Kate reached for her own drink and began fiddling with the straw. 'I've been thinking a lot this week. You see how things are.' She jerked her head in Barrie's direction. He was standing at an angle to them, still surreptitiously watching their conversation. 'My interview with you in the *Sunday Magazine* has got the press interested again, just like you said. And I didn't care before, but now as soon as we're seen together, people will have us marrying each other in no time. Or even worse, saying we were having an affair before Stuart even died.' She screwed her eyes closed. 'If that sort of rumour got out, I don't think I could bear it. It would be just too painful for words.'

Paul leaned towards her. 'You know we have something good between us,' he said quietly. 'Something worth a lot more than caring what other people say.'

She faced him then. 'There's not just me. I wouldn't care what other people say, if there was. But it's not fair to George, and to Orla, to put them through all the gossip. Not when –' She cast him a swift glance. 'Not when we're not even sure how this is going to end up.'

'I'm not going to let dross like Barrie get between us.'

To any onlooker – to Barrie, or to one of his braying friends in the corner of the garden – there was nothing out of the ordinary in Paul's expression. He still seemed relaxed, and was sitting back in his chair now, one hand wrapped loosely around his half empty glass. But close to, there was a terrible implacability about him.

'What do you mean?'

'I mean I'm not going to sit back and watch you walk away. Not now. Not without a fight. And especially not because of some dickhead from the *Shaft*.'

Kate gave a shaky laugh. 'Paul, everything's changing too fast for me. Last week I thought you were someone else. Someone predictable.' She scanned the hotel garden and the groups of Friday evening drinkers as though she'd fallen asleep and woken in a strange world. 'Now I find you're someone entirely different. Someone passionate, and determined and … and almost totally the opposite of the person I thought,' she finished helplessly. 'I need some time to get used to you.'

'I haven't changed. I've been the same person, ever since we met.'

'Then I've been a stupid idiot.' Kate swung her head towards him. 'Paul. I never had any idea –'

He shifted in his seat, resting his elbows on his knees. 'Hey,' he said gently. 'Why should you? And don't look so sad. Otherwise I'll be forced to kiss you, and slimy Barrie will have his story.'

Her laugh was half-hearted. 'You must know it came as a shock, when I read your interview.' She spread her hands. 'It just changed everything. I thought I was starting to be OK, living by myself, and now … I just don't know if I can go through all the pain of loving someone else again. Everything was just so much easier before I knew all this.'

The past few sleepless nights had taken their toll. Kate felt tears begin to form behind her eyes. Not wanting to give Barrie and his cronies the story they were looking for, she fumbled for her sunglasses.

Paul bent further forward, his head close to Kate's. 'I know you, Katerina. I don't believe you would ever settle for an easy life, when there is so much more just waiting for you.'

Kate squeezed her eyes shut behind her sunglasses. She sensed the warmth of Paul's body inches from hers. How would it be to accept him into her life? To have his solid presence with her always. To sleep in his arms every night and know he was always there for her.

Her eyes flew open. But *always* didn't exist. She had thought her life with Stuart would be for ever, but that life was smashed in little pieces.

'I know I'm not Stuart,' Paul continued quietly. 'But I love you with every fibre of my being. And if you can't return my feelings in the same way –' His voice tripped on these words, but he continued to regard her steadily. 'I know I can love you enough for both of us. And I will do all in my power to try and make you and George happy again.'

Kate closed her eyes.

'Katerina,' he said softly. 'Take a risk.'

The sound of chattering voices mingled with the muffled noise of glasses rattling and the shouted orders from the hotel kitchen. Strange how her whole world had changed, and yet other people's lives went on, indifferent. She thought of how alone she felt most of the time, and the thought of taking shelter in Paul's love was overwhelmingly seductive.

She wished there were someone there to help her; someone to give advice, as Stuart had helped her when he was alive. But Stuart was dead now, and when she spoke to him in the night, the only answer she received was silence. She thought of Orla, and knew that Orla would tell her to follow her own heart. The trouble was her heart was so crisscrossed with scars, she wondered sometimes if it had any idea any more what direction it was going in.

Her eyes flew open. 'I need some time. To get used to the different you. Everything is so new to me. And it's not just about me. There's George, and Orla, and then there's the At Home trip in a couple of weeks. It might even be awkward with Chloe, if she discovered we were in a relationship. She might wonder why I'd asked you. It doesn't seem very professional.'

The steady determination in Paul's expression didn't waver, but he nodded once, slowly.

'OK. I understand you need some time. We'll wait until we return from the girls' trip to Yorkshire, and then we'll talk again.' He lowered his voice and added with a smile that softened the steeliness in his features. 'This time we'll meet at my flat. Where I can persuade you properly.'

Kate smiled back, relieved he had understood so quickly. 'OK, at your flat,' she consented. 'But don't try anything underhand when I get there.'

Paul laughed then, and lifted his glass. A shaft of light dropped through the branches of the tree sheltering the garden, and his blue eyes gleamed.

'Once we're back from Yorkshire, I'm not making you any more promises. And I intend being ruthlessly underhand.'

CHAPTER EIGHT

The heat in London was an enervating drag on the city, slowing its movements. It was still early morning when Kate emerged from her taxi, but already warm air was rising from the pavement in a dirty haze. A gaggle of teenagers was gathered around the coach, buoyant and animated, despite the oppressive warmth. Kate took in their chirpiness and remembered with nostalgia her own teenage years, when after a night with barely any sleep she could still get up raring to go.

Kate had been up since five that morning, in a house alive with excitement. Orla was taking George for their holiday at the seaside, and they'd both leapt out of bed, giddy with high spirits. George tore round the house, racing up and down stairs, forgetting what they'd packed and unpacking everything again to make sure he'd got his lightsaber or the bucket and spade. It was brilliant to see George and Orla so happy at the thought of spending a week away alone together, but Kate was feeling the accumulation of a series of sleepless nights. The heat was relentless, and she'd spent many nights lying awake, restless and tense, trying to cool her naked body in the warm air of her bedroom, her mind whirling with separate anxieties.

One of her worries was about Orla, who was continuing to behave out of character. She would sometimes shut the lid of her laptop when Kate entered the room, and once had broken off a phone call in mid-sentence. When Kate made a mild enquiry, or asked her outright if everything was OK, Orla changed the subject. Kate and Orla had never had a secret from one another, in all their years of friendship. Kate sensed her closest friend drifting away, and felt the pain of it acutely. When she got back from Yorkshire, she was determined to try and put things right.

Kate still hadn't found the right time to tell Orla about the night she and Paul had spent together, which meant she was keeping secrets of her own. All in all, since discovering Paul's love for her, nothing in Kate's life seemed to be right any more, and her mind seemed to be in perpetual turmoil. If it weren't for George and his undimming cheerfulness, she might go crazy.

'Hey Kate!' A tall girl in a giant black hoodie waved from the group, and the other girls turned as one to chorus their greetings.

Kate waved back, giving them a sleep-deprived grin. The girls' excitement raised her spirits, bringing home to her how all Chloe's careful preparations were actually coming to fruition. The thought cheered her enormously.

She hauled her rucksack out of the back of the cab and was fishing around in her purse to pay the driver when Paul appeared at her side.

'Do you need a hand?'

Kate turned to find a very different Paul from the man who stood so silently on her doorstep all those years. Like the teenagers, he seemed full of repressed energy, and his eyes were alight with warmth at the sight of her. He kissed her cheek, but the kiss was brief and fleeting. Paul was obviously taking seriously his promise to give Kate space.

He reached to pick her rucksack from the pavement beside her, and gave a grunt. 'Good lord, what have you got in here?' He swung the bag onto his shoulder. 'Your whole nail varnish collection?'

Even his teasing seemed more laidback. A wide grin deepened the creases in his cheeks. Dressed in a white t-shirt and long black shorts, he was looking more relaxed than Kate had seen him in a long time. She returned his smile instinctively.

'Well, obviously I've had to bring a lot of stuff, because

we're going to "The Countryside".' She made quotation marks in the air. The country was an exotic place to her. 'I've brought everything I could possibly need, in case there are no shops. For all I know, we might have to tramp through fields to find somewhere that sells moisturiser. Or maybe even pump water at the village well.'

Paul looked shocked. 'Don't tell me you've never been out of the city?'

'Nope.' She threw an arm in the direction of the coach. 'Me and most of these girls wouldn't recognise a sheep if it came up to us covered in mint sauce.'

He stared at her, and the smile on Kate's lips vanished abruptly. It seemed their carefree greeting was shortlived. All her old insecurities returned in a rush, and she felt foolish and ignorant. She looked away, trying to remind herself her lack of experience was no fault of her own. After she was taken on by her agency as a teenager, she'd travelled far more than most people her age, and to cities all round the world. She'd been to New York and LA, Milan and Hong Kong, and as far as Sydney, but she'd never been out of the metropolis.

Paul seemed about to speak, when there was the sound of feet hurrying along the road behind them.

'Sorry I'm late.' Chloe appeared, out of breath, dropping her bag to the ground. 'I was just leaving the house and the dog was sick. Then my youngest started crying because she'd lost her phone, and how could she text me while I was away, so we had to have a mad look round the house for it. Turned out it was in her school blazer.'

Chloe's throaty, infectious laugh was a welcome interruption.

Kate reached out and hugged her. 'I don't think you're the last, Chloe. I definitely can't see Abi, and I think we'd all know if she was here.'

'Oh, well there's always one. And it's usually Abi.' Chloe gave another chuckle. Then she turned to Paul, holding out a friendly hand. 'Hi, you must be Paul.'

Chloe was quite small and had to tilt her head to gaze up at him. For a couple of seconds they eyed one another appraisingly. Then they both smiled at once. Paul shook Chloe's hand and bent to pick up her bag, as well as Kate's. 'Here. Let me stow these away.' He slung Chloe's hold-all over his shoulder and made for the coach.

'Wow,' Chloe breathed, watching him walk away. 'I've seen him on telly, but he's totally gorgeous in real life.' She stared after Paul, one hand pressed to her bosom. 'And the way he talks. "Let me stow these away."' She parodied Paul's deep, upper-class voice with her hand on her heart, swooning in a way that made Kate giggle. 'The girls won't know what's hit them.'

Kate gazed over at the motley band of teenagers gathered round the coach and gave a worried frown. 'Actually, Chloe, I was thinking about that. What if Paul doesn't fit in? If the girls don't take to him, the week will be a disaster.'

Chloe looked thoughtful. Paul's accent was a far cry from the voices of the rest of the group. And if the girls jumped to the conclusion he was looking down on them, as Kate herself had done as a teenager – as she'd just done that moment – they wouldn't hesitate to make their feelings known.

The girls swivelled their heads as one as soon as Paul approached. Some of the more forward were watching him with their tongues hanging out.

Chloe lifted an eyebrow and caught Kate's eye. 'Good job he's got experience in warzones,' she murmured.

As if on cue, there was a loud catcall and a lively burst of laughter from the teenagers as Paul bent to place the luggage in the hold. The muscles on his forearms were taut as he shifted the heavy bags. He straightened up, returning their attention unfazed.

'Morning, all.'

Something in the steadiness of his reply damped the teenagers' cheek. Their giggles died, and they returned the greeting with a polite chorus of 'Good mornings'. The show was over, the giddiness evaporated, and the girls went back to their previous chatter.

'I don't think you need worry, Kate. He seems like he can handle himself.' Chloe felt around in her capacious shoulder bag. 'And now I'd better take the register. As soon as Abi's here, we can be off.'

She strode off towards the coach. Right on cue from behind Kate there came a yell, and she turned to see a bony, dark-haired girl racing from the tube station, clutching a bulging bin bag.

'Thank God you're still here,' she called, pounding up the street. 'Effing housemate nicked my rucksack and went off with it.'

She propelled herself to a halt next to Kate just as her black plastic bag split at the bottom, and the contents spilled out onto the pavement. She dropped the tattered plastic and let out a fluent curse, looking round furiously at the other girls, who erupted into boisterous laughter.

'Oh, Abi.' Kate looked down in dismay at the pile of clothes and toiletries littering the ground. Abi stood rigid with anger and distress.

Paul had returned from the coach, and next minute he was crouching on the pavement, examining the split bag.

'Is this all you have to carry your stuff?'

Abi nodded, her face red. 'I borrowed a rucksack off a mate. Woke up this morning and it's gone, and all my stuff just dumped out of it on the floor. It was a good rucksack, and all. Reckon one of my housemates nicked it. I spent ages packing last night and everything.' She gave a choked, tearful curse. 'And now my mate what I borrowed it off is going to kill me when I get back.'

'Let's worry about that one later.' Paul stood. 'I've a canvas holdall inside my rucksack. Let's get everything repacked.'

Abi's face brightened. 'Thanks, mate. Who are you?'

'My name's Paul Farrell.' He stretched out his hand. Abi, who was rarely treated with such courtesy by any of the males of her acquaintance, regarded his proffered hand incredulously for a couple of seconds, before taking it with a bewildered grin.

'And you are …?' he prompted.

In the company of the girls, Paul's measured, well-modulated voice seemed to belong to another era altogether.

Abi pumped his hand, looking up at him in cheerful amazement. 'Abi Foster.'

'Good morning, Abi Foster. Now, let's get that bag.'

He returned to the coach with Abi to retrieve his rucksack, and Kate felt relief sweep through her. She'd worried Paul would act towards the girls in the same way he'd done with her all those times: aloof, a little withdrawn, joking in a deadpan way that could cause sensitive teenagers to take offence. When he returned, carrying his holdall, she watched the way he crouched by the meagre possessions strewn on the ground, helping Abi repack in a brotherly way, and felt her spirits lift. The two chatted easily, and Abi's distress melted under Paul's matter-of-fact manner. He raised his head from his task, saw Kate watching, and smiled.

Kate would have helped them both repack, but out of the corner of her eye, she could see Chloe had broken off taking the register and was now involved in earnest conversation with a man who'd just stepped out of a taxi. He was dressed in a long shirt and traditional cotton trousers, and a pair of leather sandals. Beneath the full beard, his mouth was turned down. At a little distance from the taxi stood Dashna, one of the teenagers from the group. Kate took in her dejected stance and approached her.

'What's up, Dashna?' she said. 'Is that your dad with Chloe?'

Dashna nodded, her eyes on the ground. Kate noted the girl's headscarf was pulled low over her brow, with not an inch of hair visible. Normally she wore it at a rakish angle, but not today. Kate cast another glance in the direction of the cab, where Dashna's father was still in conversation, a grim look on his face.

'He says I can't go,' Dashna said, without looking up.

'What? Why?' Kate took in the bags lying on the pavement. 'But you've brought your stuff. Why's he changed his mind at the last minute?'

Dashna turned her head to look at Paul, who was just zipping up his holdall, now full of Abi's belongings.

Kate followed the direction of her gaze, and her heart sank. 'Is it because Paul's coming with us?'

Dashna nodded forlornly. 'He thought we were all women. Now he wants to know what sort of trip we are going on.'

'But Paul's our journalist,' Kate protested. 'We need him.'

Paul caught them both looking and strolled over. 'Everything OK?' he asked, looking from one to the other. Dashna kept her head down without greeting him, and Paul turned to observe her father, still in earnest conversation with Chloe by the waiting taxi.

'This is Dashna,' Kate said. 'Her father might not let her go now. Because of you. We should have explained about you first.' Kate was mortified. It was all her fault for suggesting Paul come in the first place.

Dashna's eyes remained on the pavement. For a couple of seconds no one spoke, then Paul said, 'I recognise your father. You're from Afghanistan, Dashna, aren't you?'

The teenager's eyes widened in astonishment. She gave a brief nod.

'I thought so. But I can't quite place your dad's name.'

'Ahmal Khan.'

'Ahmal,' Paul repeated. 'That's it. I never forget a face, but after all this time, sometimes a name escapes me.'

Kate joined Dashna in staring at Paul. Did he know everyone?

'I won't be a minute.' He left them to make his way to the taxi. Ahmal, too, appeared surprised at his approach. When Paul spoke, recognition appeared to dawn. The older man smiled and offered his hand.

The two men engaged in conversation, and at one point Kate was taken aback to see Paul gesture in her direction. Ahmal looked her way, and nodded. Kate waved vaguely, unsure what was required of her. In the meantime, Chloe gazed from Paul to Dashna's father, her anxious expression gradually replaced with her usual cheerfulness. Five minutes later, Ahmal beckoned his daughter over, gave her a long farewell hug and a kiss on the cheek, and climbed back into the taxi. The vehicle pulled away, and Dashna stared after it, beaming.

There was no time to ask Paul what had been discussed. The coach driver was anxious to be off, and the waiting girls were restless. Chloe hurried over to the others, and Paul collected Dashna's bags. Soon there was much excited scrambling for position on the coach, with the louder girls rushing for the back seats, and Chloe trying to keep everyone calm.

*

Paul squashed his jacket in the overhead rack and dropped back into his seat beside Kate. Many people would have groaned at the thought of spending hours on a cramped coach with group of over-excited teenagers, but he'd been on worse journeys. He stretched one leg out into the aisle in an effort to find room for his long frame.

'How did you get Dashna's dad to change his mind?' Kate asked him curiously.

'Oh, that.' He shifted, trying to make himself comfortable. 'Ahmal is a translator. We met a long time ago, but Stuart worked with him more often than I did. I told him Stuart's widow was one of the group's leaders, and that his daughter would be in safe hands. I think I gave him the impression you were a respectable matriarch.'

'A matriarch?' she repeated. Paul returned her sceptical look innocently, and she chuckled. 'I don't think anyone ever thought that before. It's a good job he never saw my lingerie adverts.'

An image of Kate that night in his apartment flashed through Paul's mind. She was standing half-naked by his bedroom window. The light from the blinds striped the bare skin of her midriff, making her seem some sort of exotic creature in the half-light. The memory flooded his brain, and for a moment he found himself incapable of speaking. The smile left Kate's face and her lips parted. Paul forced his gaze to remain on her pupils, which had darkened so that the blue of the iris was a halo around them.

'Probably best not to mention the lingerie,' he said softly. 'Not this week, at any rate. Of course, when we get back, we can talk about your lingerie as much as you like. I'd be only too happy.'

Kate turned pink. 'Maybe you're right,' she said. 'Not a good choice of subject.'

Their warm gazes mingled for a second or two. Paul revelled in the way her feelings always showed themselves so clearly in her features, despite her reserve. The week in the country stretched before him like a glorious luxury. Even the hours on a coach were something he looked forward to. It was time with Katerina.

Then his thoughts turned to their unfinished conversation in the car park, and he said, 'I'm sorry about just now. When you said you'd never been to the countryside.'

He thought he detected a flinch, but he was relieved to see her small smile didn't fade. 'You never forget a conversation, do you?' she said. 'Must be your journalist training.'

He shrugged. 'I just want to clear things up. I thought I'd offended you, for some reason.'

'Well, you seemed surprised,' she countered. 'Really surprised. Like you thought I was an ignoramus, or something, just because I'd never stood in a field.'

So that was it. Paul wondered how long it was going to take before Kate realised there was no need to be prickly in his company. The scars of her teenage years must run deep indeed. 'That wasn't what I was thinking at all,' he said. 'And I'm sorry that's how it came across.'

'Well, what then?'

'I was surprised, but not for the reasons you think. I thought Stuart must have taken you to the country some time. To visit his parents.'

'Oh.' Her smile vanished, and she shifted her gaze from his. 'Well, that didn't ever happen. You saw how Stuart's mum and dad were at our wedding. I wasn't the daughter-in-law they'd always dreamed of.'

Paul grimaced. The chill emanating from the Hemingway family on Stuart's wedding day was impossible to miss. His parents were wealthy landowners, with a large farm and stables that had been in the family for generations. Whenever Paul had visited, they went out of their way to be hospitable. They were kind to a boy from the same background as Stuart, but with Kate it was a different matter. Stuart's parents had come to his wedding, but it was obvious they only accepted the invitation out of a sense of duty. Their conversations with Kate were impeccably polite. Their constant expressions of hope that Stuart would be happy were laden with such doubt it became embarrassing.

'Yes, I saw how they were on your wedding day,' he said quietly. 'It caused Stuart a lot of pain. He thought everyone who met you would love you as much as he did.'

'Yeah, well.' Kate picked at a piece of fluff on the seat. 'That was one of the things about Stuart. He always saw the good in everyone. All his mum and dad saw in me was someone out to spend their son's money.' She raised her eyes to Paul, with a hint of defiance. 'And you remember how much Stuart spent on me. Clothes, make-up, that sort of stuff. I didn't ask him to. I was earning my own money by then, and it wasn't anything I even wanted, but I thought if I wore the type of clothes he bought I would fit in his world, and I'd look the part, and I wouldn't let him down. All his mum and dad saw was me dressed up in Stuart's money.'

'I remember how Stuart was.' It wasn't difficult for Paul to sympathise with Kate. Stuart was generous and affectionate, but sometimes he could be impetuous, and he didn't always stop to consider how his actions affected others. 'He just wanted to spoil you. To give you all the things you'd never had. I told him at the time he was making you uncomfortable, and to stop spending so much money on you. He just laughed, and said he liked to give you presents.'

'I'm sorry,' Kate said, in a soft burst of distress.

'Sorry for what?' He stared at her, puzzled. 'Stuart was the most generous person I know. He didn't always stop to think. We both know that. It wasn't your fault.'

'No, that's not it. I'm not sorry about Stuart. It's you.' Her expression was filled with regret. 'Stuart told me what you said. He told me you warned him to stop spending money on me. But I got it wrong. I thought you were blaming me for taking Stuart's money, like his mum and dad did. I didn't realise you actually understood how I felt.' She twisted her hands in her lap. 'All along, I thought –'

Paul broke in wryly. 'You thought I was a snob. It's OK. I know you did. And I went out of my way to make you think it, too. Better that than guess how I really felt about you. That would really have been a disaster.'

Kate gave a tight laugh and turned her head, so that only her profile was showing. 'I didn't get you then, and I wonder if I even get you now. You're such a cool character.'

Paul was taken aback. Is that how he appeared to her? He'd hidden his feelings for so long, become so adept at presenting an indifferent front, maybe it was no wonder Kate struggled now to make sense of him.

He leaned back in his seat, pondering her words. If he were totally honest with himself, he knew Kate wasn't the only person who found him hard to fathom. He had learned from an early age how to retreat into himself, and to observe others from a distance. It was a self-preservation tactic that made him an excellent journalist, but gave the impression of a lack of human warmth he knew others found off-putting. Stuart was one of the few people who'd taken the trouble to dig beneath the outer front.

He observed Kate's troubled profile, and he frowned. After all these years of misunderstanding, getting to know one another without prejudice was going to take time. Still, the rest of the odds might be stacked against him, but at least time was one factor that was on his side. And just now they had a whole week in each other's company, and he clung to the delicious thought of the days stretching out ahead of them.

CHAPTER NINE

Nothing would have made Paul happier than to sit and talk to Kate for the whole of the rest of the journey, but he had an article to write, and having the whole group captive on the coach was too good an opportunity to miss.

He drew out his notepad and pen, and his tablet.

'Time to get to know everyone,' he said.

'Good idea.' Kate gave a wicked grin. 'They're all desperate to meet you. Their eyes have been out on stalks, ever since you arrived.'

He laughed. 'In that case I think I'll start with the easiest one first.'

He stood and made his way to the front of the coach, where Chloe was sitting alone, engrossed in a book.

'Hi,' he said. 'Is it OK if I ask a few questions?' He glanced at her book.

'Of course.' Chloe made room for him beside her. 'I have so little chance to read,' she said, waving her novel. 'A long coach journey would be torture for most people, but for me, it's a chance to finish a good book.'

Paul nodded sympathetically. 'I'll keep it short. I just want to go over a few things, and get some background.'

'Sure,' she said, resting her book in her lap. 'Fire away.'

He flipped to a blank page. To be honest, he'd already done most of the groundwork for the trip. He and Chloe had been in touch several times. He'd checked out details such as privacy – whether it was permissible to publish any of the girls' names, or their photos, for example. When Chloe emailed Paul to ask if he would take one of the classes, he had confounded

Kate by replying that he would be happy to.

Chloe peered approvingly at him over the top of her glasses. 'So, what else do you want to know?'

'Well, I have nearly everything I need from you, I think.' He raised his pad. 'But I was wondering what you thought about me putting a slant on my write up, so that it's weighted more from Katerina's angle. It would be something to draw the readers in.'

Chloe took off her glasses, and gave him her full attention. 'I read your interview with her. Very revealing.'

Paul lifted his hand to rub the back of his neck, and grunted noncommittally. 'Yes, well, that was just a taster for the readers.'

'Nice taster,' she murmured.

Paul was aware he'd made his feelings known in that interview, to anyone who cared to look. And he guessed Chloe was one of those people who would have read between the lines. He felt her intelligent gaze on him, and shifted a little. 'I was wondering if you could fill in a few details from your perspective. How Katerina first came to At Home, for example, and your first impressions of her.'

Chloe deliberated a second or two, her eyes fixed on Paul. Then she seemed to come to a decision. She drew in a breath. 'OK, I hope you understand how wary I am about talking to journalists about Kate's private life.'

Paul met her gaze. 'And I hope you know I'm not that kind of journalist. And that whatever I do with this article, I'm doing it for Kate.'

Chloe didn't flinch. She continued to regard him. 'You've got quite a bit of steel underneath that exterior.' Her hand touched his briefly. 'I'm glad Kate has you in her life.'

Before Paul could answer, Chloe began to tell him about how Kate first arrived at one of the offices of At Home. 'It was shortly after she'd had that trouble in school, the time she told you about. One of the police officers told Kate about us, and she just came in one day, out of the blue. I remember it well, because she had such a presence. She was thin and pale, and obviously hadn't eaten properly in a while, but despite everything she was beautiful. Not that she knew it. Kate was very prickly in those days, and slow to trust. Orla was always the outgoing one. Kate was more careful with people. She still is.'

Chloe raised her head to eye Paul closely. 'Kate has been through an awful lot in her short life. And after her husband died, I'm really sorry to say she's become even more withdrawn. She expects the worst out of life. It's not easy to gain her trust.'

Paul stopped writing. He felt Chloe's eyes on him, and the way she waited. He turned and met her gaze. 'I won't let her down.'

After a while, Chloe gave a slow nod. 'Good luck.'

A flicker of understanding passed between them.

'Thanks,' he said quietly. Then he stood. 'Now, if it's OK with you, I'm just going to chat with the rest of the group.' He glanced down the aisle and found thirty pairs of eager eyes looking back at him, alive with curiosity.

'Go ahead.' Chloe picked up her book again, her eyes twinkling. 'They're desperate to talk to you.'

He gave a short laugh and headed off down the coach. As he passed Kate, he saw she had her eyes closed and was resting her head uncomfortably on the window pane. The sun shone on her blonde hair, lighting it with dusty yellow. In repose, the lines of tiredness were gone from her face, and she looked as young as the teenagers.

He carried on to the back of the coach and squatted in the aisle, balancing his tablet on his knee.

He looked round at the expectant faces. 'I expect Chloe's told you who I am. My name's Paul Farrell, and I'm writing an article on your week away for my paper, *The World*. I'm looking forward to getting to know you all. Anyone want to tell me what they're looking forward to on this trip?'

He half expected an embarrassed silence, but instead, there was a burst of loud chatter. Paul guessed he'd attract attention as the only man in the group, and for a while he let the noisy conversation flow over and around him. Occasionally he asked one of the girls a direct question. Presently the talk became more muted, the answers more considered, and the girls waited for each other to speak. Even the shiest of them spoke up from time to time.

Paul began working his way up the coach, sitting in the empty seats, and listening to each girl individually. Sometimes one of the louder girls would butt in on a conversation, and the noise levels would rise, and then it would be back to Paul and just one of the girls again. The chatter went back and forth, and Paul made his notes and worked on remembering each of the girls by name.

Sarah's accent stood out among the Londoners. She was looking forward to being back 'oop north', even if it was only Yorkshire, and not Manchester, where her family was from. Stef was Polish and clung quietly to her best friend Anna, a Lithuanian. Both the girls regarded him with unnerving gravity until Paul tried to say hello in Polish. They burst into giggles. Jess wanted to be a bus driver because her stepdad told her there was good money in it; her friend Charlotte had never been on holiday, and hadn't slept all night with the excitement, and so on, down the length of the coach. There was an atmosphere of exuberance at being temporarily let loose from whatever problems beset the girls at home. Paul found himself swept up in their enthusiasm, and several times laughed out loud.

*

The sound of laughter penetrated Kate's doze She knelt upright on her seat to find Paul was standing in the aisle, listening to Sarah explain to him why she'd only brought high heels with her on a trip to the countryside. Paul had a look on his face she was slowly beginning to recognise. Although he wasn't smiling, the creases each side of his mouth had deepened, and his eyes were alight with mirth.

Sarah lifted up a foot and waved a wedged heel in front of him. 'I never wear anything else but heels,' she explained. 'I've worn them so long now, I can't walk in flats. My mate Carla said I could borrow her wellies off her, but I said no. Wouldn't be seen dead in them.' She gave him a cheerful grin. 'Anyway, they smelt.'

Paul caught Kate's eye as the girls erupted in laughter. Maybe someone had cast a spell over him, and transformed him entirely from the person he normally was. Kate barely recognised the reserved guy who'd come to her house to collect George a few weeks ago. She found herself beaming an irrepressible smile.

By now, the driver was pulling off the motorway and onto the slip road for the services. Paul picked up his pad and pen from the seat beside him.

'Excellent, we're stopping off. I could murder a coffee.'

The girls began rustling in their seats, searching for their handbags and slipping on discarded shoes. Kate dropped back into her seat as Paul took his place beside her.

He ran a hand through his neat hair. 'It will be good to stretch my legs.'

Kate stood, ducking her head, and clutched onto the back of the seat in front. 'I know what you mean.' She threw him a sympathetic look, taking in his cramped posture. 'It's not easy for us tall people. And I can't wait to get off and phone Orla,' she added. 'See if they've got to Bournemouth yet. Although the way Orla drives, I wouldn't be surprised if they got there hours ago.'

The morning had progressed, and the sun was now high in the sky. The heat hit them with full force as they stepped off the air-conditioned coach. The services were the usual soul-destroying stop-off point on the edge of the motorway. The traffic roared by in a filthy haze, and heat was burning off the tarmac. Kate stood in the shadow of a few dusty trees and phoned Orla.

'We got here safely,' Orla reassured her. 'We're here, we're unpacking, and then we're going straight to the beach. The sun's out, and it's gorgeous.'

'Is that Mum?' George's voice piped up in the background. 'Tell her we've got biscuits in our bedroom.'

Kate laughed, relieved to find George and Orla were still full of excitement, despite the long journey. She spoke briefly to George, who told her all about their room and how they were going to have fish and chips for dinner. She put her mobile back in her bag, not knowing whether to be happy or sad to know neither of them appeared to be missing her in the slightest.

Paul appeared from the shop, his mobile glued to one ear, and copies of all the day's newspapers wedged under one arm. Kate wondered how he would manage his workload, away from his office all week. Nothing ever appeared to ruffle him. Or outwardly, at least. She turned away, preparing to help round up the girls to continue their journey.

The group climbed back into the coach, and, once back on the motorway, the girls were glad to sit back and look at the unfamiliar landscape passing by, or else try to catch up on some sleep after their early start from London. The muted sound of music leaked from earphones, the pages of magazines rustled, and occasionally a mobile beeped. Apart from that, there was a contented silence.

Paul was leaning forward in the seat next to Kate, a pile of newspapers on his knee. His eyes were on the text in front of him, but Kate sensed he wasn't reading. She drew forward, resting her elbows on her knees.

'You really drew those girls out just now,' she said.

He turned to look at her. 'I've had far worse people to interview. It's my job, getting people to open up.'

'Yes, but –'

She broke off, and he frowned. 'But?'

There was a moment of silence while Kate tried to frame her words the right way. But the she'd left too long a pause. Paul sat right back in his seat, abandoning the newspaper on his knee. The warmth had left his expression. 'I see. You thought they'd all clam up with me because I'm not one of them.'

'I meant it in a good way,' she rushed to say. 'It's just that you've got a different accent. You're more confident. You're at ease with yourself. People can find that hard to relate to if they haven't had the same upbringing.'

'Including you.'

'Actually, yes,' she confessed. 'I used to find you a bit intimidating. I would never have dreamt of chatting to you, like the girls did just now.'

Paul didn't take offence at her words. Although he was frowning a little, she knew now that this meant he was giving them his consideration. This was one of the things Kate was beginning to love about Paul. He was never flustered by anything she said. He was such a restful person to be with.

Except that evening in his apartment. There had been nothing restful about Paul then. All of a sudden the memories of that night came flooding back, in a rush of heat. Kate pressed a hand to her face and felt Paul stir beside her. A pulse was beating loudly in her ears, and she was sure her cheeks were aflame. She tried to concentrate on the view outside, but the dry fields and dusty trees along the motorway seemed, too, to be on fire.

Paul shifted in his seat. When he rested his hand between them, next to her thigh, she saw the muscles on his arm were taut, and a vein was throbbing, in time with her own.

Kate leant back. Her face was close to his, and he was looking at her with eyes that were burning with intensity. The air between them was charged, expectant. Kate drew in a breath.

Then a mobile phone rang somewhere in the coach, and the loud voice of one of the girls broke the spell. The muscles in Paul's arm next to hers tightened and relaxed. He looked away, his expression taut.

A second or two passed, and then Paul began to continue their conversation as though nothing had happened. His voice was husky, but otherwise he carried on, exactly where they'd left off, and it was though the intense, silent exchange between them had all been an illusion.

'It's strange you should say that,' he said. 'That you found me intimidating, I mean, because the way I speak was so

different to what you were used to. When I first started at
boarding school with Stuart I was bullied for months. Stuart
was the only boy in the class to stick up for me.'

Kate turned her head sharply. Paul continued to tell her of
his memories of those early days at school, and here was
another revelation. He spoke of the time he'd gone into the
dorm and found the contents of his tuck box half-eaten and
strewn across his bed, the fruit cake his mother had baked a
wreck of crumbs, some of them shoved between his
bedclothes. His favourite sweets littered the floorboards. A
half-eaten packet of crisps spilled out on his bedside locker.
But how whenever he looked back on those days, all he
remembered was Stuart's friendship and generosity. The bleak
despair he'd felt as a child at such constant petty cruelty was
overlaid in his mind by the vision of Stuart, a pyjama-clad
crusader wielding a pillow, shouting at the other lads in the
room. 'Which one of you did this? Come on then, you
wankers!'

He was smiling at the memory, but there was so much else
beneath his expression, and Kate recognised too well the pain
of loss. She curled her hand into a fist by her side and forced it
to remain there. It was no good thinking of letting that hand
touch Paul's cheek and reassuring him with her touch. She'd
put the constraint on their relationship this week, and she had
to abide by the rules she'd made. But it seemed as though a
cloak had dropped from Paul, revealing him as vulnerable in a
way she'd never dreamt. This new understanding of his
character brought her no comfort. Instead, the core of sadness
she carried around with her since Stuart's death intensified.

'Don't,' he said. As usual, he read her thoughts so easily. 'It
was all a long time ago.'

He was sitting a little apart, careful not to touch, but
warmth radiated from him and enveloped her, almost as
comforting as an embrace.

'I don't understand,' she said finally. 'Why would they bully
you?'

'It was because I wasn't one of them.' He tilted his head in the direction of the rest of the coach. 'Just like I'm not one of this group. Ironic, huh?'

'How come?' She spread her hands wide in disbelief.

The corners of Paul's mouth turned down in a half-amused smile. 'You mean how could I not fit in with the other posh gits, when I look and talk just like one?'

'Yes.' She caught the look on his face and gave a soft laugh. 'Well, I mean you're posh, but you're not a git.'

He laughed. 'Thanks for the vote of confidence,' he said. 'Well, my family are definitely what you'd call posh. There's a house and land that's been in my father's family for ever, and my mother is related to royalty somewhere down the line. I suppose all that classes us as upper-classe. But not necessarily rich. Certainly not rich enough for me to go to one of the most expensive boarding schools in the country.'

'Oh,' said Kate, wrinkling her brow. 'I think I see.'

Kate knew Paul's father had died many years before. It was a tragedy Paul was too young to remember clearly. She also knew his mother had been left to raise Paul and his two sisters alone. Diana Farrell was a journalist herself, for a well-known fashion magazine. Kate knew of her professionally, but they'd never met. Kate had always assumed the family must be wealthy. Assumptions again.

'My problems growing up were nothing compared to yours,' Paul said. 'By most people's standards we were well off. My mother scrimped and saved everything to give all three of us a private education, but it left her with no money for anything else. I was one of those boys who went to school in second-hand uniform. My cricket whites were too big round the waist, and instead of being white they were a dirty cream. I stuck out a mile on the pitch. In the holidays the other boys went off to their villas abroad, or their rich uncles' yachts. I just stayed at home with my mother, helping her maintain the land and house, doing all the jobs my father would have done. When I was old enough to earn some money I got a summer job in a warehouse.' He gave a wry smile. 'Where I didn't fit in with anyone else because I was one of those public school toffs.'

'I had no idea.' How easy it was now to see beyond Paul's reserve. Kate understood the barrier he'd erected only too well. And of course Stuart had seen beyond the exterior, and straight to Paul's true self. Now, after all this time, Kate could finally see how Stuart had developed a bond with this most unlikely of friends. In a curious way, the realisation caused her grief to lessen a little. She felt a stirring of warmth begin to fill her where Stuart's memory was, bringing life to the numbness.

'I'm sorry,' she said.

Paul looked blank. 'Sorry for what? It was never your fault. And in any case, in some ways my experience at school made me think more carefully about things than the other boys. About social class, for example. It's easy enough to say it doesn't matter what your social background is, that it's the character inside that matters, but in reality most people make automatic assumptions. And most people feel uncomfortable outside their social group. Since I'm used to being on the outside, I find it easy to relate to anyone, which is a big advantage, doing the job I do.'

An outsider. So that explained it – Paul's easy relationship with the group of girls from At Home. He knew what it was to be on the outside of a circle. It explained his connection with Kate herself. They were both outsiders, in their own way, and both had turned to Stuart, beloved by everyone, to centre them. Now they were adrift, with only each other.

She caught hold of Paul's hand. 'That's not why I was sorry,' she said quickly. 'I'm sorry because I misjudged you all those years. Sorry I thought you were looking down on me.' She felt a twist of sadness. 'It's a waste. All those years gone by when we could have been relaxed in each other's company. We could have been friends.'

She felt Paul's hand turn, warm under hers, and his fingers return the pressure of her clasp. His expression was empty. 'We could never have been friends,' he said. 'I deliberately kept you at a distance for years. It's no wonder you found me intimidating.'

She gripped Paul's hand fiercely. His dark, solemn features were beginning to shimmer in her too bright gaze. 'No matter what happens between us now, though, we'll always be friends, won't we?' She looked up at him for reassurance, and he nodded gravely. 'Do you promise?' She squeezed his fingers until his grip tightened on hers.

'I promise,' he said solemnly. There was no hint of amusement at the childlike question. 'We'll stay friends, no matter what.'

She continued to search his face for a while, before turning away. She wondered if Paul realised just how important it was to her not to lose his friendship now she had only just discovered it. She thought of being left again by another person in her life, and went cold to the core. She needed assurances before she would take a risk with him. To lose Paul's friendship now, when she had only just found it, would be too much to bear.

His hand covered hers, and she felt the pressure of his broad knee against her thigh, and after a while, lulled by the warmth of his physical presence, she pressed her head against the window and watched the landscape of the north unfurl ahead of her.

*

The coach rumbled through the decayed Victorian grandeur of Bradford, and shortly afterwards the houses and suburbs peeled away, and there they were. 'The Countryside.' Kate stared out of the window, her forehead still pressed to the glass. Field after field rolled by, in a multitude of verdant hues. It was a kaleidoscope of greens, in a range she would never have believed possible, from almost black, through sage, to lime. After the bright neon glare of London, the sight was a fresh, glorious balm to her soul.

'Look at that,' she said. 'Isn't it glorious? I think I'm suffering from green shock.'

She felt the rumble of Paul's laughter behind her. He leaned closer, looking out over her shoulder, the warmth of him a comfort at her back.

'The moorland in summer,' he said. 'There's no sight in the world like it.'

'It's not at all how I imagined.' Kate reached a hand to the window, and pressed it there, as though trying to contain the view. 'I thought it would be all black and peaty. Wild and blustering, like in *Wuthering Heights*. But everywhere is so fresh and alive.'

'I guess it can be bleak in winter. Right now it's magnificent.'

'Yeah,' Kate breathed. 'I'm going to come back one day with George. And look. There are actually sheep!'

'Yes, let's come back with George. He'd love it.'

Kate let Paul's words sink in. Let's come back. As though Paul would be a part of her future. To her astonishment, his assumption didn't fill her with uneasiness, or make her want to draw away. Instead she felt a strange sense of contentment. She held on to the feeling, examining it in wonder. Was this how it would be to be happy again? She could picture George's excitement at the thought of Paul coming with them, and the unaccustomed feeling of gladness intensified.

And then, as soon as it began to take hold, the sensation fled, and a chill rushed in to take its place. Kate had looked forward to happiness before. Better not to expect too much.

The coach began an ascent up a bumpy side road, and then there they were, seemingly on top of the moors, and the driver was pulling in to their hostel.

Instantly the coach erupted with movement. Kate was as eager as the girls to get out and breathe in the fresh air. Her feeling of foreboding vanished in the excitement of exploring her new surroundings.

Later, she stood at the window of the room she was sharing with Chloe and stared out at the scene below her as though her soul would burst. She couldn't take her eyes off it. Acres of rolling moorland stretched for mile upon mile in a gentle haze of ferns and heather, finally meeting the horizon in a burst of startling blue. Never before had she seen the earth meet the sky without thousands of grimy roofs and office blocks cluttering the view. It was magical.

From somewhere below a bell clanged in the hostel, signalling lunch was ready. Kate barely heard it. She stood rooted to the view until finally Chloe came to drag her away from the window and down the stairs to the canteen.

A delicious smell of fresh-baked bread wafted along the corridor from the kitchen. Lunch was served through a hatch by the hostel owners, who were apparently unfazed after being descended on by a group of ravenous teenage girls. They kept up a nourishing supply of home-cooked food and cheerful greetings.

Kate collected a tray and got into line behind Abi. As she watched the teenager fill her plate, she recalled the time she'd been invited to share a casserole by the mother of one of her school friends. After weeks of surviving on peanut butter sandwiches and cornflakes, Kate had piled her plate, eyes round as saucers, much as Abi was doing now. Kate smiled at her, glad to see her eat, but Abi just turned without returning her greeting, and made her way to one of the tables.

Another similarity between them, Kate thought wryly. Abi probably assumed Kate was looking down on her because she was hungry. Kate could only hope the week away would help soften the young girl's prickliness.

After their meal, it would have been lovely to rush straight out and explore the tantalising green moors, but Chloe was determined to make the most of every moment. They had come on this trip for a purpose, and there was work to be done before the group could scatter and relax. The hostel owners had set aside a games room as a sort of informal classroom for them. According to Chloe's itinerary, the first afternoon was a 'Getting to Know You' exercise. She gave a brief introduction and then invited Paul to stand up to speak. Excited murmurs rippled round the group as he made his way to the front.

'You all know me by now.' He gave them one of his downturned smiles. 'I'm the nosy one who asks lots of questions.' There were a few friendly giggles. 'I'm a journalist, and people think asking questions is what we do. Well, that's part of it. But one of the main parts of my job is *listening*. Listening is an important skill. If we don't listen to each other speak, how can we ever hope to understand one another?' His gaze flicked to Kate at the back of the room, and then moved on over the rest of the group. 'This afternoon, as part of getting to know each other, I'm going to give you some tips on interviewing, and then I'd like you to choose someone in the group – preferably someone you don't know very well – and ask her some questions about herself, and *listen* to her answers. Afterwards you'll tell the rest of the group what you learned about each other. And it's not just an informal chat. I'd like you to treat this as a professional reporting exercise. Afterwards I'd like you to write up your interviews, and the best of them will be printed in the *Sunday Magazine*.'

There was a gasp of excitement, and Abi's hand shot up.

'Can I interview you?' she burst out. Some of the girls started laughing, and there were a few derisory whoops and wolf-whistles. Abi turned round, glaring fiercely. Paul gazed around the room without speaking, until the laughter died away into a sheepish shuffling.

'As I said, we need to listen to each other,' he repeated. 'And Abi has a right to speak and to ask questions. I want all of you to feel you can ask a question here – any question at all – without people taking the mickey.' The girls muttered their embarrassed agreement. Paul nodded at Abi. 'Yes, you can interview me.' Then he smiled broadly. 'And good for you for having the nerve to ask. Journalism's about listening, but it's also about sticking your neck out and asking that awkward question.' He eyed the rest of the group. 'Don't be shy. Have confidence in yourselves. Sometimes you need to have bollocks in life.' The girls guffawed. Paul gave an embarrassed grin. 'Well maybe bollocks isn't the right word.'

Chloe laughed. 'If we could all grow some bollocks this week, it would be brilliant. Maybe not literally, though.'

Paul leaned back against one of the tables, his hands in his pockets. 'So, think about who you're going to interview and what you want to find out about them. Next, *listen*. Try not to just reel off your list of questions. Listen to the answers you're given, and don't be afraid to forget your prepared questions and go off on a tangent. Last, and most important, I'd like you to end the interview with a couple of paragraphs on your impressions of the person you are interviewing, to sum up what you've found out. OK, let's get to work.'

Chairs were scraped back and there was a burst of activity as the girls paired themselves up. Abi bent her dark head over her notebook, preparing her questions for Paul. Kate was sitting back with Chloe on the edge of the group, ready to help out as an observer, when Dashna approached, notepad in hand.

'Do you want to interview me?' Kate asked, surprised. When Dashna nodded shyly, Kate stood, beaming. 'That's great. Thank you. There's a lot I'd like to ask you, too.'

They found a space at a nearby table. Kate drew out her notepad and was soon scribbling down her questions. It wasn't difficult to come up with a long list of things she'd like to know. For years Afghanistan was simply the country that had taken Stuart from her. Now she realised how little she understood about Dashna's homeland. She wanted to find out what it was like to grow up in a country at war, and also what it felt like for Dashna now she was in England, and her life was completely different. Her notepad rapidly filled with questions. Dashna continued to chew the end of her pen, frowning. While Kate waited for her to finish she cast a glance around the room at the other girls and noted how intensely they were concentrating. The room in which they were working had a cupboard full of board games and a table-tennis table shoved against one wall. Kate thought with a pang how so many of these teenagers had had to put away childish things too early in their lives. It was probably a long time for most of them since they had sat and concentrated in a classroom.

Then she thought of Paul, and his revelation that even he, with his privileged background, hadn't had the happy school days she'd assumed. She glanced across the room, to where his head was bent towards Abi's. He was listening to her speak, his gaze fixed on her. He was showing exactly the same involvement with Abi as he would listening to cabinet ministers on television. He raised his head and caught Kate watching him, and he smiled, the frown of concentration disappearing. For a couple of seconds there were only the two of them in the room, and Kate was filled with a sensation of *belonging* with someone, a feeling she hadn't known for a very long time.

The sound of Dashna putting down her pen brought her back to reality. She glanced across to find the teenager waiting for her expectantly, notebook poised. She had pushed back her thick headscarf, and a few tendrils of hair were escaping. She looked so eager to begin Kate couldn't resist a smile.

'Are you ready?'

Dashna nodded, and next minute questions were bursting out of her. Kate answered as best she could, and Dashna scribbled her responses down swiftly before rushing on to the next point on her list, as though frightened the opportunity to capture everything might suddenly vanish.

Why did you become a model? Do you miss your parents? Your husband? How did you feel when your husband died? How did your son feel? What will you do after your modelling career is finished? Will you train for another job? Will you marry again?

Kate leaned back with a sigh of relief when she finally put down her pen. Paul ought to take a leaf out of Dashna's notepad. She'd grilled her more thoroughly than he ever did.

Then the tables were turned, and it was Kate's time to question Dashna, whose answers proved a revelation. Quiet and reflective with the group, Dashna opened up in a way Kate hadn't expected. It was as though no one had ever asked Dashna how she felt about anything, and now that someone had at last shown an interest, her answers flooded out in an unstoppable stream.

'Phew,' she said, when Paul called time to wind up the interviews. 'Dashna, that was excellent.' She held up a hand, and they high-fived.

When Paul asked for someone to step forward and be the

first to read out her interview, there was an awkward silence, followed by giggling and shuffling of feet. The girls all looked sideways at each other, but no one stepped up.

Kate stood. 'OK, I'll go first.' Everyone shifted in their seats to gaze in Kate's direction, and she cleared her throat nervously. 'I interviewed Dashna Khan. Dashna is seventeen, and came to England when she was fourteen.'

Kate proceeded to outline how Dashna had travelled to Britain with her father, mother, and uncle. Her father was a translator in Afghanistan for foreign journalists and the British army, but the family decided to flee when Dashna's brother was killed by the Taliban in retaliation for her father's work.

There was a quiet gasp from the group. It seemed this information was new to the girls, and their eyes moved from Kate to Dashna, dwelling on her with awed sympathy. Dashna kept her eyes on the floor.

Kate went on to describe Dashna's story, which featured periods of terrible hardship and uncertainty, of trying to learn a new language and to make friends in a new country, and of battles against racism.

She finished by saying, 'Dashna told me how much she missed her homeland. How Afghanistan is the most beautiful country in the world, but because of the war, it has become the most ugly. She also told me how much she grieved for her brother.'

Dashna kept her eyes down, and Kate dropped her hand on her shoulder. 'But Dashna also told me although she had lost a lot when she left her country behind, she also found friendship at school and here with At Home. She has found kindness and made many friends in her new country. Dashna enjoys learning English, and she loves being at school here and studying new subjects. She wants to study to be a civil engineer when she leaves school. Dashna told me she's seen many buildings destroyed, and now she wants to spend her life building.'

A few of the girls clapped. Kate put down her pad. Dashna kept her head bent shyly. 'And now for my impression of Dashna. I'm glad I got to interview her. Before this interview I thought Afghanistan was a terrible place, because it's the place where my husband was killed, but Dashna told me how beautiful her country is, and how much she misses it. Dashna is quiet and doesn't talk about herself much, but with this interview I got the chance to find out how intelligent she is, and how hard she is working to make the most of her life, after everything she has been through. Most of all I've found out that Dashna is a very brave and unassuming person. I hope Dashna will find her confidence and embrace all the friendships and the new life she has discovered here.'

Kate took her seat again, and this time there was a loud round of applause. Dashna finally lifted her head and smiled broadly for the first time, a big, white beaming smile as the girls clapped.

After this the ice was broken. One by one the girls stood and revealed what they had found out about each other. Without exception they had all undergone hardships in their lives that would have sunk many, but they battled on with determination and grace, and there were often funny stories to tell amongst the bad, so that sometimes Kate laughed out loud. They also revealed a surprising range of hobbies and interests. Sarah, the girl with the collection of high heels, was questioned about her obsession with clothes. A little embarrassed, she revealed it was her dream to be a designer. She held up a sketch she had done in her notepad. To Kate's amazement it was a drawing of herself, standing hand on hip in the shorts she was wearing, but with the addition of a stylish cape flowing from her shoulders, like a sort of Superwoman on holiday.

'Wow, that's fabulous,' Kate said. 'Can I keep it?'

Sarah's face turned a fiery shade of red and she stood, tearing out the paper to give to Kate.

'We should talk some serious design later this week,' Kate said, studying the scrap of paper. She became so engrossed in examining Sarah's artwork, it was a while before she noticed Paul was standing close by. He cleared his throat, and the babble of conversation that had greeted Sarah's revelation of her skills died down.

Kate glanced over at Abi and saw the poor girl had her head bent low over her table. One hand was raised, hiding her face, and she was almost cringing in her chair. Kate understood exactly how Abi felt, having her life exposed to others in this way, and she turned her anxious gaze on Paul. Abi was the least popular girl in the group. In many ways she reminded Kate of herself at that age: a loner, a chip on her shoulder, quick to take offence. Paul caught Kate's look and nodded once, dropping his hand onto Abi's shoulder.

'Don't look so worried,' he told her quietly. 'It's all good.'

He lifted his pad and began reading from his notes.

'I interviewed Abi Foster. Abi is nineteen. She is loud, confident, couldn't care less what anyone else thinks, and has an answer ready for everyone.' There were a few mutterings from the other girls, and sidelong glances in Abi's direction. She raised her head, and returned the attention with a scowl.

Paul lowered his pad. 'Or that's the impression Abi likes to give people,' he continued. 'I've found out a lot about Abi today that makes me think she's actually a very different person. A few years ago, something terrible happened to Abi, and her mum was sent to prison.' A few intakes of breath in the room. 'This wasn't Abi's fault. It was nothing to do with Abi. But now, since her dad had already left, Abi was the head of the family, looking after her two younger brothers.'

Paul went on to describe how Abi had tried her best to keep the family together. How she had got a job, but her brothers wouldn't do as she said, and wouldn't help her round the house, and kept bunking off school and getting into trouble. How eventually social services came and told her that her brothers had to go into care.

Abi's head was low. Paul squeezed her shoulder.

'This is my impression of Abi, from what she has told me. I think Abi has taken on a lot of responsibility at a young age. She's a very caring sister and has tried to do her best by her brothers, and put her own schoolwork on one side so that she could help them. I think Abi feels responsible for not being able to look after her brothers. She thinks people look down on her and that they think it's her fault her brothers got taken into care.' Abi's shoulders wilted under Paul's hand, and he gripped it tighter. 'But my impression of Abi is that she's done more than anyone else to keep her family together. My impression is that Abi is a very brave, resourceful character, with a lot of determination. My impression is, because Abi is sometimes angry about the crap blow life has dealt her, people don't listen to her as much as they should. I also think Abi should try not to distrust people, because once people get to know her, they'll realise what a caring person she is.' Paul lifted his hand from Abi's shoulder and stepped a little further into the group. 'I'm glad I got to know Abi today. My impression of her is that she's quick-witted, intelligent, and thoughtful, and would make an excellent journalist. And I'm a little bit worried about what she has to say about me,' he added finally.

The girls giggled, and there was a generous round of applause. Abi finally lifted her head, revealing a face that was so uncomfortably red Kate could almost feel the pain of it. Kate clapped with the others, and finally the corners of Abi's mouth lifted a little. It wasn't quite the beam of happiness Dashna had shown, but for Abi, this small sign was a breakthrough.

'Your turn now, Abi,' Paul said. 'Do your worst.'

Abi unfolded her long limbs from her chair, her face still a bright crimson. She held up the tattered pages from her notebook and began reading, in a loud confident voice, at odds with her fingers, which were trembling slightly.

'I interviewed Paul Farrell. Paul is thirty-six. He's the editor of *The World*, and before that he worked as a war journalist and travelled all around the world, including in West Africa, Iraq, and Afghanistan.'

Abi went on to describe how Paul had always wanted to be a journalist, ever since seeing reports of a famine in East Africa, because he wanted to make a difference in the world. He had devoted himself to his career, ever since leaving school. Abi described how Paul studied journalism and went to work for a newspaper in America for a while, honing his craft. She described with relish every stage of Paul's work trajectory, until he reached his present position. It was obvious Abi shared Paul's enthusiasm for his career. Kate began to wonder if she had asked him anything at all about his personal life.

Then Abi said, 'When I asked Paul if he had any hobbies, he said he enjoyed his work so much, it was almost like a hobby to him. Even on holiday he reads all the newspapers. I asked him about his family, and he said he visits his sisters when he can, but one of them lives in Scotland and the other in Canada. His mother is also a journalist, and has a very busy life.' Abi looked up from her notes. Her quick gaze darted round the room, lingering for a while on Kate. She seemed to be deliberating what next to say. Finally, she took a deep breath. 'This is my impression of Paul. He is very ambitious and clever and has made a success of his career, but that's not the only thing about him.'

Kate switched her gaze to Paul, who was standing slightly behind Abi, his gaze fixed on the floor. He was listening intently, a small, self-conscious smile on his lips.

Abi still hadn't finished. She gave a small, backward glance in Paul's direction, then blurted out, 'I asked Paul if he had any family, and he said he had a godson George who he loved very much. My impression of Paul is that he would be a great godfather and a great dad if he had his own kids. He's a strong person, he's kind and he looks out for others. He's not the sort of journalist who dishes up dirt on celebs. He tries to write things about the world so that other countries can find out what's going on. He has a very strong conscience. If I got to be a journalist, I'd like to follow Paul's example, and I'm glad I met him.'

*

Paul was surprised to feel his face grow warm. Abi sat down hurriedly, and there was a burst of applause. Out of the corner of his eye he could see Kate, her slim hands a blur of clapping. He dropped his gaze to Abi to find her eyes bright and fixed on him. The girl would go far. Paul gave her a quiet nod, and, astonishingly, she broke into an answering grin.

Just one girl left to speak. Paul beckoned to Dashna, who was sitting shyly next to Kate.

Paul smiled. 'Your turn, Dashna.'

She rose to her feet, and all eyes turned to Kate, who shuffled uncomfortably, keeping her eyes on the floor. Paul was surprised to see her pick at the cuffs of her shirt in a nervous gesture.

Dashna began quietly, until a few of the girls called out, 'Can't hear you, Dash.' She gave an embarrassed cough, and began again. 'I wanted to interview Kate Hemingway because I have seen her modelling work and admired her for a long time. In my country it's not acceptable for a woman to be a model and to show off her body. I think Kate is very beautiful and I always thought she is lucky to be free to have her career.' She cleared her throat. 'As I started to interview Kate, I found out she is not lucky, like I thought. I asked her what her parents said when she wanted to be a model. She said her parents left her when she was a teenager, and they didn't care what she did.' Dashna's accented voice grew louder as she retold the tale of Kate's life, ending with her marriage to Stuart. Then she put her notepad down and addressed the group. 'I thought Kate's wedding sounded like a fairy tale ending, but then her husband died in Afghanistan, my country.'

Kate lifted her head. Paul was touched to see her reach out to Dashna, and take her hand in hers.

'Before I interviewed Kate I admired her because of her beauty,' Dashna continued. 'I admire Kate more now, because I have found out what sort of person she is inside. These are my impressions of Kate: she is very independent, she is strong, she is a loving mother. I'm glad Kate has found friends in At Home, because even though she has more freedom than I do, I think inside she must be lonely. I asked Kate if she would marry again, and she said no. It made me sad to hear her answer. We have a saying in Afghanistan, "There is a way from heart to heart". I hope one day Kate will find that way again.'

Dashna brought her final words out in an abrupt rush, and dropped back into her seat, still holding Kate's hand in hers.

Kate stared at her, dumbstruck, and the teenager gave her a quick, embarrassed smile. The whole room fell silent, their eyes on Kate, waiting for her reaction.

Kate held herself erect in her seat. She was smiling, but it was a small, constrained smile, and it was obvious to Paul she was struggling with her emotions. Her fingers were a little too tight on Dashna's, her body a little too rigid, and her eyes overbright.

In the silence that followed, Paul stood. 'Dashna, that was a great piece of interviewing.' He looked around. 'Dashna's right. Kate has good friends in At Home.'

The girls clapped, and though Kate joined in, Paul noted she was gazing at the floor.

Eventually the noise subsided. Chloe stood to thank Paul for running the workshop, and the group was finally free for the day. The girls yawned and stretched and pushed back their chairs. Within minutes they had scattered, leaving just Chloe, Kate, and Paul in the room.

'Paul, thank you so much,' Chloe said. 'That was excellent, and really broke the ice.' She looked from Kate to Paul. 'I'm going to go up to our room now, Kate. I need to write up my report for today, and catch up on a few emails. See you both at dinner.'

She left the room in her usual rush, and finally Paul and Kate were alone. The games room seemed unnaturally still now the girls had left. Kate stood under one of the high windows, and a shaft of light fell on her head, dancing with motes of dust. She raised her face to Paul's, and he saw that she was looking pale.

'Chloe's right,' she said. 'It was a great session. Thanks.'

'The girls made it what it was. They're a really bright group. It was a joy to listen to them.' He stepped a little closer, and added softly, 'And they taught me something today. "There is a way from heart to heart." Those are the most uplifting words I've heard in a long time.'

Kate hunched her shoulders, dropping her gaze.

'That was a lonely picture Dashna painted of you,' Paul

said. He reached out his hand to take hers. 'Is that how you feel?'

Kate shook her head, then shrugged. 'Sometimes. I still miss Stuart.'

'Me too,' he said quietly. He studied Kate's forlorn features, and there was a pain, like a great weight pressing on his chest. This afternoon, without the call of her job, and George, and all the surroundings of her busy life, Kate seemed no older than the others in the room. Just a lonely young woman, trying her best to battle through life. He wished more than anything he could take her in his arms, but they'd made an agreement. He studied her drooping head and was mentally saying to hell with the agreement, when his phone vibrated in his jacket pocket, bringing him to his senses. He didn't bother drawing the phone out. He knew it would be work. And just as well he'd been interrupted. If he really had broken Kate's agreement, he might have lost their fragile bond before it had even had a chance.

'It's a nuisance, but I need to get in touch with the office,' he said. 'What will you do for the next hour or so?'

'I'll phone Orla and George.' She lifted her head and her eyes met his. He was glad to see there was a smile in them. 'And then I'm going to hang around being lonely until it's time for dinner.'

'Come and sit with me while I work,' he said, reaching out a hand.

She shook her head. 'No, honestly, I really would like some time by myself. Clear my head.' She glanced at the high windows of the games room, where the sun was still pouring through despite the lateness of the day. The faint hint of a smile became a real one. 'Anyway, I'm dying to check out all that Countryside. There must be a few yokels and dairymaids I can dazzle with my city glamour.'

Paul laughed. 'You're in for a surprise. Country yokels drive expensive 4x4's these days, and the dairymaids shop online.'

The grin Kate gave him over her shoulder was cheerful enough, but Paul wasn't fooled. He gazed at the door she had

closed behind her, turning over their conversation. Then his
phone vibrated again, breaking in on his thoughts. He sighed
and drew it out of his pocket.

*

When Kate stepped outside the hostel the sun was descending
into the line of grey peaks in the distance, and the shadows
were lengthening on the ground. She took a look around her.
Not one of the girls was in sight. She guessed they'd all gone to
explore the few shops in the village at the bottom of the hill.

Kate turned in the opposite direction. A stone stile led into
a field, and she clambered over it and began to climb the steep
slope behind the hostel.

There is a way from heart to heart.

The words seemed to fit with the rhythm of Kate's feet as
she mounted the hill. She'd been longing to enjoy a walk
outdoors and to explore the views from the window. She kept
her head down and her eyes on her feet as she strode up the
dusty track. *A way from heart to heart.* The pieces of her heart
were carefully wrapped. What if she didn't want anyone to find
a way there?

She stopped halfway up the hill, suddenly feeling too
anxious to continue. It was getting darker, and the sun would
soon sink behind the hills. From the safety of her bedroom,
the scene below had seemed soft and inviting. Now Kate
stared around the unfamiliar landscape and unease threaded
through her as the shadows lengthened.

The thought crossed her mind that if Paul were with her,
she would feel fine. It would be an adventure. She dismissed
the image as soon as it had come. She turned about and
retraced her footsteps to the hostel, and the comforting lights
from the windows.

CHAPTER TEN

Next morning, Paul rose early. Already, the sun was hot in the sky, and the heat of it burned through his cotton shirt as he strolled down to the village. He took a moment to rest by a wooden gate, looking out over a field full of somnolent cows. At home in London, no matter how early he rose, the city was always awake, like a frenetic living being with perpetual insomnia. Here, in the solitude and the peace, his tension seeped away, evaporating in the hot, dry air like the dew on the ferns. He enjoyed the stillness for a moment or two; the soft sounds the cows made as they chewed; their leathery smell and the cloying scent of their dung.

Then he pulled himself away and carried on down the hill to the village shop, where he scanned the shelves for the day's newspapers. The strident headlines were an intrusion in the quiet of his morning, but after paying for them he tucked the bundle under his arm and began the climb back to the hostel. Most of the headlines were no surprise. Paul had already heard from his colleagues the night before which stories his competitors were running with. Even so, every morning he would read each one from cover to cover.

He was in the canteen with a large mug of tea and a redoubtable breakfast in front of him when Katerina appeared, looking delightfully dishevelled. She swept an errant lock of hair behind one ear.

'Can you believe I forgot my hair straighteners?'

Her blonde bob had lost its angular outline, curling in soft strands around her face. A few summer freckles were scattered over her nose and her high cheekbones, and the white vest and chinos she was wearing were creased from her rucksack.

'You look like a woman on holiday.' Paul smiled at the sight of her. 'It suits you.'

Her cheeks went pink under her freckles. She pushed her hair away from her face, and her gaze fell on the newspapers beside him. 'I suppose my bad hair day isn't really breaking news,' she said. 'And I see you're working already. The girls aren't even up yet.'

'The press never sleeps.' Paul waved a fork in the direction of the papers. 'I've been for a walk down to the village. It's a glorious day.'

'Hmm.' Katerina broke off to stifle a yawn. 'No day is glorious in the world of fashion until at least eleven o'clock. And I need several cups of tea before I can look half as cheerful as you do.'

Kate's sleepy expression and her tousled hair brought back vivid memories of the night she'd stayed with Paul. He remembered her waking, her warm limbs wrapped around him, and tried to think of a light reply, but failed. When he didn't speak, the pink in her cheeks deepened.

Eventually he cleared his throat, and shifted his attention to the newspapers in front of him. 'Is Chloe up yet?'

Kate turned her own gaze away awkwardly. 'She's gone to try and wake the girls.' Then, with an attempt to lighten the atmosphere, she pulled out one of her curls, and examined it with a sad shake of the head. 'I look like one of those shaggy sheep outside.'

She left him to collect her tray, and despite her professed tiredness could soon be heard wishing the hostel staff a friendly good morning.

Chloe was next to arrive, bustling in with her usual cheerfulness.

'How did the girls sleep?' Paul asked, as she pulled out a seat. 'Were there midnight feasts in the dorm?' He remembered his own days at boarding school, and added with a grin, 'Or worse?'

Chloe merely laughed, giving a resigned shrug. 'They're sensible girls. As long as the partying doesn't get out of hand, I don't ask.'

'They're a great bunch.' Kate arrived back with her tray. 'I expect they're all up this morning fresh as daisies.'

Chloe chuckled. 'Not exactly fresh. They spent all last night with the windows shut. And you know how hot it was. With thirty girls in the dorm, the smell this morning was pretty overpowering.'

'Can't they open the windows?' Paul was taken aback. The heat in his room had been stifling, even with his window wide open to the night air. 'Do you want me to take a look?'

'Oh, they can open them all right.' Chloe's chuckle deepened to become one of her hearty laughs, the sort that made her eyes twinkle with infectious merriment. 'They heard a couple of sheep bleating in the night, and they closed all the windows in case one got in.'

She gave way totally to giggles, her eyes watering, her round shoulders shaking. She rocked backwards and forwards, and Paul couldn't help but join in, laughing aloud with mirth.

'I don't see what's funny,' Kate said, looking from one to the other. 'I wouldn't want sheep roaming round outside my window either.'

Paul realised she was serious and tried to curb his laughter. It was a couple of seconds before he could adopt a more sober expression, during which time Kate continued to eye him askance.

'Don't worry,' he managed to say finally. 'There's no way a sheep would come inside. And even if it did, they're easy to get rid of.' He tried to keep a straight face. 'You just tell them they're baa-ed.'

This was too much for Chloe, who burst into further peals of laughter.

Kate rolled her eyes. 'Oh, haha.'

She began eating her toast in dignified silence. Paul couldn't resist. 'What about when you went for a walk yesterday? Any sheep set on you?'

She broke off a piece of toast. 'Actually I didn't get far,' she said, examining her crust without looking at him. 'It was getting dark. And there were weird country noises.'

'Weird noises?' He was curious now. 'Is that why you came back early?'

'I'm telling you they were weird. Like bats, or an owl or something.'

Paul glanced at Chloe, whose eyes danced.

'I tell you what,' she said. 'Why don't you two both go out for a walk and explore this morning? We're covering Women's Health, and I daresay Paul won't be able to contribute much to that discussion anyway,' she added.

'No,' he said, with an answering grin. 'I was going to do some work in here this morning. But a walk on the moors sounds a much better idea.'

'Is it really OK if I just go out?' Kate looked hopefully at Chloe. 'I mean, I don't want to leave you in the lurch.'

'Of course, love. The nurse from the local Well Woman clinic is coming in today, so there'll be two of us anyway.' She took in Kate's pale features. 'And if we're talking about women's health, a spot of fresh air will do you good.'

Kate caught Paul's eye, glowing with pleasure. His spirits lifted. A walk outside with Kate in the glorious sunshine out on the moors was an unexpected present. The first group of girls burst into the canteen, freshly showered, in a waft of shampoo and deodorant, and Paul found himself caught up in their surge of youthful vitality.

*

Kate pulled herself up to stand beside Paul on one of the large grey boulders that lay scattered on the moorland. They had reached the crest of the hill she'd abandoned the evening before. Below them the gentle sweep of the hillside dipped away, and the moors extended mile upon mile in soft shades of greens and lilac. Here and there dark green trees dotted the fields, like the bobbles on a woolly jumper. The sky was a glorious shade of blue, streaked with airplane trails. Kate spread her arms and turned slowly.

'This is heaven. All this space. And the glorious smell. Heather, and grass, and ferns.' She took in a deep breath, closing her eyes. 'And listen.' She tilted her head. 'Do you hear it? There's just … the breeze. And birds calling. And the weird sounds of Countryside.'

She opened her eyes with an exalted laugh, to find Paul had climbed right to the pinnacle of the boulder, and was gazing down at her. The sun was behind him, casting a bright glow around his head, and she had to crinkle her eyes to make out his features. He reached a hand to her, pulling her up easily to stand beside him, and her heart swelled with the pleasure in the moment.

'When I tried to come up here yesterday evening, I found it really spooky.' She gazed down on the peaceful scene below them. 'I think I must have been over-tired. It feels so good to be out here, away from everything – all the stresses and strains of work and home. It's like they've all been left behind in London.' She looked at Paul with a delighted laugh. 'And we're free.'

It was the closest Kate had come to a moment of pure happiness for a very long time. Paul's arm tightened around her waist, and her euphoria increased in a wild mix of joy and longing. She leaned into him, making no attempt to calm the excited thud of her heart. The heat of his body radiated through his thin shirt, and there were a few prickles of stubble at the base of his neck, which he had missed while shaving. Kate lifted her head to find him gazing down at her. The lines in his face softened, revealing a tenderness she couldn't ever recall seeing. She reached her fingers up to touch his cheek. The hand around her waist pulled her closer, into the arc of his arm.

'I wish I could break our agreement,' he said. He bent his head, and his lips touched hers. Kate had the fleeting impression of the warmth of his mouth on hers, and then he pulled back, his head blotting out the sun. 'As much as I love being with you like this, I'm looking forward to getting home. Alone, and with none of the responsibilities of this trip.'

Although Paul's tone was light, Kate was fully aware of everything he was holding in check. The years when he'd succeeded in concealing himself from her were over. She thought of how it would be if she forgot their pact; if she reached her arms around his neck and brought his lips to hers, to kiss him again with all the passion that was burning under the surface and crackling in the air around them. Her imagination moved on from kissing him, and she forced herself to take a slow breath, and to move a tiny step back on the rock, pushing against his unyielding arm.

'I can read everything you're thinking.' He reached out his free hand and touched her face. His fingers lingered, sliding down her cheek and along the length of her neck, where they came to rest. His thumb stroked the beat of her pulse. She leaned in, her eyes closing, and he bent his head, placing a soft kiss on her forehead.

'Come on,' he said, releasing her. 'I'd love more than anything to stay like this forever, but the girls will be thinking we've been eaten alive by sheep.'

He dropped from the boulder in one easy movement and turned for her, stretching out a hand. Kate slipped her fingers in his, and he pulled her lightly down.

'I'm not sure I like being an open book,' she said. The heat in her cheeks refused to subside, and her heart was beating rapidly.

He smiled. 'I can always tell exactly what you're thinking.' He brushed one of the wayward strands of hair from her brow. 'It's one of the first things I loved about you. That time in Stuart's garden. The day we met.'

His face was turned to the light now, and his eyes reflected the warm blue of the sky. Kate was transported again to the day they first met, watching the light glance off the pond, hearing Paul's footsteps approach. She frowned, troubled. She recalled the strength in Paul's arms as he caught her, and the intensity of his gaze on hers. It had been as though everything between them was open to the core, for one brief, burning moment. And then the flame was hidden.

The deserted moorland was silent. Kate had never spoken to Paul of their meeting. Now she searched his face, trying to read some meaning there.

'That day in Stuart's garden, something happened between us, I swear it. Something that threw me literally off balance. I know it sounds strange, but I swear I felt it.' She fixed her gaze on his, trying to fathom it. 'Did I imagine it?'

In the bright sunlight, all the planes of Paul's face were outlined in deep relief, as though carved in stone.

'No,' he said finally. 'It's not strange. I felt it, too.'

A bird called out in the heather close by, breaking the silence that followed. It was a lost, mournful sound, somehow discordant in the warm summer air. Kate shivered.

'What did it mean, then?' Her voice was low, the question intended more for herself than for Paul.

'I know what that day meant to me.' The lines of his face shifted and broke. 'It was the day my heart was ripped into two.'

Kate felt the pain of his words strike right through her. Paul stood unmoving, as though he were one of the boulders on the moors, holding out against the rush of his emotions. The intensity of his feelings, and the words he used to voice them, struck Kate dumb. It was as though everything about him were swept away, leaving only the core, raw and exposed.

His voice gentled as he took in her expression. 'I know I'm not like Stuart,' he said. 'Stuart was easy and open with everyone he met. And I know I kept things hidden from you. But I loved you from the start. Loved you more than I love my own happiness. More than I love my own life.'

The bird called again, and rustled deeper into the heather. Paul took Kate's face in his hands, and bent to kiss her. This time it was no gentle meeting of lips, but a mouth filled with tender, urgent passion. Kate leaned into him, and the sun beat down on them both as they kissed, easing the chill and filling Kate's very bones with heat. She wound her arms around Paul's neck, and pressed herself against him. His muscles hardened, and she could feel the strong beat of his heart mingle with her own and thrum through her body. For several long moments they clung, until Paul's kiss deepened, became more urgent, and the arms around her tightened until she felt the breath leave her body.

She broke their kiss with a gasp, and Paul released her, leaning his forehead against hers. His breath came in quick drafts.

'Katerina, Katerina.' He held her face in his hands. 'Next week you must come to stay with me again.'

Kate nodded, without speaking. He rested his head on hers for a while, gathering himself together. When his breathing had quieted, he took her hand in his.

'Come on, love. Let's go.'

Love. The Yorkshire expression filled Kate with a mixture of elation and fear, like the start of a rollercoaster ride. Her instincts told her to withdraw her hand from Paul's, to take a couple of steps away, but the light clasp of his fingers was like a spell, binding her to him.

They descended the path they had taken. All around them the heather was dry and crumbling in the heat. The way down was easier, but the sun was higher in the sky, and Kate felt the heat of it prickle her skin through her flimsy shirt. A bead of sweat trickled down her back. Paul moderated his long strides to hers, his strong hand steadying her on the dusty track.

At the bottom of the hill was a small brook, almost dry from the recent heat wave. They had crossed it easily that morning, but Kate saw with dismay that there were now a dozen large, shaggy sheep gathered around the dip. In the midday heat they were probably thirsty, and had stopped to take a drink from what was left of the stream. To Kate's city-bred gaze the sheep might as well have been a herd of hippos. The animals heard the sound of their approach and turned as one to stare.

'How are we going to get past?' She stopped dead on the path, her eyes fixed on the intimidating creatures ahead.

Paul looked from Kate to the brook, and then broke into a laugh. 'It's a few sheep. They'll scatter as soon as we get near.'

Kate eyed the group, who returned her stare with unnerving interest, and with no sign of moving.

'Why have they got horns?' Each sheep had a long, black face, and a pair of brown, beady eyes set wide apart on its brow. A set of impressive-looking horns sprouted from their heads, curling down behind their ears. On the rare occasions Kate thought of sheep, she imagined lambs – little, soft, woolly, timid creatures. These were tough, ragged animals, who were staring at her with bold curiosity.

'They're Swaledales,' Paul said. 'They're bred especially for moorland. It's a harsh environment out here in winter.'

'I suppose you've been out in the countryside since birth.' Nerves and her usual feeling of ignorance made Kate sound more irritable than she felt. 'Hunting and shooting with Lord Lucan.'

'Bingley.'

'What?'

'Lord Bingley.' Paul turned to face her. 'I went to school with Bingley's son. His father took us shooting on his estate a few times. Actually, not too far from here.'

'His name was Bingley? You're kidding me. Was Darcy there too? And Captain Wickham?'

Paul laughed. 'Listen, if you're not very careful I'm going to whistle those sheep over and get them to attack.' He caught Kate's shudder, and gave her a nudge. 'Man up, and get in the sodding chopper,' he said.

Kate eyed him sidelong and gave a nervous laugh. She was being ridiculous, and she knew it. Paul had conquered his fear of flying and climbed into a helicopter in a war zone. This was just a few sheep. What Paul didn't know was that Kate's only contact with animals had been the rats in her squat and a stray dog that had once bitten her leg. Neither of these encounters had endeared her to four-legged creatures.

'OK, we can do this,' she muttered. She eyed the sheep and straightened her shoulders. 'I'll think of the guys in my area. They were just the same. Hanging around in groups, staring at strangers. The trick is not to let them intimidate you.'

She set off at a slow saunter, head held high, just the hint of a swagger in her gait. As she approached the sheep, she looked neither right nor left. The animals scattered slowly, turning to watch as she passed them by. Their hooved feet stirred up the dust on the track, and they smelled strongly of dirt and musty wool. Kate didn't like the way their unblinking eyes followed her, but she schooled her expression into one of indifferent scorn, picking her way across the boulders on the brook. Finally she turned, deliberately taking up a stance of disdain.

'See?' she called. 'No problem.'

Paul laughed out loud. 'Next time I'm in the wrong neighbourhood I'll call you.' He carried on down the hill and leapt the brook to stand beside her. 'Good work.'

He smiled. The swell of happiness Kate had experienced standing on top of the boulder returned.

'I really showed them.' She took Paul's arm as they rejoined the path to the hostel. 'If only all our fears were as simple as a flock of sheep.'

CHAPTER ELEVEN

Paul held his mobile to his ear and gave a heartfelt curse.

'This is my fault,' he told his deputy. 'I took my eye off the ball. A rookie mistake.'

'Look, you couldn't have expected it,' John consoled him. 'Why would you?'

John was a steady, reliable man at the helm, and Paul was glad of his backup in charge, but his stomach clenched at the thought of what this news would do to Kate. In the past couple of days she'd appeared happier than she had in years. Paul had been congratulating himself on helping her step out of her shell. Persuading her to feel good about the future. Now this. His interview with Kate in *The World* had left her open to malicious gossip, and he felt the full force of the responsibility for it. Hell, he'd even known there'd be trouble as soon as he'd seen Barrie Dixon in the beer garden that day. And still he'd let it slip by.

He cursed his own stupidity again and exhaled, forcing the breath out between tight lips. 'Barrie's probably been working away at this story just to fill in column inches. It's been a damn slow couple of weeks for news.'

'Yeah, that,' John said. 'But he's a crafty bugger. It's one in the eye for you and your Kate Hemingway profile. Makes us look like schmucks.'

John was right there. The sympathetic picture Paul had painted of Kate in his interview had been undermined, and no matter how poor the aim, mud stuck.

'Maybe. But that's not my worry at the moment. It's going to devastate Kate when she reads this tomorrow.' Paul was adept at keeping his strong emotions in check, but if Barrie Dickson had been anywhere near him at that moment, he would have been tempted to smash a fist in his oily face.

He steadied himself. Anger wouldn't help Kate. Tomorrow morning she would see the papers, and there would be no concealing the story from her. In the meantime, Paul needed to remain calm, and think of a way of rectifying the situation.

'John, there's another avenue we can explore. But we need to get in first. Who do we have in Australia?'

*

'Kate.'

Kate dragged her eyes open, pulled out of a deep sleep, to find Chloe shaking her shoulder. Her friend was dressed, and was gazing down at her, bright eyed.

Kate sat up, immediately alert. 'What's up? What time is it? Are the girls OK?'

'Yes, it's not that, don't worry. It's Paul. He wants to have a word with you before the girls get up. He's in the games room.'

Kate groaned and fell back on the bed. 'Does that man ever sleep?'

'No seriously, Kate. I think it's important.'

Kate took in Chloe's expression and swung her legs off the bed in one swift movement. 'Is it Orla?' She grabbed hold of Chloe's arm, without giving her a chance to answer. 'Not George, surely. I just spoke to them last night.'

'No, no. Orla and George are fine. Paul will tell you. I'm just going to check on the girls. I'll see you later, in the canteen.'

Chloe's calm response did nothing to reassure Kate. She began to dress hurriedly as soon as Chloe left, and ten minutes later she ran into the games room, still tucking her shirt into her jeans. Paul was sitting at one of the tables, a tabloid newspaper in front of him. He raised his head as she entered. His expression was grim.

'What on earth's going on?' Kate cried. 'Is it George?'

Despite Chloe's reassurance, she couldn't prevent a surge of panic.

'No.' Paul caught her anxiety, and stood. 'No, of course not, he's fine. I didn't mean to worry you. I just wanted to talk to you before everyone got up.' He pulled out the chair next to him. 'Come and sit down.'

Kate walked round to his side of the table and sat, her heart fluttering in her mouth.

'Listen, I'm sorry, Kate. I should have guessed this would happen after I interviewed you. I let this slip by me.'

Kate's eyes widened as he pulled the tabloid forward.

'One of my competitors – that piece of shit Barrie Dickson – has been in touch with your mother. It's not good.'

Kate gave a sigh of relief. 'Oh, is that all?' She pressed a hand to her heart, which was still bumping painfully. 'I thought something really bad had happened.'

She pulled the newspaper towards her.

'Kate Hemingway "terrifying" to live with, says estranged mother.'

The sub-heading read:

'Fiona Hemingway forced to flee family home after Kate's violent outburst.'

Kate read on in silence. Paul sat back in his chair, and she could feel his eyes on her as she read every poisonous word. How as a teenager Kate had been so out of control she'd thrown a heavy glass vase at her mother, frightening her so much she'd had to 'run to a friend's'; how Kate had a habit of telling lies to get her own way; how she refused to buckle down at school; how she'd attacked a pupil and threatened to punch one of the teachers; how her mother had begged her to come to Spain and live with her and her step-father, but Kate had refused, preferring to spend her time with 'druggies' and 'drop-outs'.

And so the article went on. There was even a reference to the charity At Home, and whether the public should really be asked to donate to 'lost causes' when there were so many 'hard-working, respectable' young women trying to get by on student grants. Kate raised her brows at this.

When she reached the end of the article, she lifted her head and pushed the paper away from her, back towards Paul. She had thought she was inured to her mother's attacks and was annoyed to note there was a bitter taste in her mouth. Her hands were actually trembling a little. She shoved them under the table, gripping them together in her lap.

There were deep shadows under Paul's eyes. It struck Kate he must have known about the story the night before. He looked a little pale, and she guessed he'd spent a sleepless night.

'I didn't want to tell you yesterday evening,' he said. 'I didn't want you to be lying awake, worrying.'

Kate shrugged, holding her head stiffly. 'It's no big deal. That's my mum for you. I hope they paid her well for her story.' She clenched her mouth shut, afraid that her lips, too, might start to tremble. Paul placed a hand on her shoulder, and she shrugged it off. 'I told you, it doesn't matter.' She edged away from him slightly. If he took her in his arms, as he seemed to want to do, she would burst into tears. She could feel them gathering behind her eyes and prickling at the back of her throat.

She stood, pushing her chair back. 'In fact, I bet Mum's done me a favour. My agent keeps going on at me to raise my profile, and this is perfect. I expect job offers will flood in. That's the thing about fashion. Everyone loves a drama queen.'

Paul stood with her. 'Kate,' he said.

She ignored him. 'I'm going to get a cup of tea,' she said, walking away. 'Then when Orla's up I'm going to phone her and tell her not to let George look at any newspapers today.'

There was a definite crack in her voice at these last words. Behind her she heard Paul push back his chair, as though about to follow. She moved swiftly to the door and pulled it open. Once out of Paul's sight she ran up the stairs to her own room, where she shut herself in the bathroom and burst into tears.

At times like these the pain of missing Stuart crushed her under an unbearable weight. When Stuart was alive, everything had been safe. With Paul, everything was an unknown, spreading around her so that every step was on unfamiliar ground.

She pressed the heels of her hands to her eyes, trying to stem the flow of tears. The worst thing was, the words her mother had used in the article had an element of truth. They'd been twisted to portray Kate in the worst possible light, but there was no escaping the fact that the events had happened.

It was true Kate had once thrown a vase. She'd been fourteen at the time. As she grew older, and their relationship began to break down, her mother would often find excuses to leave Kate by herself. She spent many weekends at her boyfriend's house, and Kate became used to being alone. She didn't mind the solitude. In fact, she preferred it to the constant arguments. One time, though, days went past before her mother returned, and the weekend became a full week. Kate ran out of food, and had to ask the neighbours if she could borrow some cash.

Unfortunately for Kate, on this occasion the neighbours had taken it upon themselves to speak to her mother, and had probably upbraided her for leaving Kate alone. Her mother came into the house in a vile mood and accused Kate of spreading lies about her. Kate began to defend herself, but her mother told her she was 'nothing but trouble'. Like father, like daughter, she said. She wished she'd left Kate behind in Australia with her useless dad.

It was the final straw. The vase was the nearest thing to hand. Without thinking, Kate picked it up and threw it. It fell far short of its target, smashing into fragments on the kitchen floor with a satisfyingly loud crash. Immediately, Kate regretted her outburst, but it provided her mother with the excuse she needed. She left the house again, telling Kate not to talk to 'those sodding nosy neighbours', or she'd kill her.

After she'd gone, Kate swept up the pieces of the vase and put them in the bin. She was alone again, and to her teenage mind it seemed she had only herself to blame. Maybe if she were a better person, her parents might actually want to spend time with her.

Now Kate took stock of her mother's interview, and

couldn't help the terrible feeling returning that somehow it was all her fault. There must be something wrong with her. A feeling of panic began to overtake her. When Stuart was with her, he would laugh away her fears. He would kiss her, make her feel loved, make her feel, with his light, happy, cheerful nature, that there was nothing to fear in the world.

Kate knew Paul wanted to console her, but their relationship was all too new and strange. She found it hard to adjust to this new Paul; the man who appeared to love her for who she was. It was tempting to run back down to the games room and test his love. To feel his arms around her, and have him tell her again how much he loved her, but it was no use. She buried her face in her hands, giving way to her tears.

She brought her sobs to a snuffling halt and reached for her phone. At times like these Orla was a rock. They had cried on each other's shoulders through all the major crises of their lives.

She pressed Orla's number, and there was her voice, bright and breezy, and full of life.

'The bitch,' she cried, when Kate told her the news. 'I hope she got her thirty pieces of silver, the aul' harridan. One day your mam and my mam should go head to head.' She gave a laugh that lifted Kate's soul and covered all the pain they'd each been dealing with for years.

They went on to talk of Orla's plans for the day. There was a miniature steam railway nearby, and then a picnic, and then back to the beach, which was George's 'absolute favourite place in the world'.

Kate chuckled. The sound of her friend's laughter was an instant lift. 'Thanks so much for having him, Orla.' She sobered, and added more seriously, 'You're absolutely my best friend. I don't know what I'd ever do without you.'

There was a short silence at the end of the phone. Then Orla said, 'Sure, if I weren't here, then I'm sure you'd go on. You have lots of friends.'

'I really don't know what I'd do, Orla,' Kate insisted. 'I mean it.'

There was another uncomfortable silence. Then Orla said, 'Listen Kate, me and George are going down to breakfast. We'll phone tonight, OK?'

They said their goodbyes, and Kate ended the call. For a couple of minutes she stared at the silent phone in her hand. Talking with Orla had helped a little, until that strange evasiveness resurfaced. Orla was still exactly the same as when Kate had left on the trip. Ducking and diving, and avoiding answering things. What was wrong?

But there was no time to ponder this problem, on top of everything else. The sound of the girls talking and giggling in the hallway could be heard as they trooped down to breakfast. Kate sighed and stood to gaze at herself in the mirror. Time to face the day. Her cheeks were all blotchy with tears, but that was easily remedied. She splashed cold water on herself and proceeded to apply her make-up. Some careful use of foundation would work wonders. Playing a part was actually the only skill she'd learned in life, but at least it came in useful.

*

The staff had given Paul his usual loaded breakfast tray, but this morning he pushed the bacon and eggs round his plate without eating.

'So you think she took it OK?' Chloe pressed him.

Paul shook his head and shoved his uneaten breakfast to one side. 'She took it too well. That's the problem. She walked off as though I'd just shown her the day's weather report.' He placed his head in his hands. He knew exactly how hurt Kate had been, and it grieved him to the soul that he had been unable to help her. And it hurt him, too, that she rejected him by leaving the room. It was tempting to go after her, to take her in his arms, but he knew there was no point forcing the issue. Kate had to begin to trust him. She had to come to him of her own accord, or not at all.

Not at all. That was a terrible possibility. He shook the thought away.

The canteen door opened and Kate walked in. The room quietened. The girls were all plugged in to social media. The news would have gone round like wildfire that Kate had been *Shaft*ed by her own mother. Several heads looked her way, but she made for the kitchen hatch.

'Morning,' she called. As usual when she greeted the staff, her voice was warm and cheery. She stopped to chat for a while, asking them about the recipe for the apple crumble they'd provided the evening before, as though nothing in the world were troubling her.

When she finally approached Paul's table, she made no reference to her mother's article beyond a murmured 'Thanks for waking me' in Chloe's ear. She then sat down beside Paul, and proceeded to take small bites out of her toast. A crumb lodged in her throat, and she coughed and washed it down with a cup of tea.

She glanced briefly Paul's way. That short moment of contact was enough to tell him how much pain she was suffering beneath her composure. Her eyes were over bright, and it seemed to him she had been crying. He wished they were alone, and that he could try to draw her out, but with the curious gazes of the girls on them, it was impossible.

Chloe caught his eye and gave a tiny nod. He pushed back his chair and stood, tapping his spoon on the table. The girls fell silent.

*

Kate looked up in surprise when Paul rose to his feet. He was standing with his back to her, facing the rest of the room. The muscles in his shoulders shifted as he pushed back his chair. The girls in the group gazed at him as expectantly as Kate.

'Good morning, everyone,' he said. 'I expect you've all heard by now there's been an article in the paper about Katerina this morning.' He held up a copy of the *Shaftesbury*. The girls hummed acknowledgement. A few of them turned to look at Kate. The glances they bestowed on her were curious, but sympathetic. 'I wouldn't normally buy this rubbish, but unfortunately it's my job to read what other journos are writing, so I have to.' There were a few murmurs and one or two giggles. 'Believe it or not, the editor of the *Shaft* has actually taught us a couple of valuable lessons today. First lesson is one you all know, and it saddens me to say this as a journalist: you can't believe everything you read in the papers. This article proves it. You've all come to know Katerina, and you know she's nothing like the person they've described her. I don't know why Katerina's mother felt she had to speak to the press in this way. It's not up to me to judge, but it leads me on to the second lesson. Sadly it's a lesson a lot of you are already familiar with: sometimes your family members will let you down. I know we should be able to rely on our parents for support, but it's a sad fact that sometimes we just can't. Now, I've only known you for a few days, but already I can see how much you all support each other in At Home, and I admire you for it. I'm sure you'll all support Katerina through this. And I'd also like to say how much I admire how Katerina has responded to this article with grace and dignity. Anyway, that's a long enough speech,' he gave them a small smile, 'and now I'm going to finish my breakfast.'

One of the girls cheered, and then the rest joined in with clapping and whistles. It was all almost too much for Kate. There was a stupid lump in her throat and she knew there was a danger she would burst into tears again.

Paul pulled out his chair and sat back down, and the girls returned to their breakfasts and their gossip. Kate kept her eyes on her plate. It wasn't until she felt the touch of Paul's hand on hers that she looked up.

His eyes were hard, but he was trying to make light of things. 'I tell you what, if Barrie Dickson ever finds himself in this neck of the woods I'll round up a flock of those sheep and we'll all set on him. He won't know what's hit him.'

Kate gave a watery chuckle. '"Journalist savaged by sheep." I can just see the headlines.' She returned the pressure of his fingers. 'Thanks. It means a lot.'

'Oh, now you'll set me off,' Chloe broke in.

Kate turned her head and registered with surprise how Chloe's eyes had misted over, and she was pressing her lip together. The girls' show of solidarity had moved her to tears.

Chloe was unfailingly cheerful and down-to-earth. Her sudden display of emotion caused Kate to swallow furiously at the lump in her throat.

There was a dangerous silence for a couple of minutes, until Paul broke in. 'Well if you're both going to cry this morning, I'll have to join you.'

Chloe let out a chuckle.

'Shut up, Paul.' Kate laughed, withdrawing her hand from Chloe's arm. His deadpan humour had succeeded in relieving the tension, and at the sound of Kate's laughter some of the strain left his own features. Kate realised how responsible he must feel for her mother's article. She was about to tell him it didn't matter, that her mother's behaviour wasn't his fault, when he changed the subject.

'I'm sorry the day has started badly.' He looked at her, deadly serious. 'You need to keep your strength up, today of all days.'

She raised a wary eyebrow. 'Is that right?'

'Haven't you read the timetable? Chloe's organised a trip to a farm.' He leaned closer. 'A sheep farm. You're coming face to face with your nemesis.'

He leaned back in his chair and laughed out loud at her expression. As a joke, it wasn't the funniest, but Kate grinned back, feeling the unhappiness drain away a little.

*

Chloe had organised a coach to take the group further into the Yorkshire moors and right into the heart of the countryside. It was the perfect outing to take Kate's mind off things. They left straight after breakfast, travelling through twisting roads and climbing higher and higher. Gradually the houses and villages fell away, and the gentle, rolling moorland became more rugged. The scattered clumps of trees dwindled to just the occasional lone rowan dotted here and there. Up here, exposed to the elements, the soft green of the fields was tinged with a barren grey.

The coach rumbled past dark, brooding stretches of water, climbing steadily up onto the tops. Here, their way became just a narrow ribbon of tarmac, undulating over the hills into the distance, with the vast moorland spreading out for miles in every direction.

For the whole journey, Kate pressed her nose to the glass, drinking in the beauty of it. Chloe was right. This week away from London was a break from all her worries. Even her mother's bitter words seemed to dry up and frizzle into nothing under the bright blue sky. At first sight, the moors seemed empty, but as they travelled deeper into the heartland Kate could see rabbits hopping away as the coach passed, and pheasants collecting in pairs on the dry stone walls. Occasionally Paul would reach over her shoulder to point out a red kite, wheeling in the sky above them. And once they even startled a short-eared owl out hunting by daylight. It flapped away from the trundling coach, disgruntled and magnificent.

They left the narrow road to bump down a long potholed track and finally arrived at the farm. The girls hung back, letting Chloe, Kate, and Paul alight first.

'Do people really live right out here?' one of them asked Paul as he passed.

He gave her one of his funny, downturned smiles. 'Yes. Maybe it's quiet compared to London, but lots of people like it here.'

'But what do they actually *do*?' Sarah, the girl who loved fashion, and who was such an excellent artist, was gazing out, totally bewildered.

A lot of the other girls seemed to wonder the same thing. They were murmuring and peering through the windows as though they'd just landed on another planet. A planet with no bars, clubs, or signs of civilised life.

Kate climbed down from the coach. It seemed to her that, just as the girls thought their surroundings alien, the local farm hands must have heard that a group of young women from London was booked for the day. As soon as the coach pulled up, several men slouched into the yard. They wore peaked caps pulled low over their eyes and they cast quick, curious glances at the coach.

The girls emerged into the bright sunshine and the warm, earthy smells of the farm. The farm lads appeared purposeful, as though they had some business out there at the front of the farm, but Kate could see their interest was firmly centred on the exotic creatures flocking into the yard. The group swarmed and scattered, looking around and exclaiming. Their loud London accents hung in the air like a foreign language. When fashion-conscious Sarah descended, it was too much. The young men gave up any pretence at being busy and turned as one to stare.

Sarah had decided to go with an ironic cow-print dress that morning. The high-heeled wedges were gone, since Chloe had finally managed to persuade her they would get ruined on a walk through farm buildings. In their place were the only boots Sarah had: a pair of white leather cowboy boots with gold trim. She caught the young lads staring and glared haughtily, before picking her way over the yard to join her friends.

Paul nudged Kate's arm, and she choked down a smile. The young men stayed on one side of the yard and the girls at the other, eyeing each other as though they were at some sort of old-fashioned dance, until a man Kate thought must be the owner of the farm appeared through the barn door. The farm hands scattered like seeds in the wind, returning to the jobs they should have been doing.

The farmer was a short, square-set man in his sixties, with an alert pair of eyes under brows that bristled in a fearsome way. He introduced himself as William, and within a short space of time he had rounded up the group of girls, for all the world as though they were one of his flocks of sheep, and herded them into a dry, white-washed outbuilding equipped with rows of old wooden chairs.

CHAPTER TWELVE

Inside the old barn, hi-tech computer equipment stood on a rickety table in preparation for the farmer's talk. The large screen and laptop gleamed incongruously in the dusty, whitewashed outhouse.

Kate leaned over to Paul and whispered, 'They have broadband in The Countryside. Who knew?'

William strode over to the table in his battered wellingtons and fired up the laptop with brisk efficiency. A beautiful shot of the farm appeared on screen, seen in autumn, with the fells a glorious mixture of gold and brown rising up behind it.

'Anyone ever been on a farm before?' The farmer cast a doubtful gaze around the room.

The girls shook their heads, apart from Dashna, who raised her hand shyly. 'My uncle has a farm in Afghanistan.'

'Oh, aye?' He nodded, with the gleam of the enthusiast. 'I look forward to hearing about it, lass, after you've done our tour. Compare notes, like.'

Kate found herself having to concentrate hard on William's slow, unfamiliar accent, but he very soon had her enthralled. A series of photos flowed past on the screen. Each image showed the farm, but in the background, as if by magic, the seasons could be seen slowly changing. The greens and gold of autumn gradually became dull brown, and then suddenly there was a vast expanse of white, which caused the group to gasp. In London, snow was never white. It fell in sooty drops to lie as muddy slush on the pavements. Here on the fell, the snow spread under a virgin frost, as pristine as a Christmas card.

The photos revolved. Winter turned to spring, and then to

high summer.

'Out here we're ruled by the seasons.' William pointed to the fells on screen. 'We're exposed, we're a long way above sea level, and it can be a bleak place at times. You're seeing us at our glorious best today. In the summer, there's nowhere on earth like it. That's why Yorkshire's known as "God's own county".' He gazed round the room with a pride tinged with challenge. 'Our year starts in October, with mating season. Or "tupping time" as we call it.'

The girls burst out laughing and nudged each other.

William grinned. 'Aye, we all have different names for it. Out here, we call the rams "tups", and mating is "tupping".'

In October, he explained, during mating season, the ewes were brought down from the fells and into the lower pastures. This made it easier for the farmer to keep an eye on the flock when the ewes became pregnant.

'The ewes find it more comfortable down here in the pasture for mating than what they do up on the fell. It's a bit like checking into a five-star hotel.' He flicked onto a slide showing several ewes in a field. 'You can tell they're relaxed, because look – they're all smiling.'

This caused another ripple of laughter, and Paul nudged Kate. 'See, those ewes are just a bunch of girls out looking for a date. I told you they were nothing to be scared of.'

Kate dug her elbow in his arm and shook her head.

William explained how the rams, or *tups*, would have their chests marked with brightly coloured paint. When a tup mated with a ewe, some of his paint would be left on her back as evidence. The farmer changed the colour of the paint every two weeks. In this way, he could keep track of when a ewe fell pregnant, and when she was likely to deliver.

'Sometimes it takes a while for a ewe to fall pregnant.' A photo appeared on screen, showing a ewe's shaggy rump, branded with several different colours. 'This un's had to have several goes at it.'

More laughter. Then William's talk turned serious, telling of the lambing season in spring, and how it formed the most arduous time of year for the farmer. Occasionally they would lose a ewe, or one of the lambs would be too frail to survive. No matter how often a sheep died, the farmer was always distressed at the loss.

'It's summer now, and the sheep are back up on the fell. We can't leave them grazing in the same spot all year, though. We have to move them around, to make best use of the land. Our shepherd, Brendan, is going to give you a demonstration of rounding up the sheep. I hope you all have shoes fit for walking.' The old farmer swept a doubtful glance along the floor, raising his eyebrows as he caught sight of Sarah's cowboy boots. He made no comment, merely smiled to himself as he began to pack away the laptop.

*

Out on the fell the sun beat down from a colourless sky. The blue of the heavens seemed to have been burnt away, leaving just a pale wash. The girls picked their way up the moorland track, chattering and exclaiming at the heat. William led the way, his head bent in conversation with Dashna, and Kate followed a couple of paces behind. A few incomprehensible snippets of their conversation drifted back to her.

'*Karakul sheep ... Turkmen ... pelts ... market ...*'

Kate smiled to herself. From the way William had his head bent in concentration, she guessed he found Dashna's descriptions fascinating.

Dashna was a shy teenager, still not quite confident in her use of English, and was generally happy to sit back and let the other girls do the talking. With William's gentle encouragement, she began speaking at length, her head turned to his in her colourful scarf, her profile animated. She spoke of her uncle, who owned the farm, and then of the other members of her family. Gradually their conversation turned away from farming, and Kate caught snatches that were laced with a mixture of wistful homesickness and pride: *my uncle ... my father ... my sisters ... my mother ...*

Kate dropped her gaze to her feet and watched her boots on the track, plodding uphill in time to the soft rhythms of

Dashna's speech. She knew Dashna missed home; knew her life had not been easy. Even so, for all her troubles, Kate heard her list her relatives and felt a stab of envy. All those people to love. The only blood relative she had was George. The cloud of depression that had lifted descended again. She thought of her mother's article, and wondered if William read the newspapers. He seemed an intelligent man. What must he think of her when he read what was written about her in the papers by her own mother? When he discovered she had been rejected by her own family? A hot blush of shame washed over her, and her face prickled in the heat of the sun.

And then Paul was there beside her, matching his long stride to her slower gait. His arm brushed hers as he caught up with her, and his eyes met hers, filled with steady warmth. Some of the depression seemed to fall away, and she lifted her head.

Shortly afterwards, Abi fell into step on Paul's left. Kate took in her arrival with a quiet smile. Wherever Paul went, Abi would follow, questioning him with dogged determination about his work in newspapers. She appeared to have set her heart on journalism as a career, and she rivalled George in her hero worship. Paul shifted a little on the path to accommodate her, looking down at her with an easy-going grin. He was rewarded with one of Abi's rare smiles.

It gave Kate a deep sense of satisfaction to see how Abi had altered after just a few days away from the cares of home. The pale, angry girl who had stormed out of the tube station on the day of their departure seemed a different person. The young woman striding along beside them had a healthy glow in her cheeks, and she was gazing about her with an intelligent curiosity. The sight of her lifted Kate's spirits enormously, putting her own melancholy into perspective.

The climb was long and steep. Eventually they reached one of the dry stone walls that crisscrossed the moorland, and William brought the group to a halt.

'Now then,' he said. 'Brendan's up yonder.' He jerked his head in the direction of the flock of sheep two fields away.

'We'll wait here and let him and the dog do their work.'

William pulled a walkie-talkie from his pocket, crackled the radio into action, and gave a signal. In the distance a tall, lithe figure peeled away from the shade of a birch tree. At the sound of the shepherd's whistle a dog raced off at an angle. The young man walked steadily forward, calling out odd words and giving his shrill whistle, while his collie alternately ran and crouched. Gradually the flock began to move as one, ambling towards the gate. The collie waited beside them, bounding forward when one of the sheep strayed or lingered. In less than ten minutes the whole flock of thirty or so sheep was making its way into the next pasture, with much anxious bleating, but otherwise obedient to the dog and shepherd.

Once the sheep were in, and the gate shut, the girls began a rapt cheer.

'That was brilliant,' Kate said.

Paul smiled. 'There. Obedient and docile. Now we only have to see some sheep close up, and your sheep phobia will finally be conquered.'

She grinned back, then felt a little foolish when William halted beside her on his way back down the hill.

'Happen you don't see many sheep in London.' His grey eyes twinkled, but he added seriously. 'We've a ewe and her lamb back down in the barn. If you want to come and see them close up, nice and quiet like, you're welcome.'

*

There was a humid, earthy smell in the barn – the smell of sheep's wool, nursing ewes, and hay. Paul felt the change in temperature as they stepped inside. After the heat on the fell, the cooler air was like a balm on his skin. He leaned against a white-washed wall and felt the pleasant chill of the stones seep through his shirt.

To one side of the barn a ewe and her lamb lay in the hay. The farmer was reluctant to let the entire group come and watch, saying that the lamb was sickly, and needed quiet. So Chloe collected the rest of the girls and took them back up onto the fell, where they scattered to eat their packed lunches.

William had beckoned Kate over in the yard and told Paul he was welcome to accompany them to the barn if he was interested. When Paul nodded, Abi moved to his side like a shadow, making four of them.

Kate and Abi crouched beside the animals, the farmer standing behind them.

'What's wrong with the lamb?' Kate asked, her voice hushed as though in a hospital.

'She's always been sickly, has that 'un,' William said. 'Right from birth. She was the second twin. The first was born healthy, but with this 'un it was touch and go. Her mam was ill giving birth to her and rejected her. Then this ewe here lost her own.' He indicated the shaggy sheep lying protectively in front of the lamb. 'So we gave this ewe the sick lamb to look after, and she took to it.'

Kate hugged her hands around her knees. 'You mean the lamb was rejected by its mother?'

She was gazing at the ewe intently. Paul straightened up from his position by the wall.

'Aye, lass,' the farmer told her. 'It happens sometimes. Sometimes a ewe will abandon her lamb, and nothing we can do will make them take. But this ewe has looked after it. Taken to it like it was her own.'

'That's what happened to my brothers.' Abi's voice rang out suddenly in the echoing barn. The ewe shifted and raised her head, and Kate turned to look at Abi. 'I mean – ' Abi dropped her voice, and glanced at the farmer. 'I mean, my mum would have looked after my brothers, and everything. But she couldn't. Now their foster mum has taken to them like they were her own.'

The farmer stirred, shifting his feet on the barn floor. 'Aye, happen. Sometimes people become blood family. That shepherd up yonder, Brendan, I call him my grandson, but he's not. He's my stepdaughter's son. Not related by blood. But he's a good lad. He's like my own.'

Abi turned her attention to the sheep. Her hands gripped her knees tightly, and her back was rigid. Even from his position removed from the group, Paul could sense the young girl was battling with some strong emotion. She was a young woman who rarely opened up, and who rejected any offers of sympathy with angry pride.

Paul was at a loss what to do. He wanted to go to her side, to at least drop a reassuring hand on her shoulder, but from his experience of her that week he knew his hand would be shrugged off. Paul had noticed how she shied away from physical contact. The other girls would hug each other, and walk arm in arm, but Abi held herself aloof, reacting with irritation to anyone offering a comforting word or a touch.

Kate's head was in profile, and she was watching Abi quietly. She reached out a hand and placed it gently over the young girl's slim fingers, which were gripped so tightly around her knee. Abi let Kate's hand lie there, without shrugging it away.

'Remember Dashna's saying?' There was a gentle sympathy in Kate's profile. 'There is a way from heart to heart. Your brothers will be OK with their foster mum. And they still have you.'

Abi didn't speak. She continued to gaze at the animals. And then Paul watched as she turned her fingers beneath Kate's hand and returned her clasp. For a couple of minutes they sat there, two prickly young women united beside the ewe and her adopted lamb.

'Aye lass,' the farmer said, breaking the silence. 'Love can grow in the strangest places.'

The door swung open, letting a long shaft of brilliant sunshine into the barn. The shepherd stood silhouetted in the doorway; a straight-backed young man, with dark eyes. Abi rose to her feet, her features soft, her eyes bright with recent emotion. Her red dress made a splash of colour in the light from the doorway. The shepherd stood still at the entrance to the barn, his gaze fixed on her.

Paul glanced from one to the other, and then at Kate. She was watching the young couple's exchange. When she rose to her feet, she caught Paul's eye and gave a slow smile.

'Have you brought the lamb's feed, lad?'

The shepherd registered his grandfather's presence. 'Aye.' He held up a large bottle of milk.

The farmer glanced at Kate. 'Perhaps you'd like to help Brendan give our lamb its feed?'

Abi dropped her gaze and studied the barn floor.

'I think Paul and I will go and get our lunch,' Kate said, casting a quick glance in Paul's direction. He nodded, and she went on, 'But perhaps Brendan wouldn't mind showing Abi how to feed the lamb.'

Abi lifted her head then and regarded the shepherd, who remained motionless in the doorway, as still as one of the trees on the moorland.

William nodded briskly. 'Aye. I've work to do. Brendan, you show this young lass.'

The shepherd stepped into the barn. Kate and Paul murmured a greeting on their way out, which he barely acknowledged. The farmer headed back to the farmhouse, and as they stepped into the farmyard, Paul took in Kate's demure profile with amusement. She raised her face innocently, and he said with a small smile, 'You little matchmaker.'

She caught her lip between her teeth. 'They were just so smitten with each other, weren't they?' Her eyes were round. 'Did you see how he looked at her? Like they were the only two people in the world. You and me might just as well not have been there, for all the notice he took of us. Strange, how it happened so suddenly like that. Like Cupid's arrow.'

Her lips parted in a laugh, and for a minute or two she gazed at Paul, delight at the couple's meeting blooming in her features. He tried to speak, but could think only of the time he had first set eyes on Kate, that afternoon in the heat of summer. The intensity of that experience never lessened. He wondered if that poor shepherd boy felt the same excruciating emotion.

When Paul failed to reply, the light slowly dimmed in Kate's features.

'It wouldn't be easy for that young man, though, would it?'

she said. 'I mean if he really feels something?'

'No.' Paul breathed an assent. 'He seemed to me like a guy who feels things intently.'

'The strong, silent type.' There was no mockery in Kate's words. Her eyes on his were filled with tender warmth.

Paul studied her expression for a moment or two. Warmth was a long way from the intensity of his own emotions. He wondered if Kate's feelings would ever rival his own in strength. He knew he should be glad their relationship had come this far, but inside he was conscious of a terrible impatience. Almost desperation.

'Come,' he said. 'Let's go and join the others.'

Kate took his arm. 'Yes, it's hours since you've eaten any food. You must be ready to pass out.'

Affection and teasing. There was a time when Paul would have given anything for this sort of relationship with Kate. Now it was nowhere near enough.

*

The girls milled about the farmyard, waiting their turn to say goodbye to William. Kate took the farmer's hand, and he fixed her with his sharp eyes.

'City folk think we're remote up here, but we see a lot of life, lass. See it more clearly than maybe what they do in town.' He pressed Kate's hand. 'And we don't believe all we read in the papers,' he added in an undertone. Kate felt her cheeks redden under his shrewd gaze. 'You've a good set of folk around you,' he went on, glancing over at Paul, who was waiting patiently beside the coach. 'People need other people, lass.'

He patted her hand and released it. Kate stammered some sort of reply.

Later, she sat beside Paul on the coach, waiting for the rest of the group to board. The farmhands had all found a reason to appear in the yard again, and some of the girls were flirting outrageously. Sarah was showing off her now dusty boots, and Kate wasn't surprised to see several of the group swapping mobile phone numbers. She glanced around for Abi and made out her red dress in the corner of the yard. Abi had her back to the coach, and Kate wasn't surprised to see Brendan's dark head bent close to hers. He was addressing her urgently. Abi's gaze was fixed on the floor. The shepherd reached into his pocket. There was a scrap of white paper in his tanned fingers. He lifted Abi's hand, pressed the paper into it, and curled her fingers around it with his own. Abi lifted their joined hands to his chest and raised her head. As Kate watched, Brendan cast a quick glance around and then pulled her to him, dropping a brief, hard kiss on her lips. Then he stepped back. Abi turned away, her fist around the scrap of paper, her face flushed.

Kate gave a gasp. Paul leaned over her shoulder to see what she was looking at, and she pointed to the corner, where Brendan was watching Abi's back as she walked away. His face was dark. Kate pressed her hand to the window.

'Oh,' she said. 'What will they do?'

'He looks like a young man who will find a way.'

The shepherd's expression was stony, but there was a resolute set to his shoulders. He stood erect by the barnyard wall.

Kate turned her head. Paul's determined face was close to hers. He switched his gaze from the window, and his eyes fell on her mouth. In a swift counterpart to the shepherd's actions, he bent to kiss her, his lips hard on hers.

'He'll find a way,' he repeated.

The rest of the group clambered on board, and the quiet of the coach was broken. The driver started up the engine with a dull rattle. Last to board was Abi. As she walked past their seat, Kate noticed her fingers, still clenched around the scrap of paper.

The coach reversed out of the yard, and Brendan remained by the wall, watching until it disappeared.

They began the descent to the lower reaches of the moors. Kate stared out of the window at the birds on the horizon. They wheeled and fluttered, clusters of black dots on the skyline that grouped, scattered, and regrouped.

There is a way from heart to heart. Dashna's saying was a refrain running through Kate's mind, ever since she'd heard it. And now her words were joined by the words of the farmer. *People need other people.*

She thought of the rejected lamb in the barn, wondered how any parent could treat their child the way her own mother had treated her. A fierce well of love for George rose up inside her. Maybe it was true that people needed other people, but all Kate could see were images of the pain love could cause, rising in her mind one after another: the way Stuart had looked as he embraced her and George in the airport that last time, his usually cheerful expression as bleak as the shepherd's on the hill; the way Paul had looked, shoulders hunched with pain in his apartment; the way Abi looked, bowed with anxiety for her brothers.

It seemed everywhere Kate looked, relationships caused pain. Her back was straight as she gazed at the landscape, and she was filled with determination. That pain would never weigh George down. Not if there was anything at all in her power to prevent it.

CHAPTER THIRTEEN

The first thing Kate did when she got back to her room in the hostel was to phone Orla and George.

'Hello?' Orla shouted. 'Is that you, Kate?'

There was a crashing din in the background. Kate suffered a momentary jolt of panic. It sounded as though Orla was in the middle of an earthquake, or maybe debris from a plane was hurtling down around her. There was a terrible whooping coming from somewhere, and a rattling that rose to a repeated crescendo with ear-splitting ferocity.

Kate pressed a finger to her free ear. 'Orla? Where on earth are you? Has Bournemouth exploded?'

'What? Listen, I can't hear you. I'll just move over here. George, step over here a minute.'

'Is that Mum? Tell her I shot the alien.'

The noise diminished slightly. Of course. George and Orla could spend hours in the arcades. George would be thinking all his dreams had come true. His eyes would also be popping out of his head by now, and he probably wouldn't sleep for hours. Kate tried to subdue her anxious tendencies and force herself to relax. They were on holiday, and were having a good time.

'Are you in the arcade?' she shouted.

There was a muffled answer, and then more clearly, '… and we're just going to play one more game, before we go home.'

Kate rolled her eyes, but couldn't prevent a smile. 'One more game' was Orla and George's mantra in these places. 'I bet George is loving it.'

'George, your mum says are you having a good time?'

'Ye-e-e-a-a-h!'

Kate's pain at missing George receded. 'Orla, I can't thank

you enough,' she shouted over the noise. 'It means so much to me, you giving George such a great holiday.'

'Ach,' Orla said brightly. 'I just want to make the most of my time with him while I can, you know?'

In the background there was the noise of what sounded like machine-gun fire.

'The most of your time?' Kate repeated loudly. What did that mean?

Her friend was silent for a split second, and then, 'It's a bit noisy in here to talk, Kate. Will we speak tomorrow morning?'

'Yes. Yes, fine.'

They said their goodbyes. What on earth was wrong with Orla? The light on the phone's screen faded to dark, and Kate slipped it into her pocket. Like Orla said, it was hard to talk with all that background noise. But still, there was a bad feeling lodged in Kate's mind.

But the next morning Orla was cheerful and chatty on the phone. She sounded relentlessly chirpy as she told Kate all about the day of fun she and George had lined up. Still, Kate wasn't fooled. There was something about the way Orla wouldn't let her get a word in edgeways that only added to her feeling of foreboding. Kate knew Orla too well. All she could do was shelve the worry for the next couple of days until she could talk to her friend face to face.

There was also Paul. As they neared the end of their week, Kate could sense a shift in him. She had an impression of restlessness underneath his quiet exterior that was out of character, and made her feel a little on edge. It was the same feeling Kate sensed towards the end of a long flight, when there was a growing anticipation in the atmosphere around her; that almost palpable sense of expectation at the end of a journey. She found it impossible to relax.

Their last formal session of the week only added to Kate's feeling of tension. It should have been an uplifting session. Chloe had asked the girls to write down their dreams for the future, and to stand up and read them aloud to the group. It was an important part of the girls' development, proving that they could finally focus on the years ahead, and not just surviving day-to-day; that they could see how some of their dreams might actually be achievable with hard work and determination.

A lump rose in Kate's throat as she listened to the younger girls embrace their futures. There was an atmosphere of boundless optimism as they explained where they'd like their lives to be. She took in their eager faces, invigorated by their week away, and wished with all her heart that their dreams might be realised. She knew only too well just how hard it was to keep on going and going, when all life did sometimes was hang over you like a big black cloud.

After the session, Chloe took the group into the canteen, where a couple of careers officers from the local authority had set up an impromptu advisory service. Paul and Kate remained behind in the games room to pack away their things and restore the room to how it was before the group's arrival.

Paul closed up his notebook. 'That was an interesting day. I enjoyed hearing about the girls' aspirations.' He tapped his notebook thoughtfully. 'I might even do a follow-up piece in a couple of years. See how their lives have changed.'

'Yes.' Kate began putting her papers back in her bag, her back to Paul. 'That would be a good idea. Then you can find out if their dreams have come true.'

She stopped, looking down at the folder she was clutching. Listening to the girls talk had made her refocus on her own future. She thought about the years stretching ahead of her. She thought of how it would be to share her life with Paul all the time, and how right it had felt that weekend in his apartment. It would be like another dream to start out on a life like this. Like another chance at being happy. But in Kate's experience, her dreams came true for a short while, before being snatched away. It wasn't right to teach the girls to hope, when there was so much uncertainty in life.

A table shifted behind her, and then Paul was there.

'Katerina.' He placed his hand on her cheek and tilted her face to look at him. Then he took the folder gently from her hands and placed it on the table, before pulling her to him. He curved his hand around her head and brought it to rest on his shoulder.

'Katerina,' he said. 'Everything will be OK.'

Kate closed her eyes and allowed herself to imagine a world where she rested like this, and everything was really OK. Paul's chest rose and fell unhurriedly.

It was a good place.

*

Their last full day in the hostel. As a treat for all their hard work, Chloe had organised a coach to pick the girls up and take them for a day in Blackpool.

Kate's nose was covered in freckles after their week in the country. Paul had seen her slapping on sun cream and pulling down her baseball cap, trying to prevent a suntan ruining her next shoot, but try as she might, the freckles popped out in the most delicious way.

Today she was dressed in shorts and a sky blue vest. Her bare arms and legs glowed with a light tan, and she seemed as eager as the other girls to have fun. Paul delighted to see her like this, as happy as a George would have been on an outing.

Something was troubling Kate, but all Paul's attempts to discover the nature of her anxiety ended in nothing. The harder he tried, the more elusive she became. He had hoped that this week they would become closer, but instead, Kate seemed to be drifting away from him while he stood on the sidelines, watching helplessly.

Perhaps today, now she was relaxed and content, she might lower her guard enough to let him help her with whatever was on my mind.

'I've never been to Blackpool,' she said, peering out of the window as the coach pulled out of the car park.

Paul smiled. Kate seemed to have spent the entire week with her nose pressed to a window somewhere, drinking in the view.

'Do you think they have donkey rides?' she asked.

He laughed and shook his head. 'Blackpool's more about

hen dos than donkey rides these days.'

'I know. That's what the girls told me.' She turned towards him with a wide grin. 'They said they can't wait to see it. Some of them wanted to stay the night there. I told them I'm too old to be trawling round all the clubs.'

'I don't know about that.' Paul chuckled. 'I can just see you and Orla with fairy wings, doing your karaoke.'

Kate grimaced, but couldn't prevent herself laughing with him. 'Actually, Orla would definitely be up for that. And I expect she'd make me dye my hair pink, get us both really drunk, and I'd end up with a tattoo of a sailor on my bum.' Her chuckle became a giggle. 'Good job I didn't have a hen night before I married Stuart.'

There was a wistful note to her voice, despite her laughter. Paul thought of how young she'd been when she married. Although she had an old head on her shoulders, she'd only just turned twenty.

'Did you wish you had?' he asked. 'Had a hen night, I mean?'

'It might have been nice to celebrate with some girlfriends. I don't know. Everything seemed to go so fast.' She laughed wryly. 'You know how Stuart was. He didn't like waiting. And anyway, he was going away on a trip. He wanted us to get married before he went. We both did.' She looked down, turning the bracelet on her arm. 'Actually, I thought at the time he was just impatient. I thought it was romantic, and I got swept up in that. But now I think he wanted me to be married before he went, in case anything happened to him. So he'd know I was provided for.'

Kate twisted and twisted her bracelet. There was a frown on her face. It hadn't taken long for her excitement about the day out to vanish. She seemed to be immersed once more in anxiety. Suddenly it came to Paul what it was that troubled her. Stuart had offered her security, a life away from the day-to-day struggle for existence. When he died, security was ripped from her once again. She was plunged into a world where she had to fend for herself and George. Her mother was worse than useless – as only too evident from the way she'd sold her story – her father had abandoned her in Australia, and her only real friend was Orla.

One of the girls called out to her friend in front of him, and a loud conversation sprang up around them. There was no chance now for him to talk openly, or to dig deeper into Kate's troubles. He caught hold of her fingers, releasing them from their worrying of her bracelet, and brought her hand to rest with his on his knee. She turned her head, her fresh features close to his.

'When you get married to me, you can have the biggest hen party you want,' he said.

He sensed a jolt run through Kate beside him. He pressed her hand, willing her not to draw back, and made his voice as light as he could. 'Get drunk with Orla and get yourself that tattoo,' he went on.

The delicious image entered Paul's mind, and as though she'd guessed exactly which way his thoughts were taking him, Kate blushed. Paul kept his expression a blank, holding his breath.

Her lips curved in an irrepressible smile. 'Are you asking me to marry you?'

So she hadn't told him to stop talking rubbish. That was a good start. Such a good start he almost leapt for joy.

'Not at all,' he said innocently, and Kate laughed, shaking her head at him. 'I mean I'd like us to get married. Of course I would,' he went on. 'There's nothing I'd like better. But I'm not asking you.' He gave a grin, driving his slight advantage home. 'Not until I'm almost sure you'll say yes.'

Kate gave a shaky laugh, her colour high. 'Paul, I've never known what to make of you, in all the years we've known each other. And I still don't.'

'There's nothing complicated about me.' He lifted her slim hand in his. 'When we get back to London, I hope you'll finally get to find that out.'

Kate looked down at their joined hands, and her fingers curled around his palm. For the first time, Paul felt a stirring of hope for a future that might actually become reality.

Not wanting to lose the moment, or the softness of her hand in his, he changed the subject, and began talking of inconsequential things. They chatted lightly until the coach finally arrived on Blackpool's prom.

*

'Absolutely no way on earth.'

A hideous clanking sound filled the air, like an instrument of torture ratcheting up. They were inside Blackpool's Pleasure Beach, and several of the girls were grouped round Paul, eyes bright with steely determination, hell bent on getting him onto the theme park's highest rollercoaster. Paul had been on something called the Thrill-O-Matic (actually quite a pleasant ride, and well inside his comfort zone); he'd been chased by chainsaw-wielding zombies in a horror zone called the Pasaje del Terror, and soaked to the skin in a lurid boat ride that was aptly named Valhalla. He'd had fun, but the fun stopped when asked to hurtle down from a great height.

The rollercoaster reached its pinnacle and was about to take a sickening plunge. Gazing up, Paul knew that no power in the world could persuade him to put his vertigo to the test. Ear-splitting screams rent the air, and his stomach dived with the terrified passengers. For a heart-stopping moment, he thought he was about to endure one of his flashbacks. One of those terrible incidences when he had no control over the images playing out in his mind. But then a hand caught his, and Kate was looking up at him, a worried expression on her face.

'Are you OK?'

He nodded. 'I'm not one for heights,' he said briefly. Then, sensing he had been maybe a little too brusque, he smiled at the group of girls. 'It looks a lot of fun,' he said, in his deadpan way. 'But I think I'll just wait here and listen out for your screams.'

They gave a good-natured groan of disappointment before darting off to join the queue. Only Kate remained at Paul's side, still gazing at him in concern.

Paul looked up again at the rollercoaster, which was making

its way round for another circuit. 'Why would anyone in their right minds actually want to put themselves through this torture?'

'I've been told there's a brilliant view from the top,' Kate said. 'You can see right out to sea. Maybe even all the way to Ireland on a clear day like today.'

Paul shook his head. 'Well, I'll wait here and let the girls describe it to me afterwards.'

'*Man up*,' she murmured.

'What?' He turned to look at Kate, and she put a hand on his arm.

'*Man up and get in the sodding chopper.* You did it before. You can do it again.'

A sick feeling entered the pit of his stomach. 'I got in that helicopter because Stuart pushed me in. It was one of the most terrible experiences of my life.'

'Well, this is different.' Kate leaned into him, a look of pleading on her face that he guessed, with a terrible feeling, he was going to find impossible to refuse. 'We're not in a war zone –'

'You could have fooled me.' He shivered.

'We're on holiday,' she carried on firmly. 'It's a ride at a fun fair. The emphasis is on *fun*.' She tugged at his shirt sleeve. 'Come on. You won't regret it.'

He stood there, looking down at her without answering, his lips firmly closed.

She pulled his sleeve again. '*Man up*,' she repeated with a smile. And then, the clinching persuader, 'I braved the sheep. Now it's your turn.'

He rolled his eyes.

'Hooray,' she cried.

She dragged his leaden feet towards the ride where, to make matters worse, they had to wait for what seemed like an age in the queue. Several times Paul would have pulled out, but Kate kept a tight hold of his hand and regaled him with chat, obviously trying to keep his mind off the terrible screams above them. Paul began to answer at random. The nearer they drew to the front of the queue, the more nonsensical his answers became. The day was hot, but his hands felt like ice. Kate gripped one of them.

'You can do this,' she said, smiling at him. 'I have faith in you.'

Finally the agonising wait ended, and they were bolted in to their seats. The car began to move, the heavy metallic clanking convincing Paul he'd made a big mistake. Even Kate was looking nervous.

'Actually, I'm scared,' she said.

'What?' He turned to her in disbelief, and realised she had turned pale.

'I don't really like heights either,' she said apologetically. 'I just thought I'd –'

Their cart lurched forward and she gave a small scream. Paul caught hold of her hand, his own terror subsiding. Then he began laughing out loud, and Kate joined in, until they were both giggling uncontrollably. The cart lurched its way to the highest point of the track, and for a second or two they hung there, suspended over Blackpool and the sea. For what seemed like an eternity Paul was torn between wild euphoria at the vista in front of him – the sea stretching blue and silver to the horizon, the sands shimmering yellow in the hot sun, the warmth of Kate's hand in his and her presence next to him – and sheer terror in anticipation of the vertical drop plunging away in front of them.

Then Kate gave an ear-splitting scream that wrenched a burst of manic, gleeful laughter from his throat, and over they went, plunging down the track, their hands gripped together, his stomach floating in his chest and his mind racing and whirling with pure happiness.

CHAPTER FOURTEEN

The coach pulled into the car park in London under a very different the sky from the one they'd left. A dark yellow sun smouldered menacingly from beneath a hazy smog, and there was a clammy, sultry feel to the weather. As soon as Kate stepped out of the coach, her cotton dress clung to her in the damp heat. The girls descended, yawning and stretching, and proceeded to mill around aimlessly, waiting for the driver to unload their bags. Kate stood a little apart, the oppressive warmth of the day enveloping her and adding to her feeling of anti-climax. Only the fact that she would soon be seeing George and Orla raised her spirits.

She looked over to where Paul stood in conversation with Chloe, and her body quickened, as it always did now at the sight of him; ever since the day she sat beside him in the taxi on the way to the Afghan restaurant. How long ago that seemed, and how prickly she'd been back then. And when he'd mentioned marriage, Kate hadn't laughed it off as one of his unfathomable jokes. She hadn't agreed, but she'd taken his throwaway comment with the seriousness he intended.

Paul caught her eye and smiled, a smile that caused her pulse to begin a steady thump. Then one of the girls approached him to say goodbye, and soon they were all hugging and kissing each other, and Kate was caught up in the bitter sweetness of parting.

'Bye, Kate,' said Sarah, throwing her arm around her neck.

'I'll be keeping in touch,' Kate promised, giving her a hug.

And then there was Abi and Stef and Dashna, and all the teenagers one after another.

'Wish we could do it all over again,' Stef said. Her hands

clasped Kate's, and Kate pulled her tight.

'We'll see you soon.'

Then finally Chloe, whose husband had come to pick her up, was last to say goodbye. She at least was beaming, and delighted to be home.

'See you next week, Chloe. I'll be in to chat about a few things.'

Chloe gave her a big hug. 'Yes, do. And glad things are working out for you.' She pulled away with a glance in Paul's direction.

'Was it so obvious?' Kate was torn between amusement and embarrassment. 'We were trying to play things down.'

Chloe patted her arm. 'You were the souls of discretion. And now you can stop playing things down and find time for each other in peace.'

She gave a grin and was gone, and there was just Paul and Kate. The coach pulled out of the car park, and they were alone.

Paul had Kate's rucksack in one hand. He lowered it to the ground and stepped forward, pulling Kate into an embrace. She rested her cheek against his cotton shirt, and for a moment or two it was nothing more than a goodbye hug. Then she lifted her head, and Paul's mouth found hers. She pressed her hands to his chest and felt the heat of him beneath her fingers, and he deepened his kiss for a long, blissful moment, until finally he raised his head.

'I don't want to leave you,' he said. Kate rested her head on his chest, where his shirt was damp with the heat and his heart beat strongly. 'But I have to go home, and then to work.' His arms tightened around her, contradicting his words. 'I've a lot to catch up on, and your article to put together.'

'I know.' Kate sighed. 'Back to reality.'

'Yes.' He stepped back, dropping his arms to his sides. 'I'll have a lot to do at work next week. Will I see you next weekend?'

Kate nodded. 'Yes, I'd like that.' She tried to smile, but it was strange how things had changed. A week without Paul seemed like such a long time, when once she only used to see him briefly on the doorstep every month.

He bent and kissed her forehead, and then reached for her rucksack. 'I'll ring you later. Come. Let's get you a cab.'

*

Kate had hardly paid off the driver before George came hurtling out of the house and down the drive to meet her. She swung him into her arms and kissed him several times. 'I've missed you. Did you have a good time?'

'Awesome! We went to the beach, and I got knocked down by a wave. And Orla bought me an inflatable shark.'

He hopped up and down, tugging at Kate's hand.

At his words, Kate's heart gave a painful jerk. She knew she often reacted out of proportion where George was concerned, but the thought of him being pulled under by a wave presented an anxiety-inducing picture. There seemed to be a million and one ways she could lose her son. She pulled him into another hug and held him tightly until he wriggled free.

And then Orla was there to meet her, and in no time at all they were all in the kitchen, talking and laughing and exclaiming over each other's tanned limbs and phone photos.

'I got you something,' Kate said, opening her capacious handbag. She pulled out some football stickers, a wind-up tractor, and a woolly sheep for George.

'Wowzers.' His eyes widened, and he ran off straightaway, up to his room to check the stickers against his album.

'And I got you something too.' Kate drew out a leather notebook, beautifully bound, with Orla's name impressed in gold lettering on the spine, and a Celtic cross and eagle on the front.

'Wow,' Orla said, echoing George. She stroked the leather binding. 'That's gorgeous.' She turned the cover and began leafing through the blank pages, touching the virgin paper with the reverence of a writer. 'You didn't have to get me anything.'

'There was a craft shop in the country that embossed them. Do you like it?'

'I love it!' There was something strange about Orla's voice. She leafed aimlessly through the blank pages, and her eyes were over-bright. Kate stared at her friend, puzzled. It was only a small present. And Orla was rarely outwardly moved by anything. Tough as old boots. Perhaps she was over-tired. That made sense. A week with George could tire anyone.

'I got you this, too,' she went on brightly. She waved a stick of Blackpool rock in the air. Orla took it, and when she saw the words *Squeeze Me Slow* written down the middle, she gave a loud laugh.

'Thanks so much for having George,' Kate said. 'He loved it.'

Orla dropped her gaze and shrugged. 'It was a grand craic.'

If now was the time to ask Orla what the matter was, this was it, but outside in the hallway Kate could hear George zooming his tractor up and down the floorboards, knocking down his woolly sheep with cries of glee. It was impossible to have an uninterrupted conversation. And they both had a lot to talk about.

'Why don't you stay the night?' Kate asked. 'I've got some wine. We can get a takeaway.'

'What would you say to pizza?'

Orla looked at her hopefully, and Kate rolled her eyes. 'Usually I'd say *meh*, but for you and George I'd say OK. If we must. But I wouldn't do it for anyone else.'

George, his ears as receptive as a bat's where mention of food was concerned, rushed in, punching the air. 'Mum said yes to pizza. Yes!'

'Your mum's a darling.' Orla scooped him into a hug.

Later that night, when George was safely tucked up in bed, and nothing remained of the pizza except a couple of cold crusts, Kate and Orla sat on the settee with a bottle of wine between them.

Kate yawned. 'It's been a great week. Tiring, though.'

Orla said nothing. For the last few minutes she'd been swirling her wine, watching the liquid cling to the sides of the glass. She was looking very piratical, in wide trousers and a belt, with her tattoos visible under her loose cotton shirt. 'What are you dreaming about?' Kate said. She tugged Orla's white shirt. 'You look like a pirate in that outfit. About to sail the seven seas.'

Orla jumped, and a tiny drop of wine fell on her shirt. 'Well, now you're the one that's psychic.' She dabbed at the wine with a wet finger. 'I was thinking about travelling. Next month. I'm going to Ireland.'

'Oh.' Kate searched her face. Was this what the problem had been all along? 'Is it your mum? Is everything all right?'

'Everything's fine at home. Well,' she gave a dry laugh. 'If you can call my lunatic mother fine. The thing is Kate, I've a contract to write another book.'

'Oh, that's fabulous! Why didn't you say? We should be celebrating with more than pizza and cheap wine. This is brilliant.' Kate got up. 'There's some fizzy stuff in the fridge.'

Orla waved her back. 'No, wait a minute.' Her bangles jangled nervously, and Kate sat back down. Orla put her wine glass on the floor and turned to face her. 'The thing is, Kate, I didn't like to say this before you went away on your trip with the girls.' She pressed her hands on her knees. 'You seemed to have a lot on your mind. And I didn't want you being upset all the time you were away.'

Kate felt a twinge of guilt. All she'd thought about these past few weeks was Paul. Was it true she'd seemed abstracted? Maybe she should have tried harder.

'It's fine.' Orla took in Kate's expression and patted her hand. 'We've both had things on our minds. And what I wanted to tell you is, I'm writing a book about my ancestors and my childhood. It's a long poem, actually. And I'm going to be in Ireland doing some research. For six months.'

Six months. No wonder Orla had looked so preoccupied. Kate's heart sank. She would be lost without Orla. What was she going to do without her for six months? But it was wrong not to try and look pleased. This was an exciting moment for her, and her book would be a massive achievement.

Kate's brain told her mouth to smile, despite how she felt

inside. 'Well, Ireland's not the other side of the world,' she said brightly. 'You can come and see us at weekends sometimes. And me and George could come over and visit in the school holidays. You'll be back in no time.'

Orla shook her head, her mouth turning down at the corners. 'Actually, I won't be back soon,' she said. 'I'm writing a book about my whole family. My dad's side, too. After I've finished in Ireland, I'm going to Nigeria.'

'*Nigeria?* When? How long for?'

'I'll come home for a couple of weeks after I've been to Kildare. And then I'm going to stay in Lagos. For a year.'

Kate's mind whirled. She didn't want Orla to leave. They'd been friends for years. More than friends. They'd been each other's lifeline. And Kate didn't know what she would have done without Orla after Stuart died. Orla was the only family she had.

Her friend was looking at her now, her slim fingers gripping the folds of her trousers, her eyes welling. 'I have to do it, Kate. I want to get to know my dad. And I've a book to write. I can feel it inside me. I have to get it down.'

'But Nigeria,' Kate cried. 'It's bloody miles away.'

Then they had their arms around each other, and they were both crying.

'Look at us,' Kate said through her tears, trying to make a joke of it. 'We're like a proper cheesy sitcom. And this is the crying bit.'

Orla pulled away, sniffing and wiping her nose on her hand, trying to laugh. 'Yeah, right. Do you know what? Sometimes I think the whole of life's just a cheesy sitcom, and I'm the token black.'

Kate put her face in her hands, trying to subdue the tears. 'Yeah, you're right. And I'm the dumb blonde with ironic jokes, even when her heart's damn well breaking.'

Orla put her arm round Kate's shoulder. For a minute or two they sat there, and Kate sobbed into her hands. Then she raised her head and reached for the box of tissues on her coffee table. She blew her nose.

'I'm sorry, Orla. What a bad friend I am. It's just I'm going to miss you.'

'I know. Me, too.' Orla took a tissue from the proffered box and drew back into her corner of the settee. 'I don't like to think of you by yourself.'

Kate shrugged and wiped her eyes. 'Oh, that. You know I'll be fine. I've had loads of calls from my agent since my mum endorsed me as a bitch last week. I've got plenty of work coming in. And anyway, I'm not alone. I've got George.'

Orla looked at her. 'Listen Kate, I don't want to pry, but I thought you and Paul ... Well, ever since he interviewed you, I wondered if ...'

'If I could feel the same way about him,' Kate finished. She looked down at her wine glass. 'I didn't tell you this before because ... well, because you seemed preoccupied.' She glanced at Orla and pulled a face at her. 'But anyway, you know the last time you were in Ireland? And George was at Stuart's parents? I slept with Paul.'

Orla's eyes widened. 'So it's serious? Oh Kate, I can't tell you how happy I am.'

'Well, Paul is definitely serious. Can you believe he even mentioned marriage?'

To Kate's surprise, Orla nodded. 'I can believe it, hon. I never would have done, but since that interview of his, everything's fallen into place. He's totally in love. But what about you?'

Kate cast her mind over the past few weeks, to the evening Paul had interviewed her, and how suddenly the atmosphere became charged. She thought of Paul with his face in his hands, crying in his apartment; the way she'd felt when she woke up beside him, the light playing over his sleeping form; the way he smiled when his gaze rested on her ...

And then she remembered with a jolt the pang she'd felt when they'd said goodbye that morning. And they would only be apart for a week. Imagine if Paul were going away for a year. Or what if it wasn't even just a year, and he went away just as Stuart had done, and she never saw him again?

A cold sliver of fear trickled down her spine.

'I don't know,' she said curtly, leaning forward. 'Maybe it's all going too fast.'

'Too fast?' Orla gazed at her, astounded. 'He's been in love with you for ever. I don't understand why it's taken him this long to say anything.'

'Paul's always known he was in love. But I'm only just finding out about him. And I'm just not sure I'm doing the right thing. Maybe it's better for me and George to be alone, you know?'

Orla opened her mouth to speak, but Kate drew back in the settee, pulling her knees up and hugging them. 'Anyway,' she said with a smile, 'I want to know all about your project. What are you going to do in Ireland? And where are you staying when you get to Lagos? And what about your dad? Are you staying with him?'

Orla gave Kate a worried look, but her plans were so exciting it was very easy to divert her. Soon she was telling Kate all about how her book contract came about, how her father had told her she could stay on the campus where he was a lecturer in return for giving English and creative writing lessons, how she was looking forward to meeting the family she'd never got to know.

'I've got two half-brothers and I've never even met them,' Orla said. 'Apart from on Facebook.'

'At least your dad always stayed in touch. My half-brother must be fifteen or so by now. I wonder if he even knows I exist.'

'You never thought about getting in touch?'

Kate screwed up her face. 'No. Sometimes I wonder what they're doing. But if my dad wanted his kid to know about me he'd have contacted me by now.' Kate had no intention of making the first move. There was a limit to the number of times she could put herself forward to be rejected.

'It's your dad's loss.' Orla reached forward and pressed Kate's hand. 'And think what he's missing with George. You couldn't ask for a lovelier grandson.'

'I know.' Kate's eyes began to fill again, and she blew her
nose. 'Do you know what? I often think it's good that I don't
have anything to do with my mum and dad. Good for George,
that is. At least if my parents keep out of my life there's no
chance of him being hurt.'

Orla's lips twisted. She cast Kate a worried glance. 'You
know, you can't protect George forever. There's always a risk
of being hurt, no matter what the relationship. He needs to
have other people in his life.'

'George was hurt enough when Stuart died. I'm not
exposing him to any more.' She waved her empty glass at Orla
and said cheerfully, 'Anyway, enough sadness and crying. Let's
finish this bottle and talk about when me and George are going
to come and visit you in Lagos.'

They resumed their conversation about Orla's plans, but
Kate was aware her friend wasn't totally side-tracked. From
time to time Orla would give her an assessing, concerned look.
Kate knew she wanted to bring up the subject of Paul again,
but she refused to talk any more about her worries. Orla had
an exciting time ahead of her, and a wonderful opportunity,
and so Kate kept the conversation as light as she could, until
both she and Orla were yawning, and their wine bottle was
empty.

*

The next day was Sunday. Despite her late night with Orla,
Kate was up early to take George to the gym again for their
weekly swim. She was in two minds whether to appear there so
soon after Barrie Dickson's article in the *Shaftesbury*, but
George was eager to get out of the house. It seemed unfair he
should suffer just because his grandmother was a nutcase and
tabloid journalists were unscrupulous, and so after their swim
Kate pulled her baseball cap down over her forehead and
braved the canteen.

As it happened, no one took a great deal of notice of them.
The offending article had been only a small piece in a paper
that heaved with other much more exciting and libellous
stories. There were far more famous fish to fry than Kate. That

very morning the headlines in one of the Sunday papers were all about a professional footballer and his affair with a judge on a reality TV show. Kate was already old news, which was how she liked it, no matter how much it upset her agent. She and George tucked into a plateful of pancakes with only a few curious glances cast in their direction.

It seemed as good a time as any to tell George that Orla was going travelling. Kate wasn't looking forward to starting the conversation, and she tried to break the news in as light-hearted a way as possible. But George wasn't easily fooled. He bent his head over his plate and concentrated on capturing the last remnants of syrup with his spoon.

'You mean we won't see her for ages,' he said.

'Well, it will be a long time, but we can Skype her lots. And Orla says we can go and see her in Africa when she gets there. That will be exciting!'

George licked the back of his spoon. 'Will there be snakes?'

'Well, I'm not an expert, but I don't think there are any snakes where Orla's going to live, in the city. But we could go travelling round Nigeria, and we're bound to find some. And Orla says there are elephants, gorillas, and lions.'

'Cool.' He deposited his spoon on his plate and pushed it away. 'Why don't we go and live there, too?'

'Well.' Kate half-smiled at her son's logic, and tilted her head on one side, giving his question due consideration. 'You would have to leave your school and all your friends. And I would have to leave my job. And then we wouldn't have any money.'

'I'm not bothered about my friends,' he said. 'Orla's much more fun than they are.' Then he pursed his lips, struck by a thought. 'Actually, Paul's my friend. I don't think we should leave him.'

'No,' Kate said faintly. 'Quite.'

'And he's your friend. I think he'd be sad if we went.' He slurped up the last of the milkshake and wiped his mouth with his hand.

'Yes, Paul would be sad.' Kate handed George a serviette.

'So that's settled then. Orla goes to Ireland and Africa, and we wait here with Paul until she gets back.'

'Yeah.' He stood, pushing his chair back. Then he looked down at the table. 'What if Paul goes travelling, too?'

'Oh, I don't think he will. He's got an important job in London. He needs to stay here.' Kate took in George's downcast face, and felt again that terrible stab of anxiety she always carried for him. The loss of Stuart was a tragedy he would have to bear for the rest of his life. He was taking the news of Orla's leaving with a maturity beyond his years. If Paul, too, were to disappear for any reason …

Kate gave a gasp. Her heart was beating in her ears, and her hands were clammy. She took a swig on the cold dregs of her coffee.

'Are you all right, Mum?' George was looking at her curiously.

'Yes, I'm OK.' She huddled into her fleece and gave George a smile. 'Think I got a bit of a chill in the pool. Let's go and see if Orla's up yet. She can tell you all about her brothers in Nigeria.' She stood, stacking their things on the tray. 'One of them's got a restaurant. He cooks shark meat.'

'Woah.'

They made their way home, cheerfully discussing all the animals in Africa it was possible to kill and eat, whether they would taste good, and whether it was right to eat them. By the time they got home and found Orla in the kitchen, immersed in the Sunday paper and the salacious doings of professional footballers, Kate's moment of anxiety had passed. The seeds of unhappiness were firmly rooted, however. Later, she watched Orla and George lying side by side on the settee, laughing together over the cartoon channel, and her heart almost burst with sadness.

CHAPTER FIFTEEN

Paul rang, as he'd said he would. He called a couple of hours after they'd returned from Yorkshire, and then again that same evening, as Kate was lying in bed. She told him about Orla leaving and listened to his quiet breathing as he took in the information.

'Eighteen months isn't a long time.' His voice was reassuring. Kate lay back on her pillow, pressing her phone to her ear. She felt dizzy with tiredness and the wine she'd drunk, and from crying.

'I wish I were there with you,' he said.

'Me too.' The words were out before she realised.

She heard him take a deep breath. 'I'll see you next weekend. It'll be a long week.'

He phoned every evening on his way home from work. Kate heard his footsteps as he crossed Southwark Bridge and the sound of the traffic passing by. It was good to hear his voice, and to feel a part of his life.

'I've been thinking of you.' A text message he sent her on Wednesday afternoon. It said no more than that. Succinct and to the point. Kate held her phone up with a smile.

And then on Friday, the day before she was due to meet him at his flat, Paul phoned her first thing in the morning. She had just dropped George off at school and was on her way to work. She pulled in to the side of the road.

'Morning,' she said. 'This is an early call.'

'Are you busy?'

'Well, I'm on my way to an appointment.'

'I won't keep you long,' he said. 'It's just tomorrow.'

Something's come up.'

There was a strange note to Paul's voice. Like he was actually nervous about something.

Kate swallowed. 'I see,' she said brightly. 'Can't you make it?'

'Yes. Of course. It's just ... Look, can you meet me somewhere else? There's a bed and breakfast near King's Cross.'

'What?' Kate caught sight of her own astonished face in her rear view mirror, and closed her mouth with a giggle. 'Do they charge by the hour?'

He gave a laugh that still had a touch of edginess about it. 'No, that's not it. Although I wish it were,' he muttered in an aside. 'There's someone who wants to meet you.'

'Oh.' Kate frowned. It was the last thing she was expecting. 'This is all very mysterious. Do I get to find out who?'

'Look, I've got to go,' he said hurriedly. 'I'll email you the directions. I'm sorry. This isn't how I'd planned this weekend. But you will come?'

'Yes, if it means so much.'

'It does. I'm sorry it's all such a rush. It's come as a surprise.'

'Well, I hope it's a nice surprise,' she said.

'I'll see you tomorrow.'

'See you tomorrow,' she repeated faintly.

Paul clicked off the call, and Kate sat there by the side of the road, brow furrowed. Why all the mystery? And why the B&B? Was it someone she knew from her homeless days? She cast her mind back, and could think of no one who would even care where she was now, or what she was doing. Maybe someone who wanted some help through At Home? That was more like it. Although why they wanted to contact Kate through Paul was a puzzle.

She shrugged, dropping her phone on the passenger seat. All would become clear tomorrow.

That evening, Paul didn't phone after work. Kate felt a surge of disappointment so strong, it unnerved her. She picked up her phone several times, on the verge of phoning him herself, then put the phone down again, unable to go through with it. Perhaps he was staying late at the office. Or out for a drink with his colleagues. She couldn't bear the thought of the phone ringing and ringing, and Paul not picking up.

This isn't good, she thought. When did you start to rely on him?

She went into the kitchen to make herself a hot drink. As she was about to carry it up to bed, her phone buzzed a message.

Sorry not to phone. I've been tied up this evening. Thinking of you a lot. See you tomorrow.

Succinct again. Kate sighed. What did this elliptical text mean? It was typical Paul: deadpan, reserved, uncommunicative.

She was about to type in a reply, but found she could think of nothing to say. She replaced her phone on the kitchen counter and went upstairs to bed, where she spent another sleepless night.

*

The next day Kate took the tube to King's Cross, following Paul's directions. The sky overhead was dark and threatening when she stepped out of the station. For days now the weather forecasters had been predicting an end to one of the longest heat waves on record. The atmosphere was sticky and sultry. There was a gust of warm air, and the litter on the pavement made an angry swirl around Kate's feet.

She made her way across the lanes of traffic outside the station and into a quieter side street. At the bottom of a row of rundown houses was the Lawnswood Hotel. Kate checked Paul's email on her phone. This was it. Like every other B&B on the street, the evocative name bore no relation to the grubby setting.

The heavy glass door was unlocked. Kate pushed it open. There was an untidy reception desk and a bell, and a small table littered with leaflets for London's sights. Paul sat on a scruffy chair against the wall, staring grimly at his phone. When

Kate stepped in, he rose to his feet.

'Hi. What's all the mystery?' she said, trying to smile. 'Are you undercover reporting?'

'No,' he said. He spoke quickly, making no attempt to acknowledge her levity. The receptionist appeared behind the counter and stared at them. Paul took Kate's arm. 'Let's step outside a moment,' he said. Then under his breath, 'There's nowhere to talk privately in this damn place.'

He pulled the door open, and Kate found herself back outside on the gloomy street. The sky was an ominous charcoal.

'What's all this about, Paul?' She was beginning to feel uncomfortably anxious. Paul himself seemed nervous, which unusual state of affairs only heightened her own tension.

'Look, I didn't want this to happen.' He ran his hand abruptly through his short hair. 'Remember that article your mother wrote?'

'How could I forget?' Kate began, and then blanched. 'Don't tell me Mum's in there.'

'No, no. God, no,' he said. 'Nothing as bad as that. At least I don't think so. It's just that when that article came out, I felt responsible.'

'I told you, it's not your fault –'

He shook his head sharply. 'I'd interviewed you, and I should have guessed Barrie Dickson would follow it up. Or any one of the others,' he added. 'So I was determined not to let that happen a second time.'

'How do you mean?'

'Well, someone from Barrie's paper got in touch with your mother and paid her to say what she did. If anyone was going to print your father's side of the story, I wanted it to be me.'

Kate felt the ground sway under her feet. A large drop of rain fell from the heavens and splattered beside her on the warm pavement, drying instantly. A few more drops followed swiftly afterwards, chilling her neck, and bringing her to her senses.

'Are you telling me my dad is in that hotel?' She enunciated every word, standing stiffly as the rain began to increase.

'Yes. One of my reporters finally managed to track him down in Australia. It took a while, because it seems he's anglicised his name. He's now called Steven Rudd. I didn't ask him to come to London. I had no idea that's what he intended. He got in touch yesterday and said he was about to board a flight, and would I meet him at the airport, and bring you to see him.'

Paul's normally steady voice grew ever more uncertain as Kate stood rigid, waiting for him to finish.

'You bloody journalists,' she said. Her voice was quite calm, but anger radiated and pulsed through her body. 'It's absolutely none of your damn business. Paul, did you never consider that I might not actually want to see him?'

'Yes, of course! Of course I did. I didn't bloody well ask him to come here. But now he's here and I've talked to him, and ... Please, Kate.' Paul put his hand on Kate's arm, and she stared down at it, icy with rage. 'Please. It's important. Come inside and give the guy a chance.'

She shook off his hand. 'Like he gave me a chance, you mean?' She turned on her heel. 'I can't even believe what I'm hearing.'

The rain was falling in sheets now, dripping from her hair in wet streaks. Kate blinked the water out of her eyes and stumbled as she walked away. Instantly Paul was at her side, steadying her. His shirt was soaked, plastered to his frame.

'Kate, if not for your dad, then for his kids. They're waiting inside to meet you.'

Kate stopped in her tracks. 'Them?' she said. Her voice was brittle. 'How many has he got?'

'Two. He's brought his son and daughter.'

A brother she'd only met once as a baby, and a sister she didn't even know existed. Kate's teeth began to chatter in the rain. Paul stood over her, the rain rolling down his forehead and into eyes full of urgent anxiety.

'Why?' she said. 'Why do you care?'

He caught hold of her arms and turned her to face him.

'Because I care about you,' he said. The rain was now a torrential downpour. Paul raised his voice above the sound of the water beating hard on the rooftops. Raindrops ran in rivulets down his face and over his lips. 'I might be an idiot. I might have done this all the wrong way. But I care about you. This is your only family. You have to give them a chance, before it's too late.'

Her body was shaking, but she forced her mouth open to speak. 'It's not fair. Not fair of you to ask. Not fair of him to come here after all this time and blackmail me with his children like this.' She gave a violent shiver, half anger, half misery. 'And it's especially wrong that you even thought about contacting him without telling me. I cannot believe you did that.' Her anger consumed her so that she could barely articulate herself. The words stuck in her throat, and she heaved great breaths.

Paul gripped her arms. 'No, I know. Nothing about it is fair. And I shouldn't have contacted him without letting you know. But I didn't want to see any more lies printed about you. I thought I was looking after you.'

For a moment he held her, bending his head over hers in a vain attempt to shelter her from the rain. Then he dropped his hands to his sides. 'Come on inside.' He made an attempt at a smile. 'In case you hadn't noticed, it's raining.'

Kate followed Paul back to the door with feet that dragged at every step. The man on reception eyed them coldly.

Paul stepped up to the desk. 'Hi. We're here to meet the family in Room 23. We got caught in the rain. I don't suppose you could give us a couple of dry towels?' He indicated their soaking clothes with a sweep of the hand. The man shook his head and began to type into his computer terminal, without speaking. Paul drew out his wallet and took out a note. 'We'd be very grateful,' he said dryly, lifting the note between his fingers.

The receptionist left the desk, and Paul looked around him wearily.

'Welcome to the world I used to live in,' Kate told him.

'Where no one trusts anyone.' She swept her gaze over the dreary reception room and shivered in her wet clothes. 'I thought my dad was doing well for himself.'

Paul shrugged. 'Maybe he is. He just booked everything at the last minute, and got on a plane. It can't have been cheap to get three tickets to the UK.'

The enormity of her father's action began to make itself felt in Kate's mind. She wrapped her arms around herself, staring down at the floor. At last the man returned with two towels which, although threadbare, at least seemed clean. Paul and Kate dried their hair and clothes as best they could.

'Right, we'll go on up,' Paul said. 'Ready?'

Kate shrugged.

The staircase was narrow. There was the smell of damp bathrooms and stale burgers. They reached number 23 and Paul knocked. The television playing inside the room fell silent. A man's voice bade the come in, and Paul pressed the handle and stepped inside.

Kate followed. Over Paul's shoulder she caught a glimpse of a handsome, tanned man, sitting in a small chair by the window. He stood as they entered, and his eyes went straight to Kate. It was like looking in a mirror. They were her own eyes, a clear blue. He stood tall, stooping a little in the small room. Kate searched his creased features for the father she'd known, and found nothing.

'Little Katya,' he said quietly. There was a note of marvel to his greeting. The Czech accent Kate remembered was still there, overlaid with an Antipodean twang.

There was a movement from the double bed, and Kate turned silently. A boy and a girl sat upright, their backs against the headboard. A packet of crisps and a remote control lay between them. The boy was about fifteen, stocky and dark-haired. His solemn gaze met Kate's. Next to him was his sister. Kate stiffened in shock. Her own features gazed back at her hesitantly from the girl's face. Blue eyes, a little grave; a clear complexion dotted with freckles; blond hair cut short over an elegant head. Most of all, the girl was tall. As tall as her brother, already, Kate could tell, even though they were both sitting. Her thin legs stretched down the length of the bed, and she shifted self-consciously. Despite her own turmoil of emotion, Kate felt for her. She gave her a small, reassuring smile and was oddly gratified when the girl smiled back shyly.

Paul looked from Kate to her father. 'I thought I'd take the children to a café for an hour or so. To give you both time to talk.' He raised his brows questioningly at Kate's father, whose eyes were still on Kate.

'Is that all right with you, love?' the older man asked.

Kate's eyes narrowed at the affectionate pet name, but she nodded. Her father turned to the two children. 'This is Rob and Lou – Louise. Say hello to Kate, guys, and then get your things. Paul's going to take you for something to eat.'

'Can we get fish and chips?' Rob asked.

His sister pulled a face at her brother's request, but stood quietly and began fishing for her shoes.

'We'll see,' Paul said. 'We'll find somewhere Louise would like, too. And better put your coats on. It's raining.'

'That's right, we're in England now,' Kate's father joked. 'I told you you'd need your gumboots.'

The children bustled to put on their outdoor clothes, casting Kate a brief, curious glance as they bid goodbye, and Paul shepherded them out. As he passed her, he placed a hand on her shoulder and pressed it. Then he was gone, and there was just the sound of their feet moving away down the worn carpet.

Kate and her father eyed each other. Kate leaned back against the door, determined not to be the first to speak.

'I expect this is a shock,' her father said. Kate resisted the temptation to snort. 'Here,' he added quickly, 'what am I thinking? Have a seat.' He pushed forward the only chair in the cramped room. Kate skirted the bed and sat down in it. Her rain-soaked leggings clung to her legs uncomfortably.

'You look like you got drenched,' her father continued.

Steve Rudd, Kate thought. The change to his name alienated him still further from her. She stared at the tall stranger filling the room, and wondered how it was possible they were related.

'We've got some coffee,' he was saying. 'Would you like some? Or tea?'

Kate nodded, and he turned to busy himself with the tiny kettle.

'I bet you're wondering why I've come,' he went on quickly, his back to the room as he made their drinks. 'I had no idea …'He stopped, his large brown hands fastened around the chipped cups, swallowing them in his grasp. 'I hope you'll believe me when I say that all these years I had no idea what had happened to you. No idea you'd been forced out of your home. Your mum wrote to me and told me –'

'Wait,' Kate said, her eyes widening. 'Mum *wrote* to you?'

He turned. 'Yes. I asked her to keep in touch. To tell me how you were doing.'

'So you wrote to each other. She never told me. You didn't ever think of writing to me.' Kate said the words flatly, emphasizing the *me*, making it more of a statement than a question. She'd long since resigned herself to the fact that her father hadn't wanted her in his life.

'I did,' he said. 'I did write. I wrote every week for months after you left. You didn't answer.'

Kate stared at him, the implications of his words sinking in gradually. Her father kept his eyes fixed on Kate. They reached the same damning conclusion together.

'She didn't ever give you the letters.'

Kate shook her head slowly. Her father's letters to her must have landed on the doormat every week in their terraced house in north London. What happened after that, Kate could only guess at. Her mother must have opened them, standing there in their narrow hallway, and read all the words that were meant for Kate. And then she must have thrown them away.

Kate's eyes filled with tears.

'My God,' her dad said quietly. 'I had no idea. She wrote to me and told me you weren't interested in hearing from me. That it was best not to write any more. That my letters only upset you. That when you were ready, you'd get in touch. She wrote every few months and said how great you were doing at school.'

Kate gave a bitter laugh.

'How you were doing well in your exams,' he finished. He stood there, the cups clenched in his bear-like hands. Behind him the kettle puffed furiously, steam clouding the air, until it switched itself off with a noisy click. He didn't move.

'Do you want to know what else she said?' he asked. Kate stared at the ground without answering. 'She said she was going to Spain with her boyfriend, but you were staying in England to go to college. She said she wasn't going to write any more, now you were older it was up to you. She gave me an address for you. Somewhere in Hampstead. I wrote, but it got returned. "Not known at this address."'

Kate lifted her gaze. 'You could have looked me up. Didn't you even try?'

'I did. Found out you were a model. Married some rich guy. I thought if you'd wanted to find me, you would. But I never heard from you.'

There was silence in the room as they stared at each other. Kate tried to make sense of her father's words as her life history tilted and altered around her. She found it hard to grasp the enormity of what he was actually saying.

'It wasn't until Paul's journalist guy got in touch that I started to think maybe I'd got it all wrong. It seemed incredible, but maybe your mum hadn't told me the truth. I decided the only way to find out was to see you for myself. I brought Rob and Lou along because I thought –' He struggled with his sentence for a few seconds and turned finally to make their tea. 'I thought even if you didn't want to see me, maybe you might want to get to know them, because they want to get to know you. They're your family, too. They're good kids, and they didn't do anything wrong.'

Kate sat in perfect silence. Her father put the tea bags in their cups and poured in the water. Then he added sugar, although Kate drank it without, and stirred the cups. He looked down at the spoon, turning it round and round for far longer than necessary. 'I heard you got a little boy.'

'Yes.' Kate wanted some time to think. She watched the spoon, tiny in her dad's massive hand, and wished she could just sit quietly for a while. As though guessing her thoughts, her father passed her the tea, saying, 'I put sugar in it. It's supposed to be good for shock.' He then sat on the end of the bed, bending his head to blow on his drink, and relapsed into silence.

For several long minutes they sat there. Steven Rudd stared at the floor. The rain beat down on the window, washing it clean. Kate took a sip of the hot, sweet tea and it warmed her a little. She cast a few surreptitious glances at her dad. He looked worn and tired, and was probably jet-lagged. There was a deep frown on his forehead. She wondered what he had said to his children before they came away, and to his girlfriend. Was she now his wife?

Then she began wondering what to say to George. How to tell him he suddenly had a family. She knew he would be wildly excited and curious. Despite her father's explanation and his dramatic gesture, she was still bitter and angry. She'd love to walk away. That would be the easy option. And leaving would just perpetuate useless discord down the generations.

She sighed, and her father looked up. 'All right, Katya?'

'I'd rather you didn't call me that,' she said coldly. 'And no, of course I'm not all right.'

Her father flinched. Kate dropped her gaze, and there was a knock at the door.

'We're back, Dad.'

Steve rose from the bed and went to the door.

'Hi. D'you get wet?' he asked. His voice was over cheerful.

'Yeah.' The children seemed to think rain was an adventure. Their faces shone with vigour. 'We saw loads of red buses. Paul says there's a cool museum nearby with real Egyptian mummies in it. Can we go?'

'Yeah, course.' He pulled Louise to him in a hug.

Kate rose abruptly. 'Can I use your bathroom?'

Steve turned, and his son said, 'We have to share a bathroom here. There's a key.'

The boy went to the bedside table and picked it up. Kate took it from his outstretched hand, and his fingers felt warm under hers. He smiled at her, his eyes eager on hers as she thanked him.

'It's down the corridor at the end, love – Kate.' Steve corrected himself awkwardly as she passed him by. Kate felt Paul's eyes on her, but kept her face averted.

She went down the gloomy corridor and pushed open the bathroom door. Inside some washing was drying over the bath. The atmosphere was steamy, and there was water on the floor and a dirty towel. Kate closed the toilet seat and sat down, putting her face in her hands.

CHAPTER SIXTEEN

The morning had a nightmare feel to it. Like one of those interminable and pointless dreams where you're rushing to meet someone but they keep changing the venue, and you constantly find yourself in the wrong place. Then when you finally catch up with the person you're looking for, you discover he's changed into someone else entirely.

Kate thought of the look on her father's face as he pulled his daughter to him in a hug. She pressed her fingers to her head, digging them in. This was how he used to look at Kate, all those years ago. *Little Katya*. She'd forgotten the nickname. She'd forgotten her father. Put him to the back of her mind, where the thought of him couldn't hurt her any more. And now here he was, living and breathing and real, with two children.

She brought her hands down and stood to look in the mirror. There wasn't much of her father's little Katya remaining in her reflection. Her mascara had smudged a little in the rain. She tore off a piece of toilet roll and wiped the fragile skin under her eyes. Her face looked back at her, hard and unfeeling. That was good. Unfeeling was good.

She dropped the tissue in the toilet and flushed it.

When she returned to the bedroom, the children were back on the bed, and the television was showing cartoons. Paul and her father were standing by the window. They turned as she entered the room.

'So, how long are you planning on staying?' Kate asked.

'We're here a week. We would have stayed longer, but the kids, and school ...' His voice trailed away under Kate's gaze.

'Are you staying here?' She held one hand out, indicating the room.

Steve followed the direction of her arm. There was a double bed, which Kate guessed he and Rob had shared. A Z-bed was folded up in one corner, which she assumed was for Louise.

'I know it's not a great place,' he said. 'We might try and find somewhere else. Not easy to find somewhere affordable in this city. And my wife –'

He stopped, not meeting Kate's eyes. Suddenly everything fell into place. His wife hadn't wanted him to come and see her. Or to bring the children. Her father was trying to spend as little money as possible, so as not to exacerbate a difficult situation. Kate assimilated this new aspect of the situation, and realised her father had finally put her first, before his wife's wishes. It must have cost him more than money to fly over here.

She came to a decision. 'Well, there's no need for you to stay here. I've got room at my house. You can come and stay there for the week. Get to know George.'

Steve's eyes lit up. He stepped forward. 'Are you sure, love? I mean, Kate?' She nodded. 'That's great. Hear that, kids? We're going to stay at Kate's. You can get to meet your nephew.'

The children shuffled, embarrassed, but Kate sensed they were pleased. Louise was smiling.

'I'll need some time to sort things out,' Kate said. 'And to talk to George. Maybe you could come over tomorrow.' She picked up her bag. 'I'll leave you my mobile number.'

Kate sensed the joy radiating from her father. He seemed a quiet man, contained, like Kate was herself, but his feelings flowed from him. Kate remembered what Paul had told her once, that everything she felt was easily read, and she wondered if this was something she and her father had in common. She glanced over to where Paul was still standing by the window. Unlike her father, as usual his emotions were hidden. The pale light from the window was behind his head, casting his face in shadow and making it doubly difficult to tell what he was thinking.

Kate scribbled down her number and passed the scrap of paper to her father. When he took it, she noticed his fingers were trembling a little, and for the first time she felt a stir of pity.

'Thanks,' he said, looking down at the paper as though fascinated by her handwriting. 'I'll text you, so you have my number.'

He looked up then, his eyes alight with this small symbol of contact. Despite her mixed feelings, Kate found herself giving him a tiny smile in return. 'OK,' she said. She looked at Paul. 'And now I think I'd better go home. I need to get the house ready for you, do some shopping, and tell George he has a grandfather, an uncle, and an aunt.'

The two children chuckled. Her father smiled. Paul's face was impassive. He made his way round the double bed. 'I'll come with you to the tube station.' He offered Steve his hand. 'Good to meet you.' Then he waved at the children. 'Thanks for lunch. Hope you get to see those mummies.'

Kate backed towards the door, not wanting to face the awkwardness of having to choose between hugging her father or shaking his hand. She opened the door wide. 'See you all tomorrow.'

And then she and Paul were out in the corridor. They walked down the dingy staircase and past the now-empty reception in silence. Back on the street, the rain had stopped. Unbelievably, the downpour had failed to clear the heat. The atmosphere was still sultry, and the steam rising from the streets added to the humidity. Kate's clothes clung to her, damp and clammy.

Neither of them spoke until they'd almost reached the busy main road. Then Paul said, 'Katerina, what you did was magnificent.'

Kate stopped and turned to face him. Her insides still felt hard. She stared at Paul, knowing her features were frozen. 'I don't think it was,' she said. 'If it hadn't been for you, I wouldn't have gone in there. I would have quite happily walked away.'

'Happily,' Paul repeated. For the first time, his impassive features melted. His eyes on hers were shadowed. 'Nothing about this situation is happy. I wish it were. I wish we were having the weekend we'd planned. I wish you were coming home with me, to my apartment, and I could make you dinner and we could talk. Alone. Where I could do my best to try and make you really happy.'

Kate shrugged. 'Yeah, I was looking forward to seeing you, too. But you know things can't be like that. Life always gets in the way.' She turned to walk on.

Paul caught her hand, whirled her around, and next minute he was kissing her, and Kate was kissing him back ferociously. The feelings she'd tried to bank down, everything she'd tried to unfeel, burst forth into her kiss, and her mouth met his with desperate urgency. She wrapped her arms around his neck, his shirt hot and damp under her fingers. His kiss deepened so that she arched back, holding on to his strong shoulders. He wrapped his arms around her waist, pulling him to her, painfully close.

He broke their kiss, and even through her own numbness Kate registered the anguish in his features.

'I'm sorry,' he said. 'Sorry all this happened.'

Kate lifted her hands to his face for a moment. 'It's not your fault.' Then she dropped her arms and pulled herself free. 'I wish things were different, too, but this is how it is.'

She pulled away, creating a gap between them that would have continued, except Paul reached for her hand. His fingers warmed hers as they continued their walk. When they entered the rush of traffic and people on the road outside King's Cross station, Paul gazed ahead, his face now stony. Even in this part of London, where no one ever looked anyone in the eye, people glanced up as they passed. Kate wondered if any of the passers-by recognised the two of them and realised she no longer cared.

At the steps leading down to the tube, Paul pressed Kate's hand in his before releasing it. 'Looks like we're back where we were last week,' he said. 'Saying goodbye.'

Kate nodded. 'I'll be spending all week with my dad.' She hesitated, then added, 'If you want to come over one evening for dinner, to get to know him ...'

He looked away. 'It's not easy. I've so much to do at work in the evening. By the time I got over to you, it would be late.'

Kate nodded again and looked down. Paul reached out and lifted her chin. 'I'll come over next weekend. Drive them over to the airport.'

'Thanks.' She lifted her eyes to his. 'And thanks for making me see them. I think,' she added, with the ghost of a smile.

He ducked his head and kissed her lips briefly. 'I hope it goes well this week. I'll phone you.'

'Yes.' She smiled properly this time. 'I like your phone calls.'

He dropped his hand and stood back. 'I love you,' he said.

Kate was already turning away. She raised a hand in farewell, and a crowd streaming out of the tube station engulfed her, not giving her time to reply. Maybe it was for the best. She couldn't bring herself to tell Paul she loved him back. Everything inside was still a hard, unfeeling knot.

She made her way down the soulless corridor to the platform and onto a waiting train.

*

Kate reached home just as Orla and George were about to leave the house. They were in the hallway, putting on their shoes. Orla did a double take as Kate pushed the door open.

'I thought you were staying at Paul's. What happened? Who was the mystery B&B guest?'

'Well, he definitely was a surprise.'

'Was it a good surprise, Mum?' George looked up from the Velcro fastenings on his trainers. As usual, Kate's feelings must be clear to see, especially to a perceptive five-year-old.

'It was the best surprise ever,' she said, fixing her face in a smile so wide it hurt. 'Are you and Orla going to the park? Shall I come as well?'

'Yeah,' he said. 'You can go in goal. Orla's rubbish.'

Kate and Orla laughed. 'I'll just put my trainers on,' Kate told him, 'and then I'll tell you all about my morning. We're going to have visitors, and you'll soon have loads more people to go in goal.'

They set off to the park, and on the way Kate told them the incredible events of the morning. For George's benefit, she played down her shock and distress at her father's reappearance after so many years. Instead of the major emotional trauma it had caused her, she made it seem merely like an exciting visit from some Australian relatives.

George was massively enthusiastic at the thought of a new aunt and uncle. His only other relatives were Stuart's parents. Another grandfather, though, presented him with something of a dilemma. Was it possible to have two granddads? And if you have two granddads, what do you call the second one?

Orla suggested Granddad Oz, with a wicked laugh, and George thought this a brilliant idea. By this time they had reached the park. George's burning question had been answered to his satisfaction, and he raced off to take advantage of an empty slide.

As soon as George was out of earshot, Orla turned amazed, worried eyes on her friend. 'Wow, Kate, this is fecking huge. Turning up after all this time. What did he have to say for himself?'

'Actually, not much.' Kate shrugged. 'In a way, I felt a little bit sorry for him.'

'*You* felt sorry for *him*? Kate, I think it's incredible you're letting them come and stay with you, after all the years of nothing.'

Kate eyed her friend with a small smile. 'Yes, that's just what Paul said. He said it was *magnificent*.'

'Who's magnificent?' George asked, charging back from the slide.

'Your mum,' Orla said. She picked George up and swung him round. 'Your mum is totally magnificent.'

This made Kate laugh properly for the first time that morning.

'Shall we play football now?' George asked.

The three of them headed onto the grass, squabbling amicably about who should provide a fleece for the goalposts.

After their trip to the park, Kate spent the rest of the day getting the house ready for her father's visit. When she finally collapsed into bed that night she felt a little feverish, and her throat prickled uncomfortably. The drenching that morning in the rain was taking its toll.

Despite her tiredness, sleep refused to come, and so she lay there for a while, staring at the night sky through her window. The stars were concealed by black clouds, which the morning's storm had failed to clear. There was a muffled feel to the city.

Kate reached out a hand to pick up the photo of Stuart from her bedside table.

'My dad's here, Stuart.' As she spoke the words in the dark, she finally realised the enormity of what had happened that day. Of how her father had dropped everything and crossed the world with his children as soon as he realised Kate might actually agree to see him.

Then she thought of how Stuart would never now have the chance to get to know her father, and how her dad and his children would never have a chance to get to know the man she'd loved. The prickling in her throat intensified, and became a burning behind her eyelids. She tried to think of something more uplifting to say.

'And I kissed Paul again,' she blurted out. She felt the ridiculousness of telling her husband she'd kissed his friend, and expecting him to be cheered by that thought, but somehow she knew that he would. It was an odd thing, but she felt Stuart would even be comforted by it.

'I'm going to put your photo downstairs tomorrow, Stuart,' she told him. 'I hope you don't mind. But talking to you makes me feel sad.'

Stuart smiled at her as if this, too, was something that gladdened him. Kate laid the frame back on the table and curled up, her eyes on the night sky.

*

Kate and Steve sat on the settee in her living room, turning the pages of a photo album. The children were outside in the garden and Kate could hear them calling to each other.

'George, not like that. Watch me.' Rob's shout was followed by the sound of a ball being booted up the garden. Kate's father had brought George some presents – a toy kangaroo and a half-size rugby ball – and his children were showing him how to throw and kick it. From the moment the three children met, they had bonded, in that simple way children had. Kate heard their playful cries, and envied them. At what stage did childhood simplicity get left behind, she wondered, and everything between adults become so much more complicated?

'So that's Stuart's parents, right?' Steve drew her attention to an unsmiling couple in Kate's wedding album.

Kate nodded. 'George goes to stay with them at least once a month. They have a farm in Gloucestershire.'

If Steve thought Kate's reply was a little stilted, he didn't remark on it. He merely flicked her a glance before turning the next page in the album.

Getting the photos out had been a bad idea, Kate thought. It only reinforced her sense of loss. Her only friend at the wedding had been Orla. There were a few girls from her agency, but no one she was particularly close to. At the time it hadn't mattered. She'd been about to start a new life with Stuart, and Stuart was everything to her. Why would she need anyone else?

And after Stuart died, well, as Paul had indicated that night in Adeeb's restaurant, Kate had retreated into herself for a long time. Even with Chloe and the other girls from At Home, she always held something of herself back. It was safer that way. There was only Orla she was totally herself with, and now Orla was …

Kate pressed her fingernails into the palm of one hand and dug in deep. The pages of the album swam in front of her eyes. She tried her best to keep nodding as her father pointed to the people in the photos – but her shoulders began to shake. The next minute, her father had his arm around her. He pulled her to his chest.

'Hey,' he said, his own voice quivering. 'Little Katya. I'm sorry. I'm sorry.'

He brushed a hand through her hair in a gesture that brought back memories of Kate's childhood. The time she'd tripped in the park and banged her head on the kerb. The time she'd fallen out of bed in the night, and her dad had been there. Her sobs began in earnest. Her father cradled her head to his shirt and continued to soothe her, patting her shoulder.

'*Neplač, zlatíčko.*' He rested his cheek on the top of Kate's head. She felt a tremor run through him, and wondered if his relapse into his native Czech meant he was battling his own emotions. She put a hand to her face, trying to still her sobs.

'Don't cry,' he said again. 'What can I do? What can I do to help you?'

'There is nothing, Dad. Just sometimes I get upset about Stuart, and now my friend Orla is going away, too, and it just all gets a bit too much sometimes.' She choked down her sobs and drew herself upright, fishing for a tissue in her pocket.

'I should have been here for you.' His voice was full of anguish.

Kate reached over and touched his hand. 'Don't worry, Dad.' She gave him a tremulous smile. 'You're here now. I'm glad you've come.'

Her father took her hand in his. 'I'm so glad, too. Really glad. I was frightened you wouldn't see me, but Paul said he thought you would. We talked a lot about you after he collected us from the airport. He's a good guy.'

'Yes.' Kate looked away. 'He was very good to George after Stuart died.'

'And to you, too.' Steve's gaze held a question.

Kate nodded, withdrawing her hand slowly. She didn't want to think about how she had started to depend on Paul. She missed him. Her feelings for him had deepened, but instead of this being a source of comfort, it only seemed to add to her pervading sense of foreboding.

'Come on, love.' Steve stood. 'Why don't we go in the kitchen, and you can show me where you keep everything. And then for the rest of the week, I'll do all the shopping and cooking, and me and the kids will take George to school. You have a rest.'

'Thanks, Dad.' Kate stood with him.

'It's the least I can do,' he said. 'Absolutely the least I can do. I only wish we had more time —'

'Oh, don't worry.' Kate opened the door for him. 'Now you've offered to help out, I'm going to take ruthless advantage. You'll soon be wishing you were on that flight home.'

It was an attempt at making light of things. Whether it fooled Steve or not, Kate couldn't say.

In the event, it was lucky Steve was there to help run the house. Kate's tickly sore throat refused to go away. That week she was involved in a shoot for winter coats. It was September, and although the heat wave of the summer was finally over, the days were still warm enough to make wearing a thick coat enervating. Luckily all that was required of her was to tramp through a wood looking moody. Since Kate felt utterly miserable, this didn't task her too much. The day was long, though, and there was a lot of standing around. She came home feeling more exhausted than ever.

Steve was as good as his word and wouldn't let Kate lift a finger in the house all week. He seemed to be making up for lost time as a father and grandfather. He ferried George to school and back, and every day when Kate returned from work she found he had fixed another small DIY problem in the house — a drawer that wouldn't shut properly, a loose tile in the kitchen, the shower head that had begun to leak.

And every evening after dinner, he would play with George, teaching him how to play cards, or kicking the rugby ball in the garden with Rob and Louise, or learning the names of all the footballers in George's treasured sticker book. By the time the end of their week's stay arrived, it was as though he'd always been part of the family.

The night before his return to Australia, Steve and Kate sat together in her living room after the children had gone to bed. Steve had an early flight, and Paul had promised to come and pick him up bright and early.

Kate was sitting in her dressing gown. Her face was flushed, and she was drinking the hot toddy that Steve had made for her.

Steve took a sip of his beer. 'Just as well you're not coming to the airport with us, love. You need to get some rest tomorrow.'

Kate swirled the drink in her hand, watching the warm whisky cling to the sides of the glass. She didn't know when it had begun to be natural for her father to call her 'love'. She liked the sound of it, in his part Czech, part Australian accent.

'George is excited about going with you,' she said. 'And he's dying to see all the planes. But I don't like airports.' She closed her mind to the image of Stuart disappearing through the departure gate, his hand raised in farewell, his kiss warm on her lips. Then she lifted her glass and drained the whisky in one go, and the liquid settled in a heated lump in the pit of her stomach.

Steve's next words came out hesitantly. 'Kate, I know it's too late to change the past. God knows, I would if I could. But it's not too late for the future. I've been thinking – I wondered if you and George would like to come and spend Christmas with us?'

Kate looked up from her empty glass in shock. Had she heard right? 'But what about – ? I mean, I thought your wife – ?'

'Miranda had her moments before we set off here. But that was just her insecurity. I think you might get on once you get to know each other. And it would be great for George to have a real family Christmas.'

His final words were definitely true. This Christmas there would be no Orla to share it with. Kate thought about Paul, and dismissed him just as quickly. She expected he would want to spend the holiday with his family, as he usually did.

'I'll think about it, Dad.' She registered the disappointment in her father's features and added with a small smile, 'Thanks for asking me. It means a lot. And thanks for coming all this way to see us.' She stood. 'Now we've got an early start. I'd better get to bed and try and sleep off this stupid fever.' She put down her glass on a side table. 'Shall we say our goodbyes now?'

Steve stood and pulled her into a hug. 'Bye, love,' he said. His arms tightened. 'Thanks for being such a magnificent daughter.'

'Magnificent,' Kate repeated with an attempt at a smile. 'Have you been talking to Paul? That's just what he said.'

'I told you, he's a good guy.' He kissed the top of Kate's head. 'And think about what I said about Christmas. Bring Paul, too, if you want.'

Kate pulled out of his embrace and reached up to kiss his cheek. 'One step at a time, Dad.'

CHAPTER SEVENTEEN

It was as well Paul came over next morning. Kate had spent the night in a heavy sleep, and when George burst into her bedroom at dawn she'd opened her eyes sluggishly, shivering and drenched in sweat. She forced herself into a cool shower. When she arrived downstairs she found her father in the kitchen preparing breakfast amidst scenes verging on chaos. Louise was hunting tearfully for a miniature London bus, bought as a souvenir for a school friend, and in the meantime George and Rob were outdoing each other in massive high spirits. Kate got herself a couple of aspirin and a glass of water.

'All right, love?' Steve eyed her, concerned. 'You're looking peaky. Still not feeling good?'

'It's OK, Dad. Just a bit of a headache. It'll clear up.' She put an arm round Louise, who was frantically searching through their hand luggage. 'Lou, didn't I see you playing with that bus in George's bedroom yesterday? Do you think it might be up there?'

There was no time for any more conversation with her father. The rest of the morning was a mad scramble to get the children their breakfasts, and to make sure nothing else had been forgotten. By the time Paul knocked on the door to collect everyone, Kate was exhausted and ready to fall back into bed.

As the children scrambled for their seats in the car, and Steve loaded the luggage, Paul took Kate aside.

'Katerina, you look shattered.' He placed his cool hand on her forehead. 'And you're burning up.'

She squinted up at him. The sun rising over the rooftops

was painfully bright. 'I might go back to bed for a couple of hours while you're out. Sleep it off.'

'Why don't I take George out for the day?' he said. 'Give you a break. I could take him to a football match.'

Relief swept through Kate in a welcome wave. 'Thanks, Paul. I didn't want to ask Orla. She's really busy packing and sorting out her flat.'

'No problem. I like having him.' He leaned in to kiss her damp forehead and Kate closed her eyes, but then her father's footsteps sounded on the drive and Paul stepped away, beating a tactful retreat to let them say their goodbyes.

Steve pulled Kate into an embrace and held her. 'Thanks for everything, love. Thanks for having me and the kids. A guy couldn't ask for a better daughter.' He spoke steadily, but his arms were rigid around her. 'And George is a wonderful little boy. He's a credit to you.'

Kate hugged him back. 'Thanks, Dad. I'm glad you came.'

Her father lifted his head. Kate saw his eyes were moist, and felt her own lips tremble. 'Remember what I said,' he told her. 'About you coming over.'

'I'll think about it.'

'Do.' He pressed her hand. 'I'll phone you when we're back.'

He pulled Kate into one last brief, hard hug and turned away, pinching the bridge of his nose. Paul started the car, and all three children waved furiously. Kate could hear their cries of goodbye even through the closed windows. She smiled and waved, her head aching painfully in the bright light.

When she walked back into the house, it was horribly quiet. She tidied away the breakfast things and wandered from room to room, righting everything that had been scattered in the rush to get packed. Then she mounted the stairs, took off her clothes, and fell shivering under the bedclothes.

*

When Paul returned in the early evening, George was tired and over-excited by the week's events. He would have raced inside, but Paul caught hold of his hand.

'Not so fast, mate. Your mother isn't well.'

'OK,' George whispered. He pressed a finger to his mouth and tiptoed through the door, exaggeratedly quiet, and Paul followed him into the living room. Kate was lying on the settee in her pyjamas, a blanket pulled up around her. She looked exhausted and flushed. Her hair was fluffed around her head in a golden halo, and her eyes were large in her face.

'Are you all right, Mum?' George asked. He ran up to her, and Paul's heart lifted to see the smile of welcome on Kate's face. Whether the welcome was directed solely at George, he didn't know, but when Kate's eyes met his he basked in their warmth.

'Much better, now, George,' she told him. 'Just a bit tired.' George wrapped his arms around her, and Kate smiled at Paul over his head. 'Thanks for having him,' she said. 'I've had a good sleep this afternoon. Think I'm better.' Paul approached the settee and noted the black shadows under her eyes. Her face was pale. 'You look tired, still,' he said. 'I brought me and George some fish and chips.' He waved the packet, and Kate recoiled. He smiled down at her. 'Take it, you haven't got your appetite back. Want me to stay and put George to bed?'

'Yes!' George cried, leaping up. Kate opened her mouth to speak, but Paul, too, forestalled her.

'That settles it, then,' he said. 'I'll get George his supper, and bring you a cup of tea.'

Kate's response indicated just how weak she was feeling. Paul had half-expected her to insist on getting up herself, but she merely lay looking up at him, her eyes over bright. 'Thanks, Paul.'

In the kitchen, George took great pride in showing Paul where the plates and cutlery were kept. When it was time to run his bath, he ran to fetch clean towels and pyjamas for himself. Half an hour later he was clean and dry, and ready to say goodnight to Kate.

'Oh, you smell lovely, George,' she said, kissing his cheek. 'Did you show Paul where everything was?'

'Yes, and I didn't even make a mess in the bathroom,' he

said, full of pride.

Kate glanced over at Paul with an awkward smile. 'Is Paul staying the night?' George continued, looking at his mum hopefully.

Paul said nothing. Colour mounted in Kate's pale face. 'Paul hasn't brought his things with him,' she said.

'Oh.' George perched on the settee next to Kate, and looked down sadly at the carpet. 'He probably wouldn't stay very long, anyway.'

'What do you mean?' Kate stared at her son's averted profile, and Paul was shocked to see how much anxiety there was in her expression. There was an unhealthy flush in her cheeks. 'Why should Paul stay? He doesn't live here.'

'I know.' George kicked the rug aimlessly with his bare foot. And then the happenings of the day finally hit him. His face turned scarlet. He turned a quick, embarrassed glance in Paul's direction, obviously biting back tears. 'I didn't want Louise and Rob to go home. Now we'll never see them again.'

Kate sat up and patted his hand matter-of-factly, but Paul could see the unhappiness sweeping through her. 'We'll see them again. Granddad said he'd Skype. Then Rob can show you his table-tennis table.'

'Yeah, but that's not the same as playing with them.' George's head was down, and his voice was rising.

'I know. It's a long way to Australia, but Granddad said we could both go and visit.'

George brightened a little. 'They've got a swimming pool.'

Kate laughed, and ruffled his head. 'Yes, they do, don't they? You can learn to swim properly then.'

'Yeah.'

Paul watched their exchange from the doorway. There was a painful lump in his chest. George continued to gaze at the floor, and Kate's eyes were fixed on him with a look of utter helplessness. Paul pulled himself upright.

'Come on, old chap,' he said. 'Come and show me your sticker album before bed. Then I'll read you a story.'

George stood and took Paul's hand. 'Night, Mum.'

'Sleep tight.' Kate laid her head back down. 'And just one story, mind.'

*

Kate heard their footsteps mount the stairs and stared up at the ceiling. Paul's deep voice could be heard talking steadily as they made their way to George's bedroom. Her son's answers were quieter, more subdued than normal.

Kate squeezed her eyelids shut. She should have guessed this would happen when her father re-entered her life. He'd got George all excited about his new family, and then everything was taken away. And next weekend would be even worse, when they had to say goodbye to Orla. She pressed her fingers to her eyes and turned her face towards the back of the settee. Her shoulders shook, causing a stab of pain to shoot through her head. She was hot, and she ached all over. She remained in this position for a while, holding back the tears, until she heard Paul's steady tread descending the stairs. Then she shifted herself upright.

Paul pushed the living room door open quietly. 'He's asleep already, poor chap,' he said. 'He's had a tiring day.'

Kate nodded, not risking speech. Paul crossed the room and stood, gazing down at her. 'I'll fetch you another cup of tea,' he said. 'Are you sure you don't want anything to eat?'

Kate shook her head and he left for the kitchen. She heard the sound of the kettle boiling and the dishwasher being filled, and then he was back, carrying two steaming mugs. Kate sat up properly, swinging her legs off the settee and onto the floor, her head swimming a little. Paul sat down beside her.

'Here,' he said, passing her a mug.

For several minutes they sat without speaking, drinking their tea. Then Paul placed his mug on the table next to him. He turned to Kate and surprised her by taking the half-empty cup from her hands, and setting it down next to his. His action forced him a little closer. She could smell the scent of George's shampoo, and there was a damp patch on his dark T-shirt from when he had given George his bath. His pulse beat strong and slow in his throat.

He turned to face her. 'Katerina, I know George is upset about your father leaving. And about Orla. And I can guess how hard it is for you, too, that they're going. But I want you to know that even though other people might move on, I won't. I won't ever leave you.'

Kate didn't answer. How could Paul possibly tell in advance that he wasn't going to leave? Stuart had made the same promise when they married. She returned his gaze without speaking.

'You know by now how much I love you.' He reached out a hand, and took hers in his. His clasp was warm and strong. Kate let her fingers lie there, without returning his pressure. 'And I'm asking you to marry me.'

Kate let out a gasp. Paul's hand covered hers, and the heat of it seeped into her, banishing the chill of fever. Yet despite his comforting closeness, a knot of fear closed her throat, as though in some sort of nightmare.

'Don't answer yet,' Paul said quickly, although she was incapable of speaking. 'Listen to me. If we married, you'd never have to be alone again. I could look after you. Look after George.' He placed both his hands around hers, holding her fingers tightly. 'I know you'll never feel for me the way you felt for Stuart.' Here his voice lost its steadiness. 'But I promise you I'd do all I could to make you and George happy.'

Kate began to tug her hand away, but Paul held it close.

'Say yes.' He reached out to cup her cheek, forcing her to meet his gaze. 'What do you have to lose?'

'Everything!' she burst out, with such vehemence that he dropped his hand to his side, startled. Kate tugged her fingers out of his and got to her feet. 'I wish you hadn't asked me.'

Paul stood and caught her to him. His chest was hard, but his body trembled against hers. 'Katerina, don't tell me you feel nothing. That night –'

'That night was a mistake. It ruined everything.' She wrenched herself out of Paul's embrace, almost staggering with the mental effort to break free. She saw the hurt flare in his eyes and looked away. She couldn't allow herself to feel his pain. She took a hurried step back and wrapped her arms around herself. A picture flashed before her of a future with Paul, of waking up in his embrace every day. The warmth of him, his solid presence, his body beside her in the night ... The images were so hard to fight, the effort of it caused pain to shoot through her temple. She placed one hand against her ribcage, breathing heavily.

'I won't believe there's nothing between us.' Paul struggled to keep his voice under control. 'I refuse to believe that that night meant nothing to you. I –'

He reached for her, and Kate smacked his arm away.

'Don't tell me what I think!' She stood, panting, and they stared at each other in mutual horror at the violence of her response.

'Katerina,' Paul said, his voice low. 'Tell me what you're so afraid of.'

Kate flinched. 'I'm not afraid.' She drew herself upright. 'Thank you for having George today.' She was going to add 'and for helping me meet my dad', but the words crowded in her throat. She swallowed, her throat on fire. 'But I'd like it if you left now. I know you want to help me, and look after me and George –' She stopped a moment, clenching her fingers. 'But I think it's best for both of us if we go back to how we were. If you just come to see George once a month.'

The colour drained from Paul's face. 'You're making a mistake.'

'Please just go.' She reached out a hand, as though she could physically push him away. When he didn't move, she cried out, 'Go!'

He nodded once, and turned to pick up his jacket from where he'd left it slung on the back of a chair. 'I'm going now. But that doesn't mean I'm giving up on you, Katerina. I told you I won't leave you. I mean what I say.'

Kate stood rigid. His words were meant to be reassuring, but the fear inside her only intensified. She watched him turn and fumble with the door, then listened to his footsteps on the wooden floor of the hallway, and then the front door closing gently. He was gone, and Kate had got what she asked for. She threw herself face down on the settee and into uncontrollable sob. For a long while she lay there, her face in her hands, weeping useless tears until finally she had exhausted herself. Then she crept upstairs to bed.

Despite her fatigue, sleep eluded her for a long time. Her temperature had risen again with the heat of her emotions, and when she finally dropped off into a fitful sleep she dreamt she was in the dusty heat of Afghanistan, under a raging sun, with sweat seeping from her pores. In her fevered dream she heard a rustling overhead, and when she looked upwards she found a helicopter hovering just above her. The blades made no sound, and the aircraft bobbed gently. In the open door she could see Paul sitting on the floor, his feet dangling in mid-air, with George beside him. They were laughing.

Terror rooted Kate to the ground. She wanted to go to Paul, but dread immobilized her. He and George were chatting happily, unaware of her fear. Beside her she felt a movement, and when she turned, there was Stuart. He was smiling, as joyfully as Paul and George. He touched her face.

'Man up,' he said. His expression was gentle. She wanted to answer him, to tell him she was too frightened to get in the helicopter, but his form began to dissolve before her eyes.

'Stuart, come back.' She tried to say the words, but her throat closed around them. She struggled to shout, for Stuart to help her, and woke to find herself calling aloud in the dark, in her own bedroom, alone.

She sat, hot and shivering, her heart pounding. She turned to her side table automatically, to look at Stuart's photo for reassurance, and remembered she had taken it downstairs. There was an empty space where it should have been.

She lay down heavily, and the image of Paul in the helicopter floating gently above her swam before her again. The picture was safe and serene, and Paul's expression was a tender smile of welcome.

It was then that Kate remembered how frightened Paul was of flying. Yet in her dream, he was perfectly at ease. It was

Kate who was terrified.

*

By Monday Kate's fever had lifted. Physically, she was better, but emotionally she was worn out. She'd heard nothing from Paul. He'd been in the habit of phoning every day, and texting at least once, but there'd been nothing since he left her house. She'd asked him to go back to how things were – to seeing George once a month – and he was obviously taking her at her word. The thought should have satisfied her, but it only deepened her unhappiness.

She dropped George at school and made her way to the offices of At Home, where she had an appointment to meet Chloe. There were a few things she wanted to ask her, about Sarah in particular, and she was looking forward to catching up on how the girls were doing now they'd all returned home. A brush with the normal world would do her good.

It was such a relief to see Chloe's round, cheerful face greet her as she walked into her office that she almost felt tears rising.

Chloe stood and gave Kate a hug. 'Good to see you, love,' she said. 'How are you doing?' She held Kate at arm's length. 'You look a little tired.'

Kate gave her a twisted smile. 'I know. Good job there's a couple of days until my next job.' She filled Chloe in on her eventful week, concentrating on the extraordinary arrival of her dad and his family, and omitting Paul's dramatic proposal and departure.

'Oh, Kate.' Chloe's round eyes brimmed with sympathy. 'It's wonderful your dad got in touch, but what a dreadful shock it must have been, just arriving like that.' She eyed Kate in concern. 'It was good Paul was there with you.'

Kate shrugged, fiddling with the handbag strap on her lap. 'Yes, I'm glad he was there.' She thought of Paul's steady presence beside her in the poky bedroom that day, the way he'd taken the teenagers out to give her some privacy with her father, his rocklike support at her side. If Chloe guessed how her weekend with Paul had ended, and how Kate had sent him away, she would be stunned.

Luckily Chloe had other things on her mind. 'I spoke to Paul last week,' she said, full of excitement. 'Did he tell you? His article's been submitted, and we're going to hit the newsstands in the *Sunday Magazine* a week on Sunday. I can't wait!'

Her news brought a smile to Kate's face at last. Paul hadn't mentioned the date to her, and she hadn't realised it would be so soon. For a while she and Chloe discussed Paul's article, and the publicity it would generate for At Home.

'Oh,' Kate said, suddenly remembering. 'It's such a shame Orla won't be here with us when it comes out. She's off to Ireland at the weekend.'

'Oh, of course. I'm so thrilled for her.' Chloe beamed. 'After everything you both went through together, she's done so well for herself. It's going to be a great adventure. She really is a special person.'

Kate dropped her gaze. Her distress must have been obvious. Chloe reached forward and touched her arm. 'I'm sorry, love. First your dad, now Orla. What a terrible week this has been. Paul must be a tremendous support.'

Kate's lip trembled and she blinked once or twice. 'Paul's been a great help,' she said. Then she changed the subject quickly. 'Actually, Chloe, I've come to ask your advice. It's about Sarah.'

Her diversionary tactics were successful. Chloe opened her eyes in surprise. 'Sarah? The girl who's the artist and makes all her own clothes?'

'Yes, that's the one.' Kate smiled at the description. 'She's got the makings of a great designer, and not just in the world of fashion. You know Dashna is going to study engineering?'

Chloe nodded. 'Yes, and I saw how she and Sarah got on like a house on fire that week. Such an unlikely friendship, but they really were inseparable.'

'I know. It was lovely to see them together. Anyway, Dashna put it into Sarah's head that she could use her design skills as an architect.'

Chloe whistled softly, drawing back in her chair. 'Well, that would be a great career, but I mean ... Dashna's lucky. She has her family to support her. But it's a totally different thing for Sarah. It takes so long to train up, and Sarah struggles as it is, trying to support herself from her job. I'm sure that's why she flunked her 'A' levels She'd have to redo them, and how would she manage?' Chloe shook her head. These were the types of obstacles that put the girls at a disadvantage before they'd even started.

'Well, this is what I've been thinking.' Kate leaned forward. 'Orla used to help me out a lot with George. I'll really miss her babysitting when she's gone. And I've got a big house for just me and George to rattle round in. I thought about offering Sarah a home for as long as she wants. She's great with kids. She can help me with George from time to time and I'll support her for as long as she needs. That way she won't have to worry about bills while she studies. I was wondering what you thought? Could it work?'

'Well, yes, I suppose.' Chloe wrinkled her brow. 'But have you thought about how long you'd have to support her? It's many years before she'd qualify. And what if – I mean, you could remarry. Would Sarah carry on living with you?'

'I'm not remarrying.' The words were clipped and cold.

Chloe didn't answer straightaway. She continued to study Kate, a tentative expression on her face. 'I hope you don't mind me bringing this up, but I thought there was something between you and Paul. Perhaps I was jumping the gun.'

Kate shook her head vehemently. 'There's nothing between us.'

Chloe seemed disappointed, but she didn't press Kate any further. 'I'm sure Sarah would be absolutely delighted. I'll ask her to come in and see you, and we can talk about it together.'

'Great.' Kate sat back, a tight smile on her face.

Chloe tapped her pen on the table. 'Well, even if there was something between you and Paul, I'm sure he wouldn't have any objections. Not with the way he's helping Abi. You and he have a lot in common.'

'Abi?' Kate stared at her, puzzled. 'Paul never mentioned anything.'

'No? Well perhaps he thought you had a lot on your mind. Abi's going back to live in Yorkshire.'

Kate's jaw dropped open as Chloe explained how Paul had talked to the farmer they'd visited, and as a result how the farmer had agreed to have Abi to live with his family for a year. In return, Abi would help with the farm work, and she would also complete a long-distance course in journalism which Paul had paid for. And – most excitingly of all – every week Abi would write a blog post for *The World* online, about a city girl's life on the farm.

'So everybody wins,' Chloe finished. 'The farmer gets free labour and publicity for his farm visits, and Abi gets a home, she gets to study and to write her first assignment.'

'And she gets her shepherd,' Kate said. She grinned, her first smile of real delight in what seemed like weeks. She told Chloe how Abi and the shepherd had met in the barn, how they'd fallen head over heels at first sight, and how Kate had thought they would never get a chance to see each other again.

'There is a way from heart to heart,' Kate murmured to herself.

Chloe caught her words, and patted her hand. 'There always is a way,' she said with a smile. 'Sometimes it just takes a little courage.'

*

Orla was sitting on Kate's settee in her dressing-gown, a glass of wine in one hand, a chunk of Dairy Milk chocolate in the other, and a look of total disbelief on her face.

'So tell me again. You'd been lying in bed all day with a temperature, feeling crap. And probably looking it.' She ignored Kate's perfunctory protest. 'Your dad had just left, you were miserable, and the house was a mess. And Paul decided that was a good time to propose.' Orla clapped the hand holding the chocolate to her forehead. 'Men! Why are they such fecking eejits?'

'You've got chocolate on your face,' Kate said.

Orla popped the chocolate in her mouth and then dabbed at her forehead with a tissue. 'Mhm mgrrh,' she said, her mouth full.

'That's exactly what I said to Paul.' Kate gave a watery laugh. 'Oh, Orla, I'm going to miss you so much.'

Orla reached out a hand sticky with chocolate, and pressed Kate's fingers. 'The time will fly by, hon, you just wait and see. I just wish – I mean, I really thought you and Paul were starting to have something between you. A future together. If you're looking for a real friend, Paul's always been there for you.'

Kate took a sip of her wine. 'I'm much better by myself.' She drained her glass and reached for the bottle. 'Anyway, let's not talk about Paul. It's your last night in London. Drink up.'

Orla stretched forward with her glass for a refill. 'OK. But I'll just say this, and then I'll shut up. You can't live in fear for the rest of your life, Kate. Don't hide yourself away. You're much too good for that.' Her brown eyes glistened and she bit her lip. 'Here's me, getting all maudlin.' She raised her glass. 'Here's to Kate Hemingway. Best friend ever.'

'To Orla.' Kate clinked her friend's glass, giving her a smile that was only half-sad. 'And to her many adventures.'

CHAPTER EIGHTEEN

Both Kate and Orla were feeling the worse for wear next morning. Kate's head gave a dull throb when she woke, but she crawled out of bed before sunrise to see Orla into her taxi. Her friend had told her the night before that she wanted to get up and leave, with no fuss. And definitely no breakfast, unless Kate wanted her to bring it all back up on her drive.

When Kate arrived downstairs, Orla was already in the hallway, surrounded by luggage. A subdued George sat beside her on her staircase, still in his pyjamas and dressing-gown.

Orla blinked sleepily when she saw Kate. 'You look like a tree full of owls.'

'You don't look so great yourself. Your mum will be telling you she knew you should never have gone off to that London.'

They both attempted to laugh. Then the taxi's horn sounded outside, and next thing the driver was loading Orla's bags into the boot, and they were all hugging.

'Remember what I told you,' Orla murmured in Kate's ear. 'Don't hide yourself away.' She held her tight. 'Embrace life.'

Then George was demanding a hug, and Orla whisked him into her arms, and then she was in the taxi, waving furiously out of the window, and then the taxi turned the corner and all of a sudden she was gone.

George kicked the gravel. 'I don't want Orla to go.'

To Kate's great consternation, he buried his face in his hands and burst into tears.

'Hey, George.' She caught him to her in a fierce hug. 'It's not a sad day. Orla's going on an adventure. And we can go and visit her.'

'We're always having to visit people,' he protested, the sobbing muffled in her embrace. 'Granddad and Rob and Louise and Orla. I don't want to visit them. I want them to stay here with us.'

Something inside Kate hardened. It was all very well for Orla to tell her to embrace life. She didn't have a child to look after.

She dried George's tears and told him she'd thought of a special treat. They would go to Hamleys toy shop and then have a burger and chips and milkshake for lunch. That would cheer them both up.

George agreed, and as the day progressed his usual high spirits returned. With the resilience of a child he was able to turn his attention to the future, and when Kate promised him he could have some school friends round for a sleepover, he went to bed much more cheerful than he'd woken. Which was more than could be said for Kate. After George had fallen asleep, and she was finally alone, she fell into a fit of crying that lasted until she crawled into bed.

*

The week dragged, and Kate's spirits with it. She tried her best to shake off her deep depression, but the evenings when George was asleep and she was alone with her thoughts were the worst. She would lie on her settee, a cushion clutched to her, and try to watch a film, but instead of the images on screen a picture of Paul filled her mind. He would be crossing Southwark Bridge on his way home from work. She thought of all the evenings he'd phoned her, and wondered if he was thinking of her at this time, too, and whether he now despised her. This last was a very lowering thought, but the look of hurt on his face as he left her house that day played in Kate's mind over and over again. He had made no attempt to get in touch with her. His next visit with George wasn't for a couple of weeks, and Kate looked forward to it with a mixture of dread and longing.

The only highlight in the week was her visit to At Home, and her conversation with Sarah, who was so overwhelmed by

Kate's offer of support she burst into tears. Her reaction, strangely, helped Kate keep a lid on her own emotions, forcing her into the role of calm good sense. She and Sarah had a long discussion, and the upshot was that Sarah would move in once she'd worked out the notice on her present flat. Sarah was euphoric. Her lively company would be good for George, Kate thought, and for Kate, too, if she were honest. So really, she didn't need Paul at all.

Yet with the best will in the world it was hard to put Paul from her mind when all Chloe could talk about was his forthcoming article. She had arranged for the group to meet the following Sunday, and booked some tables at a local pub for lunch. That way they could read the article together. Only Abi would be missing, as she'd already left London for Yorkshire.

When Kate walked into the pub the first person she saw was Paul, leaning against the bar. He turned his head when Kate entered, and the blood drained from her face.

Paul pulled himself upright. 'Katerina.'

His face, too, was pale. Kate found her voice, the words escaping her before she could prevent them. 'I didn't know you were coming.'

His expression hardened. 'I see.'

Kate stood without speaking. The awkwardness was even worse than her imaginings. She was saved from answering by a great scream from the other side of the bar.

'Kate! Come and look at this!' One of the girls was brandishing a copy of the *Sunday Magazine*. 'It's bonkers!'

Kate nodded and smiled. 'Be there in a minute.'

'Hope that's bonkers in a good way.' Paul was regarding the group with one of his dry, quizzical expressions. Kate caught his eye and chuckled. He still had the ability to make her laugh, despite herself.

She hitched her bag onto her shoulder. 'I'll go over and join them.'

'Can I get you something to drink?'

Now she smiled again. Paul's innate courtesy never slipped,

even in the most awkward situations.

'Thank you.' Kate eyed the group of girls. 'I'd better have a whisky and ginger. It might be a long afternoon.' Then she caught Paul's expression, and blurted out, 'I don't mean – I mean, it's not because of you.' She felt her cheeks redden. 'I just thought some of the girls seemed over-excited.'

Then it was Paul's turn to smile. 'I know exactly what you mean,' he said. 'It's written all over your face. It always is.' He gestured towards the girls, who were moving to occupy a long table against one wall. 'Why don't you go and join the others? I'll bring your drink through.'

Kate slipped away, her heart beating uncomfortably fast. The sight of the girls, heads bent together and chattering over their copies of the magazine, raised her spirits. She met Chloe's eye and waved.

'Kate, I'm on the *front cover*!' Sarah hissed, drawing out a chair for her. 'Me and Dashna. Look. It's mad!'

She shoved the magazine under Kate's nose. There on the cover was Sarah's blonde head, pressed close to Dashna's headscarf, each of their faces split by an enormous smile. In the background was the barn. The sun shone down from an intensely blue sky, creating a halo around their heads, and turning the green of Dashna's scarf into a vibrant glow of colour. Above the photo was the title 'Escape to the Country'. And then in smaller print, 'The Londoners from At Home discover themselves'.

'Wow,' said Kate. 'That's amazing. How fabulous you look.'

'You're in it, too.' Dashna reached over the table and turned the pages excitedly. 'Look!'

Kate was used to seeing photos of herself, but she went through the motions of being as excited as the girls. There was a picture of her leaning against the coach in her shorts and vest top, in close conversation with Abi.

Sarah turned away to speak to Dashna, leaving Kate to read the full text of the article. She bent her head, absorbed. Paul placed his warm hand on her shoulder, setting her drink by her elbow. There was an empty chair next to her, and Kate thought for a moment that he was going to pull it out and sit down. She stiffened, but Paul straightened up, moving away from her to the other side of the table, taking a seat beside Chloe.

Kate felt a contrary pang of disappointment, and told herself sharply to stop being ridiculous. She immersed herself once more in the article. It was easy to let Paul's words sweep her away. The noise and chatter continued all around her, but Kate remained engrossed until the final paragraphs.

'Chloe told me, "Sometimes these girls feel as though they are battling alone against an unending sea of problems. If we do nothing else at At Home, we can at least make them feel that someone is standing there beside them."

'When we finally arrive in London, the girls shoulder their meagre belongings and make their way back into the familiar streets, to face whatever difficulties await them. Their heads are held high.'

Kate finally lifted her gaze from the text in front of her, blinking away tears. Paul had captured the girls' spirit exactly. Her eyes met his across the table. He was leaning back in his chair, beer in hand, watching her. She gave him a small smile, and he raised his glass.

Then Sarah tugged Kate's arm, diverting her with another question, and the rest of the meal passed by with cheerful gossip and catching up with the girls' activities. Kate tried not to look too often in Paul's direction. Once, when her gaze drifted despite herself, she was surprised to see Chloe's head bent towards Paul in earnest conversation. Paul caught Kate's eye and looked away, his expression uninviting.

Kate's temples began to ache with the effort of smiling all the time. As soon as politely possible, she pushed back her chair. There was a chorus of disappointment.

'Sorry to leave you all so soon,' she said. 'George is at a friend's house, and I need to pick him up.'

It was only a half-lie. There were still a couple of hours before she needed to collect him. She bent to pick up her bag, and Paul rose from his chair.

'How are you getting home?' he asked.

'On the tube.'

'I'll give you a lift.' He picked up his jacket from the back of his chair.

*

Paul noted the high colour in Kate's cheeks. She'd frozen when he offered her a lift, but he knew she wouldn't protest in front of curious onlookers, no matter how much she wanted to avoid his company. He bent to shake hands with Chloe, who scraped back her chair and stood, giving him a close, affectionate hug.

'Remember what I said,' she murmured. 'Don't give up.'

He nodded. Then he lifted his hand in a wave to the girls, and they gave him a loud chorus of thanks and goodbyes. He smiled, their affectionate farewell raising his spirits momentarily.

Then he stood back, allowing Kate to precede him outside.

'There was no need for you to leave early,' she said, glaring up at him in the car park. 'I'm happy to get on the tube.'

Her face was tilted to the sun, the light playing over her stubborn features. Paul said nothing, merely taking her arm gently, steering her towards his car.

Kate fastened herself in and stared stiffly ahead. Paul reversed out of the car park, and for the first ten minutes of the journey neither of them spoke. When Paul glanced to his left, he could see Kate hunched in her seat, a ball of misery. He turned his gaze back to the road, his fingers tightening on the wheel. He tried to think of something to say, some way to start the conversation. When they reached the traffic lights he turned his head.

'Do you – ?' he began.

'It was –' Kate started at the same time.

The both broke off, laughing awkwardly.

Kate spoke, Paul thought. That was good. 'Go on,' he said. 'You first.'

'I was saying how brilliant that is about Abi going back to Yorkshire. And everything you did for her.' She smiled. It was a small, downturned smile, but a smile nonetheless. 'I'm sure her shepherd must be pleased to see her.'

Paul moved the car into gear as the lights changed. 'I'm sure he is.' He gave a low laugh. 'Although I got the impression that young man is quite capable of sorting out his own love life, without any help from me. I did it because Abi is tenacious and has a great insight. I think she has the makings of a good journalist.'

'Tenacious.' She stole him an uncertain look.

'That's right,' he said, meeting her gaze. 'We journalists don't give up easily.'

There it was again. That unmistakable flicker of fear in her eyes. Kate didn't move, but he sensed the anxiety welling below her rigid exterior. He forced his eyes back to the road.

After Kate's rejection of him, Paul had been consumed with pain, unable to think clearly. For the first few days he'd barely slept, wondering if he might even be going out of his mind. As the week passed, and he was able to look on their conversation more dispassionately, a realisation took slow hold. He remembered Kate's overwrought terror as he'd reached out to touch her. It was a fear out of all proportion, and he began to suspect it was not himself that she was rejecting. She had begged him to leave because she was terrified of suffering further loss and pain. A few seeds of hope began to ripen inside him. Even so, it had taken Chloe's urgent advice, murmured over the table that afternoon, to conquer his self-doubt and bolster his resolve.

He cleared his throat. 'Katerina,' he began. 'There have been some times as a journalist when I was truly frightened. When you're holed up in a hotel for weeks, and everyone else is leaving. When you hear gunfire in the streets outside. When people tell you you're mad to stay, that you'll be killed. You go to bed alone in that silent room and your fear becomes a part of you.' He felt her eyes on him. 'There was a guy I met in West Africa once who never seemed to fear anything. He'd talk over the noise of gunfire as though we were in a pub in Soho. When I was at a really low ebb, he told me that fear came of trying to fight against yourself. The secret was to accept whatever you were afraid of, and work with it, not against it.'

'It's easy to live with fear if there's only yourself to think about,' Kate countered swiftly. 'What if it's not just you in that hotel room? What if you've got a child to look after? Do you accept fear then?'

So that was it. Paul felt an icy sliver enter his gut. The car came to a halt at the lights, and he closed his eyes for a second. Here was the reason she was so afraid. It wasn't for herself, but for George. A deep, primeval fear. And if he couldn't succeed in loosening its hold, what then?

He glanced at Kate as the lights changed. She was sitting stiff-backed, staring ahead, her whole being radiating tension. He thought of the blows life had dealt her, and how hard it would be to convince her that by shielding George for the rest of his life, she was harming him rather than protecting him. That it was better to show her son the way to embrace life with courage, not to keep him cocooned.

Paul slipped the car into gear, and felt his own fear knot and harden at what he was about to do.

'Next Saturday is my day to visit George,' he said. His gaze met Kate's briefly. 'I'd like you to come out for the day, too. There's something I want to show you.'

'Oh?' She lifted her head at last. 'What is it?'

'You'll have to wait and see.' He tried to smile, but his lips froze.

'Is everything all right?'

'Yes,' he said. The terror roiled inside him, but his voice was utterly calm.

*

During the week that followed Kate was so overwrought by nightmares, she wondered if she were actually going crazy. Her nights were filled with stark terror, leaving her drained and exhausted. And the dreams were always same. She would be gazing up at a helicopter, mostly in the heat of Afghanistan, but in one particularly frightening dream she was standing on the Yorkshire moors. Stuart, Paul, and George were all sitting in the aircraft doorway, their feet dangling almost at Kate's eye level. Everything was real and vivid. Stuart had on a pair of dark jeans she remembered, and his climbing boots. George had on his blue socks, and as usual his trainers were unfastened. Paul's shoes shone black, and he was smiling at her, all stillness and calm.

Kate's terror made no sense. All three in the aircraft waved down to her, beckoning her in. The helicopter bobbed gently, serene and welcoming, the blades making just the faintest rustling in the air. And yet her horror for George's safety made Kate scream at them, begging them to come down. Once again she woke, calling out in the dark.

'This can't go on,' she told herself, pressing the heels of her hands to her eyes.

The worst and most stupid thing was that throughout her exhaustion, Kate longed to see Paul again – the very person she was frightened of seeing. His solid and reassuring presence was the only thing that could comfort her. Need of him caused her anxiety to increase all the more. With these thoughts battling each other, she told herself, it was no wonder she was going crazy.

By the time Saturday arrived, Kate was exhausted. Paul had told them it would be an early start, and she opened the door to him at six in the morning. The first thing she noticed was how pale he looked. He reached forward and kissed her cheek, his lips chilly despite the warmth of the day.

'Hey, Paul.' George rushed through the door and threw himself at his godfather, wrapping his arms around his legs. 'Where are we going?'

'Hello, George.' Paul ruffled his head. 'It's a surprise.' He smiled, but Kate noticed his smile was confined to a mechanical movement of the lips.

'Is everything all right?' she asked, searching his face.

He was about to answer, and then he tilted his head on one side with a wry smile. 'I could ask you the same thing.' He ran his eyes over her. 'You look like you haven't slept.'

'Thanks,' she protested, half-laughing at his directness.

His eyes gleamed amusement for a second, and then the

light died. He took George's hand. 'Are we ready to be off?'

'Are you going to tell us where we're going?' Kate asked.

'I'll tell you on the way.' Paul threw his answer over his shoulder, already turning, his hand still clasped round George's.

'I like adventures,' said George, tugging on Paul's hand as they headed for the car.

'Me, too,' Paul said. Then added dryly, 'Most of the time.'

He strapped George into the car seat he'd bought for him, and then held Kate's door wide.

'This is very mysterious.' She slid into her seat. He tucked in her trailing jacket without answering, and closed the door.

For a while George chattered in the back of the car, and Kate answered sporadically. Paul took them along the North Circular, before heading north out of London. When she glanced in his direction, she noticed his hands were gripping the wheel more tightly than necessary. There was a pallor about his features that seemed to be more than ordinary tiredness.

They joined the motorway, and Kate asked, 'Are you going to give us a clue now?'

'We're going to an airfield. It's not far.'

'Oh? Is there a show on?'

He glanced over at her then, a wry smile on his lips. 'Sort of. I'm doing a parachute jump.'

'*Woah.*' George's voice filtered through from the back of the car. Kate stared at Paul in astonishment. His eyes were back on the road now, and the tension in his hands on the wheel seemed to have eased a little with his revelation.

'A parachute jump,' she repeated faintly. 'You? A real one? Jumping out of a plane in the sky?'

A spasm crossed Paul's face, but he answered steadily enough. 'Yes. A parachute jump. I'll be jumping out of a plane. With a parachute.'

'But I mean how? Don't you have to train to jump? They can't just let you do it, surely?'

He looked over at her quizzically. 'I have trained. I did a

whole day of training yesterday. I'm reliably informed that's all I need, and I'm ready.'

'Ready?' she repeated, aghast. 'You're nowhere near ready. Look at you. You're terrified! Didn't you tell the instructors you were frightened of flying?'

'Yes. They seem to think I have the "mental toughness" to go through with it. That's their expression, by the way,' he added apologetically. 'I don't want to seem big-headed, or anything. They seemed quite impressed with my "attitude". Told me the jump would "leave a smile on my face".'

Kate stared at him. When she failed to answer, Paul turned to her with a tired grin, adding, 'Anyway, I can't back down now. I've raised quite a bit of money for At Home. Chloe will kill me if I don't go through with it.'

Kate's eyes widened.

'Are you frightened, Paul?' George's awestruck voice came from the back of the car.

Paul glanced in his rear-view mirror. 'Yes. Some people don't like flying, and I'm one of them. But sometimes when you face up to the things you're afraid of, they become less scary.'

'I wouldn't be afraid of flying,' George said wistfully. 'I wish I could jump out of a plane.'

'Well, you can. When you're older.'

Kate drew in a breath. 'Over my dead body', were the words about to leave her mouth. Then she caught a glimpse of Paul's profile. Resolute, set, his eyes on the road ahead. She twisted her fingers round and round in her lap. Was this what it was all about? Confronting your fears? Was she wrong to want to keep George safe? A flurry of thoughts jumbled round in her head. She wanted to do the right thing, to protect her son, but maybe she was doing everything wrong. She turned her head to the window. Everything was confusing and miserable.

Then she felt Paul's hand cover her agitated fingers briefly, before he returned it to the steering wheel.

'Hey,' he said quietly. 'I'm the one who's supposed to be

scared, remember?' He gave her one of his deadpan smiles. 'You're stealing my thunder.'

Kate was forced to chuckle. 'I can't believe you're actually going to go through with this.'

'Oh, but I am.' His knuckles showed white on the steering wheel. 'And I'm going to "reach the ground smiling".'

CHAPTER NINETEEN

It was just as well George was with them, rattling out his excited questions in the back of the car. Without his chatter, Paul would have driven up the long ribbon of tarmac and onto the airfield in total silence, the fear a tight knot in his chest. A small plane in garish yellow and green colours stood on the airstrip. In a couple of hours he would be inside this metal machine, thousands of feet above the earth, standing in the open doorway. He tried not to battle with this image – tried to let it become an exhilarating picture instead of a terrifying one –but the fear inside him swelled, rising into his throat.

He pulled into a parking spot and leaned back stiffly in his seat, his hand still clutching the handbrake. Kate reached forward, and her warm fingers closed over his.

'Paul,' she said softly. 'I know why you're doing this. It's a truly magnificent gesture. But please don't go through with it.' She lowered her voice, checking that George's attention was fixed on the aircraft outside. 'I get it. I'll try and stop hiding away. You don't have to put yourself through this – this torture, just to convince me.'

Her eyes were fastened on his, wide with anxiety. Paul caught up her hand and squeezed it. 'You're not supposed to worry for me. Everything's going to be OK.' The seeds of hope inside him unfurled with the warmth of her fingers on his. Without thinking, he reached his free hand to her face, pulling her to him. He pressed a swift kiss on her parted lips. When she responded, her mouth seeking his, his heart leapt.

'You kissed Mum.' George's tone was half-curious, half-surprised.

'Yes, I did,' Paul answered matter-of-factly. 'And do you know what? I'm glad I'm jumping out of a plane.' He gave Kate's hand a final squeeze and twisted his head round to his godson. 'They've got a games room and a café. Do you want to check them out while I get ready?'

'Yeah!' George unfastened his belt and stood.

Outside in the airfield a group of onlookers huddled around one of the sheds. Paul cast a quick glance at the sky. A few wisps of cloud hovered high up, motionless in the pale blue.

'Perfect flying conditions.' He caught Kate's eye with a grin. 'What a shame.'

Kate put her hand on his arm. 'Back out,' she urged. 'It doesn't matter.'

He shook his head. 'Yes, it does.' He slowed to a halt, looking down at her. 'Don't think I haven't thought about backing out. There'd be nothing easier. But when my nerves are worst, I picture Stuart standing with me in the doorway, laughing. Telling me to "man up".'

'And laughing and smiling.' Kate's mouth opened, and she breathed in quickly. 'My dreams,' she said. She turned wide, amazed eyes on Paul.

Paul wanted to stop and ask her what she meant, but his instructor had seen them and was bearing down on him like a relentless executioner.

'Take care,' Kate murmured. She reached up on tiptoe to kiss Paul's cheek, and he caught her to him in a fierce hug, feeling a rush of euphoria as she clung to him.

The instructor spoke beside them. 'The condemned man bids a last goodbye.' There was a cheerful, unworried smile on his face; the insouciant look of a man who thought nothing of throwing himself from great heights.

'Morning, Duncan.' Paul was pleased to note the steadiness in his reply.

Duncan squatted down next to George. 'There's a mini airplane for kids inside. You can climb in and fly it. Want to have a go while I help your dad get ready?'

Kate opened her mouth, perhaps to explain that Paul

wasn't George's father, but George's eyes merely widened. He did a standing jump. Then Duncan was shepherding them all towards the sheds, and Paul moved along with them, his feet weighing him down with each step.

When they reached the group outside the training hanger, a young man stepped forward. Surely this couldn't be the pilot? Paul thought wildly. He seemed barely old enough to shave. But introductions were made, and Paul shook his hand. The fresh-faced youth began to lead Kate and George away into one of the other sheds, where there were games for George, and refreshments.

'Good luck,' Kate mouthed.

Paul nodded, unable to reply. In his mind he was wondering what would happen if he kitted up with the others and found himself paralysed with fear, unable to exit the training hanger. For a heart-stopping moment he felt as though he was about to experience one of his occasional flashbacks. The world slowed down around him. Sounds and conversations floated and retreated. Paul closed his eyes, and an image came into his mind of Kate, her hand pressing his in the car, eyes wide, her love for him unhidden. His heartbeat slowed, his breathing became more regular. Then someone tapped his shoulder, and the group was moving inside the training hanger, taking him with them.

Paul headed straight for the toilets, where he was quietly sick.

After that, he went through the steps of preparation feeling numb. He stepped into garish blue overalls, his parachute was strapped on, and he was handed goggles, helmet, and altimeter.

'How are you feeling?' Duncan asked.

'I've felt better.'

Duncan grinned. 'You're not going to regret it.'

Paul thought again of Kate and this time felt a different kind of apprehension. One that ran deep into his bones. He merely answered, 'I hope not.'

And then his jump partners were there, running through the radio procedure one more time. After that, he wasn't sure how, he was outside in the sunshine, his feet taking him inexorably towards the aircraft. He turned his head, trying to make out Kate and George, and saw them standing outside one of the sheds. George was waving frantically. Paul waved back, and he even managed to laugh when his jump partners, too, waved to George.

Despite his heavy harness, a feeling of lightness came over him. The propellers on the plane were turning, but the sound was gentle compared to the helicopters he'd flown in on assignment. He looked up at the sky before boarding the craft. The clouds had vanished. He felt for the rungs of the ladder. One step, and then another. His jump partner was behind him, and now he was inside and had passed the point of no return. The door of the aircraft swung shut.

The other, experienced skydivers talked and joked among themselves in the plane, which began to manoeuvre bumpily down the runway, the engines accelerating.

Duncan tapped his knee. 'How are you feeling?' he asked again.

Paul nodded and swallowed. 'OK,' he rasped.

It was impossible to articulate how he was feeling, even to himself. The plane lifted off the ground, and his fear of the jump evaporated. He could think only of Kate, and how she was waiting for him below, and his terror at losing her. What if he failed to persuade her? What if she insisted on returning to their previous stilted existence, with him knocking on her door once a month, waiting for George to appear? He didn't know if it was humanly possible to bear it.

The plane banked and climbed, and he opened his eyes, checking his altimeter. Ten thousand feet already. How could they have climbed so high? There was a stirring of anticipation amongst the skydivers. Paul glanced at the window, but wasn't seated near enough to make out the ground. Only the milky blue of the heavens. His heart lurched up and plummeted again with sickening force. His hands were rigid inside his gloves.

His jump partners rose from their seats. One of them nodded at him. Was he going first? He wasn't ready. Crazy thoughts whirled through his mind, and then his terror escalated, and the door of the aircraft was open, letting in a sickeningly cold blast of air.

'Door!' His jump partner gestured to him, and Paul rose, certain his limbs were too heavy to carry him forward.

He reached the door and fear froze his brain, leaving his body to perform the practised manoeuvres with mechanical precision. A strong smell of petrol wafted to him. This wasn't in the least like he'd imagined it. His jump partners had him in a firm grasp, and before he could think, he was outside, freefalling, the side of the plane a metallic green blur disappearing rapidly above him.

The rush of air whipped into his face, flattening his flesh against his skull. He tried to breathe, and failed. His jump partners were indicating the release on his parachute. He reached behind. It was there, thank God. He nodded. They made him check again. He checked his altimeter. Still too high. Christ. Could a man die of fear? He checked again and gave the signal. His jump partners released him, he struggled with the cord at his back, and shot skywards, his legs flailing.

And then the parachute filled out, and everything slowed. Paul began to breathe. The adrenaline surged through his body, and he had the urge to laugh out loud, as he'd laughed in the helicopter with Stuart, that time years ago.

Stuart. He gazed at the horizon, the green fields meeting perfect blue. Down below was the airfield, the thin ribbon of runway, the sheds like tiny matchboxes. The ground appeared to remain static, as though he were really floating, and would never descend. His breathing slowly returned, and with it a feeling of deep peace. He was above the world. Below him the fields were intersected with roads and housing estates, and in the houses and cars were hundreds of people, all going about their lives, each carrying their own hopes and dreams and tragedies. For this instant, Paul was above it all, free of worry.

A way from heart to heart ... Out of nowhere, he heard Kate's soft voice. He thought of how taken she'd been with Dashna's saying, and his fear floated away. Suddenly, he was filled with the conviction that everything would be well.

The green fields grew larger. Then his radio crackled, and the instructor on the ground was telling him to begin guiding his chute. He tugged on the strings. The ground was approaching more rapidly now, but Paul remained calm. He knew which way he should steer himself, his movements falling into place with instinctive ease. He was in control.

The air around him became warmer as he neared the ground, and there was the smell of grass and dug earth. Then there was his instructor below him, jogging lightly towards his landing spot. The ground approached. Paul bent his knees and leaned backwards, hitting the ground with unexpected force, but remaining on both feet. His parachute crumpled to the ground in soft folds behind him.

He smiled.

*

Two hours later Kate and Paul were leaning back on the bonnet of his car, faces turned to the sunshine. They were on their way home from the airfield, and Paul had promised George they would stop off for a picnic beside a lake he used to swim in as a child. But George had fallen asleep in the back of the car, worn out by the excitement of the morning.

Kate turned her head. The car windows were wound down, and a light breeze ruffled George's curls. His head lolled forward. He was sleeping soundly.

'He's had a grand day out,' Paul murmured.

'Oh, I know. When your pilot told him he could get inside the plane, I thought he was going to explode with happiness.'

The pilot had been much taken with George. While Paul was getting changed, he'd allowed George to climb inside the empty plane and sit in the cockpit. Ever since they left the airfield, George could talk of nothing else.

'He told me he doesn't want to be a bin man anymore,' Kate continued. 'Which amazed me, because watching the bin men haul the rubbish into the truck used to be an obsession. But now he's decided he wants to be a pilot. And he definitely wants to have a go at throwing himself out of a plane.'

Paul glanced down at her sidelong, his face creasing in a smile. 'It must be wonderful to have no fear.'

'Yes, it must be.' Kate dropped her gaze to her feet. 'I can't believe you went through with the jump. When we were in Blackpool, you didn't even want to get on the rollercoaster.'

'No. But I did it, though,' he said softly.

Kate could feel his eyes on her, watching. She edged a stone on the path with the tip of her foot, rolling it back and forth. 'If you're frightened, and you still do the thing you're frightened of anyway, I suppose that's being brave. I wish –' She raised her eyes to his. 'I wish I didn't feel frightened for George, all the time. I worry all the time. Ever since Stuart died, I just … And now Orla going, and my dad.' Her lips trembled, the sensation travelling right to the back of her throat, choking the words.

Her quiver touched Paul, and he reached for her, pulling her to his chest, tucking her head under his chin. He caressed her hair with his warm fingers for a while, and Kate leaned in to his embrace. And then he said, 'Would you let me share some of the worrying?'

Kate stood stiffly, unable to untangle his words.

'Katerina,' he continued softly. 'I think everything is going to be all right. I can't promise it will be. But I think it's worth the risk.'

His words vibrated in his chest, the sensation soothing Kate as she leaned against him, easing the tension in her body. For a while there was silence. A breeze ruffled the surface of the lake, and a bird flew low over the water. Kate moved her head, and Paul lifted her face towards his. His eyes fastened on hers, and he stroked her cheek with the tip of one finger. And then he bent his head and kissed her. She shifted in his embrace. His kiss deepened, became more urgent, and her lithe body bent in his arms.

There was the sound of the car door being pushed open, and small feet approaching.

'Are you kissing again?' George stood in front of them, eyes wide and speculative. Paul's laugh was rich and infectious.

With a swift movement he reached down and pulled George up to join them.

'George, this is one of the best days ever,' he said. 'And everything's going to be all right.'

Kate watched them both – George's fresh, young face alight with carefree pleasure and Paul grinning back at him – and then she tilted back her head, the sound of her laughter bubbling over and mingling with theirs.

THE END

Thank you so much for taking the time to read *The Summer of Love and Secrets*. I hope you enjoyed Paul and Kate's story. If you did, please consider telling your friends or posting a short review. Word of mouth is an author's best friend, and much appreciated.

More by Helena Fairfax ...

If you enjoyed *The Summer of Love and Secrets*, why not try another of my feel-good romances?

FELICITY AT THE CROSS HOTEL
A quaint hotel in the Lake District. The Cross Hotel is the perfect getaway. Or is it?

Felicity Everdene needs a break from the family business. Driving through the Lake District to the Cross Hotel, past the shining lake and the mountains, everything seems perfect. But Felicity soon discovers all is not well at the Cross Hotel ...

Patrick Cross left the village of Emmside years ago never intending to return, but his father has left him the family's hotel in his will, and now he's forced to come back. With a missing barmaid, a grumpy chef, and the hotel losing money, the arrival of Felicity Everdene from the notorious Everdene family only adds to Patrick's troubles.

With so much to overcome, can Felicity and Patrick bring happiness to the Cross Hotel ... and find happiness for themselves?

OTHER BOOKS BY HELENA FAIRFAX

Penny's Antique Shop of Memories and Treasures

The Silk Romance

In the Mouth of the Wolf

Come Date Me in Paris (a novella)

Miss Moonshine's Emporium of Happy Endings (an anthology)

If you'd like to get in touch, I'd love to hear from you! You can find all my social media links on my website www.helenafairfax.com, or just email me at helena.fairfax@gmail.com. I look forward to hearing from you!

ABOUT THE AUTHOR

Helena Fairfax was born in Uganda and came to England as a child. She's grown used to the cold now, and these days she lives in an old Victorian mill town on the edge of the Yorkshire moors. She finds the wild landscape the perfect place to write romantic fiction.

Helena's novels have been shortlisted for several awards, including the Romantic Novelists' Association New Writers' Scheme Award, the Global Ebook Awards, the Exeter Novel Prize, and the I Heart Indie Awards.

When not writing, Helena loves walking the moors with her dog, enjoying the changing seasons and dreaming up her heroes and her happy endings.